ALL RELIGIONS ARE GOOD IN TZINTZUNTZAN

ALL RELIGIONS ARE GOOD IN TZINTZUNTZAN:
EVANGELICALS IN CATHOLIC MEXICO

PETER S. CAHN

UNIVERSITY OF TEXAS PRESS
AUSTIN

Requests for permission to reproduce material from this work should be sent to
Permissions, University of Texas Press, P.O. Box 7819, Austin, TX 78713-7819.

♾ The paper used in this book meets the minimum requirements of ANSI/NISO
Z39.48-1992 (R1997) (Permanence of Paper).

Library of Congress Cataloging-in-Publication Data

Cahn, Peter S., 1975–
All religions are good in Tzintzuntzan : evangelicals in Catholic Mexico / Peter S.
Cahn.—1st ed.
    p.   cm.
Includes bibliographical references (p.) and index.
ISBN 0-292-70538-7 (cloth) — ISBN 0-292-70175-6 (paper)
1. Tzintzuntzan (Mexico)—Church history—20th century   2. Sociology, Christian—
Mexico—Tzintzuntzan.   3. Catholic Church—Mexico—History—20th century.
4. Evangelicalism—Mexico—Tzintzuntzan.   5. Catholic Church—Relations—
Evangelicalism.   6. Evangelicalism—Relations—Catholic Church.   7. Church and social
problems—Mexico—Tzintzuntzan.   I. Title.
BR1642.M6 C34   2003
306.6'77237—dc21   2003006704

CONTENTS

Threats of interreligious conflict have replaced cold war tensions as the major source of global instability in the twenty-first century. From Northern Ireland to Kashmir to the West Bank, the irreconcilable coexistence of two faith traditions has the potential to spark bloody confrontations. Motivated by doctrinal exclusivity, religious partisans see the destruction of nonbelievers as the only way to ensure the purity and survival of their way of life. On news broadcasts, journalists track the latest arrests of religious extremists plotting to do the United States harm. On college campuses, pro-Israeli and pro-Palestinian factions hurl punches along with invective. The regular reports of religious violence from around the world moved my eighty-seven-year-old grandmother to ask, "Wouldn't we all be better off without religion?"

In this book, I answer her and others who blame religion for fomenting violence and promoting intolerance. I argue that conflict is not a necessary outcome when adherents of different religious backgrounds live together, and, when disagreements do arise, religion is only a proximate cause. Taking the example of a region where new evangelical Protestant congregations have emerged to challenge the dominance of the Roman Catholic Church, I show how members of both groups adopt beliefs and practices of the other so as to minimize denominational discord. This mutual borrowing does not diminish the fervency of a person's chosen faith but rather strengthens it by connecting the spiritual realm with the conditions of daily life. Seen in this light, religious affiliation is not a fixed category but a vibrant, lived experience that responds to specific social, economic, and political contexts over the course of a believer's lifetime.

Between 1998 and 2001 I conducted fieldwork in Tzintzuntzan and its neighboring communities on the shores of Lake Pátzcuaro in the central-western Mexican state of Michoacán. Previous studies of conversion from Roman Catholicism to evangelical Protestant denominations in Latin America have taken place in countries with a high proportion of converts, such as Guatemala or Brazil. When scholars have conducted such research in Mexico, they have tended to focus on the southern states, which have the largest number of evangelicals. This approach allows the field-worker to participate in a full range of churches, but it also can produce overly deterministic conclusions about why Catholics have left their natal church. Talking to the many evangelical converts in Chiapas, for instance, one would get the impression that the only explanation for remaining in the Catholic Church is ignorance.

This skewed perspective ignores the continued vitality of the Catholic Church in most of Mexico. Moreover, it does not take into account the interactions between Catholics and their converted relatives and friends. During my fieldwork around Lake Pátzcuaro, the phenomenon of evangelical churches was still recent and relatively limited. Because this area remained a predominantly Catholic community, I was able to document both why converts have left the Catholic Church and why most Catholics have not. The Tzintzuntzan area also afforded the additional advantage of more than half a century of ethnographic data. As a result of the ongoing presence of anthropologists in Tzintzuntzan, of which I am the third generation, nearly everyone in the community is a willing collaborator with inquisitive outsiders. Their familiarity with anthropological methods enhanced my access to expressions of personal spirituality.

For most of the fifty-five years that anthropologists have studied in Tzintzuntzan, the Catholic Church has been the sole organized religion. Despite the arrival of missionaries from mainline Protestant denominations during the nineteenth century, serious challenges to the dominance of the Catholic Church in Mexico have appeared only in the last few decades. The non-Catholic Christian faiths that began to register since the 1960s in government census figures were not mainline churches like Presbyterians and Methodists but evangelical ones like Pentecostals and Jehovah's Witnesses. These more successful churches proselytize enthusiastically and rail against the perceived sins of the secular world. Their proportion of the Mexican population consistently remained under 2 percent until 1980, when it reached 3.3 percent.

Then, by the 1990 census, evangelicals totaled nearly 5 percent (Giménez 1996:230–242). By 2000, the number had reached 7.4 percent. With an overall population of nearly 100 million, this meant more than 7 million adults self-identified as evangelicals in Mexico. In Tzintzuntzan, a county seat with three thousand residents, eleven extended families have left the Catholic Church to join an evangelical church.[1]

The pattern of community harmony that I observed cannot be attributed to the relatively small number of evangelical converts. Most of the evangelicals and Catholics whom I introduce live or pray in Tzintzuntzan, but I draw on examples from the surrounding lake communities to show how they represent larger regional trends. Given the very public nature of Catholic worship and the efficiency of small-town gossip in Tzintzuntzan, conversion cannot be disguised. Even in larger cities nearby like Pátzcuaro and Quiroga, people know which of their neighbors attend Catholic Mass and which do not. Some Protestant churches around the lake have amassed sufficient resources to build highly visible places of worship. Since evangelical doctrine enjoins its members to bring salvation to the unsaved, converts tend to be open about their beliefs. Not all knock on doors to encourage Catholics to convert, but they do proselytize in some manner. Every member of the community belongs to a religion, and everyone else knows what it is.

Although there is diversity within both groups, I will treat Tzintzuntzeños as belonging to two basic religious affiliations: Catholics and evangelicals. This categorization reflects the perceptions of Tzintzuntzeños themselves. Since atheism is unheard of, even the most alienated believers claim membership in some church and recognize the distinctions between their religious group and the other. Catholics call converts "evangelicals," "brothers" (in reference to their habit for calling fellow members "*hermanos*"), or "hallelujahs" (a reference to their ecstatic forms of worship) without respect for denominational differences. In turn, most converts call all Catholics "*católicos*," and a few use the term "*romanistas*" to refer to their foreign origin. The converts are not that rigorous about applying distinctions between their own denominations either, calling all fellow non-Catholics "Christians," which is a generic term in Spanish for "human beings." For the purposes of simplicity, I will use "convert" interchangeably with "evangelical." The churches use the term "Protestant" less frequently because it does not adequately convey their diverse spiritual lineages. "Evangelical," with its emphasis on spreading the gospel, best describes the non-Catholic religious groups I visited.

Catholicism in the Lake Pátzcuaro area resembles the blend of rural European belief and pre-Hispanic elements that characterizes the majority church in other parts of central Mexico (see Ingham 1986). For most Catholics in this part of Mexico, the figure of the parish priest embodies the institution of the Catholic Church. He oversees daily Mass, though few Catholics attend more than the Sunday service. His role in administering the sacrament of communion and officiating at events such as baptisms and weddings places him in an intermediary position between the lay believer and the divine. Catholics rarely pray independently to God; they convey their thoughts to God through a layer of saints, powerful statues, and the merciful Virgin Mary. Instead of reading the Bible, they rely on the priest to interpret Scripture. The priest also presides at the liturgical celebrations that punctuate the religious calendar and affirm the sanctity of the church through a combination of solemn processions and raucous merriment.

Converts from Catholicism to evangelical churches typically frame their autobiographies in terms of a total transformation in which the misery of life "before" (sin, chaos) gives way to a peaceful "after" (harmonious, re-ordered). Evangelical pastors signal this life change by asking new members to make a personal decision to accept Jesus into their hearts.[2] For evangelicals, salvation comes through faith, in which they deliver themselves sincerely and repentantly to the Lord. This direct relationship with God contrasts with the mediation by priests in the Catholic faith and requires the adoption of a rigid code of behavior. Accepting Jesus means following all of his directives, as interpreted by each church. The variety of new activities and beliefs, from reading the Bible to rejecting the Virgin Mary, often bewilders recent converts. Staying in the church demands an even greater commitment to the prescribed rules, which govern converts' lives down to their wardrobe. Consequently, many women and men who start to attend evangelical services drop out.

Those who remain active in evangelical churches consider themselves to be born again. Only adults can take part in the ceremony of baptism, which confirms their rebirth as "creatures in Christ." Rebirth is so central that even the relatively few adults who have been born into an evangelical church usually go through a period of rebelliousness, only to return to the faith with renewed vigor.

In their new lives, converts accept certain tenets of faith that distance them from the Catholic religion. First, they consider the Bible the holy and inerrant word of God and interpret it literally. Evangelicals reject the cult of the saints and the institution of the papacy, pillars of Catholic belief that lack explicit grounding in the Bible. Second, they come to believe that they are living in the final days before Judgment Day. Predictions from the Bible have come true; warning signs have manifested themselves, making the Apocalypse imminent. Third, because of the impending Judgment Day, it becomes imperative to spread the "good news" of Jesus to as many souls as possible, converting them to the true faith before they receive final judgment.

Conversion also entails an overhaul of everyday behavior. Whereas Catholic priests tend to tolerate many practices as human foibles or expressions of untutored faith, evangelical pastors direct their followers to eliminate drinking, smoking, dancing, fiestas, rodeos, profanity, and other "worldly sins" from their lives. Evangelical churches also place a much stronger emphasis on reading Scripture than the Catholic Church does. Every member brings a Bible to evangelical services, flipping to the suggested passages and reciting verses aloud. In other respects, converts also participate more vigorously in church worship. Evangelical services (with the conspicuous exception of the Jehovah's Witnesses) merge ecstatic prayer with frenzied music. Often the electrified ambience induces wailing, flailing, and speaking in tongues. Since the pastor claims no special access to the divine, any member may lead any part of the service. A charismatic leader cannot contradict a member's visceral connection to the divine, whether manifested in tongues, prophecy, or faith healing.

In the traditionally Catholic community of Tzintzuntzan, where evangelical churches have become part of the religious landscape only during the past two decades, I sought to look behind the static, self-identifying labels of Catholic and evangelical to examine the process of mutual accommodation that characterizes religious life. I show how evangelical conversion arises from familial crises like alcoholism, not coercion from zealous missionaries. Whereas evangelical leaders portray their congregations as embattled minorities seeking to transform what they perceive as a sinful secular world, converts are more concerned with individual healing. Their energetic brand of faith has not erupted into violence because they continue to participate in communal life. Converts contribute financially to traditional Catholic celebrations and retain the structures of Catholic worship. Catholics, in turn, temper their disapproval of converts by attending evangelical ceremonies and importing Protestant principles into parish activities. Even if it means contradicting the universalizing doctrines espoused by the priest, Catholics value community harmony over blind allegiance.

Throughout Latin America, a flowering of religious diversity has replaced the centuries-old spiritual monopoly of the Catholic Church. There is debate among scholars about what the impact of these new churches will be. In places like Chiapas, where religious differences overlay struggles for political control, the result of evangelical conversion has been forced expulsion and unchecked violence. Around Lake Pátzcuaro, social and economic changes set in motion by increased out-migration to the United States have made peaceful coexistence possible. Alone, the presence of competing religious traditions in a single place is not responsible for creating conflict. As my experiences from Tzintzuntzan demonstrate, followers of different faiths can incorporate elements of the other into their religious beliefs and practices. When people told me that "all religions are good," they affirmed that it was less important to belong to a specific group than to share a common belief in God. Far from provoking conflict, evangelicals in Tzintzuntzan have fostered community solidarity.

In researching and writing this book, I borrowed freely from the advice and generosity of people of many different faiths, even if I did not always convert to their way of thinking. The National Science Foundation and the UC Berkeley Center for Latin American Studies funded my travel to the field. At Berkeley, I am grateful to Stanley Brandes, Laura Nader, and William Taylor, who encouraged me with their prompt, careful readings and their informed suggestions. Nancy Scheper-Hughes and the members of my dissertation writing group offered both a friendly space to sharpen my prose and the blessing of externally imposed deadlines. Richard Rodriguez helped me appreciate the vitality of Roman Catholicism.

   A postdoctoral fellowship at the University of California Humanities Research Institute provided a peaceful place for revision. I am especially appreciative of the incisive comments on my drafts by Jerry Miller, Mimi Saunders, Mark Wild, and Chiou-ling Yeh. Ramón Gutiérrez guided me through the publishing world, and Christine Eber and David Stoll, readers for the University of Texas Press, gave constructive advice on how to improve the manuscript. A small portion of Chapter 3 appears in *Chronicling Cultures: Long-Term Field Research in Anthropology* (2002: AltaMira Press). Annie Decker, who has written a scholarly paper on acknowledgments, merits special mention; I thank her for her meticulous editing.

   The category of "acknowledgments" does not seem profound enough to convey the debt I owe to the people of Tzintzuntzan. I could not have chosen a more congenial or stimulating place to conduct fieldwork. As much as my university colleagues, Tzintzuntzeños and friends in Santa Fe and Pátzcuaro clarified concepts, challenged my assumptions, and gave me confidence in the project. Dr. John Cook kindly read an early version of the manuscript and gave me permission to use his name. Estela, whom you will meet in the following pages, integrated me into her household with aplomb and good humor. Protective yet affectionate, she made sure my parents did not worry about me any more than they usually do. It did not surprise me at all when Estela turned up on the front page of the *Washington Post* explaining the realities of undocumented migration to a newly inaugurated President George W. Bush on his first visit to Mexico. He would be wise to listen to her.

I dedicate this work to El Doctor and Mariquita, who first brought me to Tzintzuntzan and gave me the best ethnographic methods course an anthropology graduate student could desire.

ALL RELIGIONS ARE GOOD IN TZINTZUNTZAN

ONE

SHARING THE BURDEN OF FIESTAS ACROSS BORDERS

WHEN George Foster began his ethnographic research in the central-western Mexican community of Tzintzuntzan in 1944, he heard a common refrain. Tzintzuntzeños answered any question about who were the wealthiest families or the most macho men in town with a denial of differences: "Here we are all equal" (Foster 1967:12–13). The physical landscape tended to reinforce that idea. Surrounded by steep hillside on three sides and bordering Lake Pátzcuaro on the other, Tzintzuntzan had no room for the acquisition of large-scale landholdings. The population of twelve hundred lived in one-story adobe houses with tile roofs, all resembling one another. Every Sunday, they all worshipped at the parish church, a whitewashed, domed building visible from clear on the other side of the lake.

In their access to resources, Tzintzuntzeños could claim equal—albeit limited—opportunities. Pottery making via the traditional method of molded clay fired in wood-burning kilns provided the main livelihood. Any artisan could find the necessary components for clay and logs for burning in the immediate vicinity. Agricultural production also sustained many Tzintzuntzeños, but no one practiced it on a scale large enough to allow significant reselling. Using canoes and enormous nets, men caught a regular supply of fish in the blue waters of Lake Pátzcuaro. Few men or women worked outside the "village," as Foster called it. Schooling beyond the sixth grade required traveling to another city, so most Tzintzuntzeños inherited the occupations of their parents. The *bracero* program contracted Mexican men to work on farms in the United States, but they usually returned home after a few months.

Foster contended that the claim to homogeneity stemmed from the villagers' implicit assumptions about a healthy society. In the model of "image of limited good," Tzintzuntzeños perceived that all desirable elements of life, tangible and intangible, existed in finite quantities that could not be increased (Foster 1965). Therefore, if any single member of the community acquired more land or wealth, for instance, he deprived others of valuable resources. To counter this threat of imbalance and perpetuate the fiction of uniformity, Tzintzuntzeños devised several strategies to maintain equilibrium (Foster 1967:136–141). Assertions of "here we are all equal" reinforced the illusion of the ideal state by masking differences between villagers.

DISRUPTING THE EQUILIBRIUM

Returning to Tzintzuntzan in 1958, Foster began a longitudinal study of the community, regularly tracking population changes, occupational data, prices of commodities, and migration patterns. By the time he revised his monograph, *Tzintzuntzan: Mexican Peasants in a Changing World* (1979), the community scarcely resembled the one he had come to know in the 1940s, which had claimed that all its members were equal. He explained in the preface that the population had more than doubled, and some families had acquired televisions, pickup trucks, and washing machines:

> Accompanying these material changes has been a striking shift in world view, particularly among the members of the younger generation. . . . They recognize opportunity, believe that with hard work they can exploit it, and demonstrate through their collective achievements the accuracy of this perception. Increasingly well-educated, these young people in aspirations and outlook are broadly Mexican and not narrowly Tzintzuntzeño. (Foster 1979:preface)

If the image of limited good had ever guided the actions of what were once conservative peasants, it no longer did. By the third edition in 1988, Foster had concluded that the terms "peasant" and "village" no longer applied to Tzintzuntzan; rather, the people there had come to resemble city folk: "They are Mexicans who happen to live, geographically, farther from Mexico City's central plaza than do their fellow countrymen who live and work in the capital city" (Foster 1988:398). Tzintzuntzeños no longer attempted to maintain the appearance of equilibrium. They had become sufficiently integrated into

1.1 Seen from the archaeological site above the community, Tzintzuntzan is hemmed in on three sides by mountains and on the fourth by Lake Pátzcuaro. Income earned in the United States has fueled construction of two-story homes.

a larger pattern of international migration and capitalist participation that they could no longer plausibly claim homogeneity.

Tzintzuntzan without the refrain "Here we are all equal" does indeed resemble any larger Mexican city (Figure 1.1). The population had reached three thousand inhabitants by the 1990s. All the streets are paved and lined with sidewalks. Many homes have abandoned the traditional design of a single story around a central patio in favor of an enclosed plan with two stories, balconies, wrought iron railings, and a satellite dish. Nearly all families count on the services of piped water, electricity, and drainage. Although every household has gained access to more material goods since Foster's first visit, those improvements are not distributed equally. Alongside the double-decker homes with stained glass windows and garages stand sagging adobe homes with dirt floors. Some teenagers wear the baggy pants and plaid shirts that symbolize hip-hop cool, while others make do with torn jeans and hand-me-down T-shirts.

The same class divisions appear in how a family earns a living. The highway that bisects town supports two pharmacies, a hardware store, a restaurant, four small food markets, a video rental business, a butcher shop, and a stationery store. The larger and better stocked the business, the more successful the owner. The most affluent storekeepers own pickup trucks, which they drive to buy produce at the wholesale market in the state capital of Morelia. The expansion of educational opportunities also reveals differences in status among Tzintzuntzeños. Students can attend school in the community through ninth grade, which most do. If they choose to continue on to high school in the neighboring cities of Pátzcuaro or Quiroga, their families have to bear the cost of transportation, uniforms, and books. The most comfortable families can afford to send their children to enter university or even medical school in Morelia or Mexico City.[1]

Different classes of artisans also have become conspicuous. Three potters have invested in high-temperature gas kilns that produce a more even firing and a lead-free glaze. They experiment with fanciful colors and designs, earning the attention of galleries in Mexico City and the United States. All other potters continue to use the traditional method of low-temperature wood firing or have branched into weaving ornaments from wheat straw. Some sell their goods at a weekly market near the entrance to the churchyard, but most prefer to sell to intermediaries at unfavorable yet secure prices. Along the highway across from the town hall, the community built a craft market with about two dozen stalls where resellers cater to intermittent tourist traffic. Nearly all the homes that line the highway next to the market have turned their ground floors into showrooms for pottery, wood, or wheat straw artisanry.

Artisans who live farther from the main highway and do not rely on resellers have to transport their pieces to distant markets at considerable expense. On vacation in the beach resort of Puerto Vallarta, I encountered a family from Tzintzuntzan selling straw Christmas wreaths to passengers from cruise ships. I knew other artisans who resorted to bartering items in Pátzcuaro in exchange for food staples. Still other artisans without access to tourist commerce have relocated their homes to plots of communal land astride the highway connecting Tzintzuntzan to Pátzcuaro. In what has come to be known as La Colonia Lázaro Cárdenas in honor of the former Michoacán governor who became president, artisans exchange the comforts of paved roads and sewage systems for guaranteed access to passing visitors.

However, for as much as Tzintzuntzan has shed its peasant village mentality and adopted the trappings of big-city life, it remains very much marginalized from the decision-making centers of the country at the start of the twenty-first century. Tzintzuntzeños rely entirely on others to determine their political and economic well-being. Ceramic artisanry, still the primary industry, is a key example. Pottery making requires arduous work for little remuneration. Most locals use metal cooking pots or Tupperware containers in

1.2 On weekends, this potter sells directly to tourists who visit Tzintzuntzan. Her white pottery, or *loza blanca,* is distinctive to Tzintzuntzan and has attracted orders from galleries in San Miguel de Allende and Mexico City.

their own kitchens and depend on the arrival of tourists to purchase their colorful dishware. Trouble is, outside of Day of the Dead and Easter, which the state bureau of tourism promotes heavily, few tourists venture to Tzintzuntzan. For the woman shown in Figure 1.2, who bypasses the intermediaries by bringing a wheelbarrow full of her plates and bowls to the crafts market every weekend, it is common not to sell anything for two entire days. And when she does sell, the prices are so low—about $1.50 for a bowl—that she can barely earn back her investment in materials.

The glazes that give the plates their attractive green, white, or brown luster after firing contain lead. In the early 1990s, an ecological organization initiated a campaign to remove lead from consumer goods sold in Mexico, including traditional artisanry. With added pressure from strict laws against the importation of products containing lead into the United States, the Mexican government agreed to phase in a prohibition. While manufacturers of paints and items like juice cans can easily find substitutes for leaded products, no suitable replacement exists for the leaded glazes the potters used. Gloria Cáceres Centeno, a researcher I spoke with at the Casa de Artesanías, the government-sponsored center for artisanal promotion in Morelia, blames much of the outcry against lead to irrational anxieties. She cites the instance of the United States ambassador to Mexico who claimed his young daughter had contracted lead poisoning from drinking water out of a ceramic pot. This accusation fanned consumer worries, but Cáceres points out that lead is soluble only in acids, not water.

Still, the government announced in 1994 that potters had three years to eliminate lead from their wares, even though the substitute lead-free glaze they were formulating would not become available until 1996. When the Mexican company MACECA began distributing the lead-free glaze, it did not immediately catch on for several reasons. Although it can be used in the same wood-burning low-temperature ovens, potters cannot simply substitute the new glaze for the old one without specialized training. Also, the resulting shine is less brilliant than the old glaze and therefore less attractive to tourists. Most important to potters, the new glaze is not cost-efficient. Despite little difference in price, much more of the new glaze is required to bathe the pieces in each oven load. Wary of the disadvantages of the new glaze, most potters in Tzintzuntzan continue using the old leaded glaze. Rumors circulate that the secretary of health will launch surprise inspections of workshops or halt the sale of the old glaze, but several potters simply stockpile the glaze, storing it discreetly in the rafters of their workshops.

When I conducted fieldwork in 1999 and 2000, past the original deadline for eliminating leaded glazes, only three potters in Tzintzuntzan made lead-free ceramics. The rest continued using the techniques inherited from their parents and denounced what one woman called "all the propaganda" that had been scaring off tourists from purchasing pottery. She insisted that her family had been eating from the glazed plates for years without suffering any ill effects. But the impact of the rules already can be felt; many potters are ceasing production and very few children take up the craft or even want to help in their parents' workshop. Cáceres predicts that survival of the fittest will prevail among the potters, leaving only a few resourceful artisans who have access to intermediary exporters. During the 1990s she witnessed a decline in the number of potters throughout Michoacán and a concomitant rise in out-migration.

The demise of pottery has forced both men and women to seek alternate ways to earn income. With minimal employment opportunities in Tzintzuntzan or even the larger Mexican cities, crossing the border into the United States remains as attractive as it was for the braceros during World War II (Galarza 1964). Unlike during the bracero program, however, obtaining legal documents to enter the United States is nearly impossible for someone from

Tzintzuntzan. In 1999, I spoke to Valentina,[2] an older woman who lived off the pension of her husband, a retired teacher, and the profits from her small general store in Tzintzuntzan. A year before, she had obtained a visa to visit the United States, where her sister, a naturalized citizen, had fallen ill. While Valentina was visiting, her sister's condition worsened, and she died. When Valentina went to renew her visa in 1999 to visit other siblings in Chicago, it was costly. She had to close her store temporarily and pay for transportation to the American Embassy in Mexico City. She brought with her bank statements, the forty-five-dollar application fee, and letters from her siblings in the United States. She took a number, then patiently waited for her turn at one of the teller windows. Valentina expected to get approval since she had obtained a tourist visa before and since given her age she was not likely to seek work in the United States. However, when her turn came, the clerk asked her if her sister was still ill. Valentina, believing candor was the best route, said that her sister had died. Without further explanation, the clerk denied her application. When Valentina tried to argue, a guard came over to usher her away from the window. To increase her frustration, she was not entitled to a refund of her application fee.

As Valentina recounted these events to me, she seethed. She understood why the embassy limited visas, but she had no intention of remaining to work in the United States. Upset at the time and expense she had wasted, she accused Bill Clinton of needing money to silence Monica Lewinsky. Turning more serious, Valentina said: "It's no wonder people cross illegally. I can re-apply for a visa in one year, but there's no guarantee I'll get it then. I know a *coyote* (border guide) who takes up to thirty people across the border and charges twelve hundred dollars. If I have an urgent need to go to the United States, I'll cross with him." In fact, very few Tzintzuntzeños try to secure the proper documentation before crossing the border; they have every intention of working in the United States and lack the evidence of assets in Mexico that will persuade officials that they intend to return promptly (see Conover 1987).

As a result, the majority of Tzintzuntzeños enter the United States without documents and with the help of a coyote. Several coyotes from other parts of Mexico work with representatives in Tzintzuntzan, who earn fees for alerting the community of imminent departure dates. After several years of such crossings, certain coyotes have earned reputations as either being careful to see that everyone crosses safely or being more likely to abandon people in the desert. Living in Tzintzuntzan, I would occasionally hear word that a coyote was planning a trip to the border. Then, one morning I would find that up to forty people had left during the night. With coyotes charging their passengers from twelve to fifteen hundred dollars, migrants are obligated to work in the United States for long periods of time to repay their loans and to earn extra money to bring home. The cost and danger of repeated border crossings means that once a migrant enters the United States, he or she will likely stay for several years (Jordan 2001). The handful of documented workers I knew in Tzintzuntzan would work in the United States just a few months a year and then return to live off their earnings in Mexico.

Similarly, Rouse (1991) traced "circuits" of migration between Aguililla, Michoacán, and Redwood City, California. Workers who moved to the United States managed to maintain ties to their Mexican roots by using employment opportunities in California to finance retirement dreams in Mexico. Similarly, Tzintzuntzan is a community spread out over several sites; as many Tzintzuntzeños live outside the lake region as in it (Kemper 2002). Both news and remittances from the migrants contribute significantly to community life. When I left the field briefly to participate in a conference in Chicago, I made more telephone calls to relatives of my Tzintzuntzan friends than to members of my own family.

Crossing the border into the United States is not as easy as it used to be. In the 1970s, with few INS agents patrolling the border, a migrant could walk unobserved from Tijuana to San Diego, California, in just twenty-four hours. Beginning in the 1990s, both xenophobic ranchers (some of whom have shot migrants crossing their land) and armed federal agents have been patrolling the southern border of the United States. With the buildup in vigilance, undocumented migrants seek increasingly more remote stretches of land to cross, such as the Arizona desert, which takes days to traverse. The number of deaths caused by dehydration or starvation led the Mexican government in 1999 to air a series of radio ads advising potential migrants how to cross the desert safely.

Tacoma, Washington, forms the main node of the circuit radiating from Tzintzuntzan. A group of men from Tzintzuntzan arrived there in 1979 after performing contract work picking asparagus, apples, and cherries in Yakima, Washington. They heard of a field in Tacoma that no one would work because the immigration authorities came by every morning at 8 A.M. to check the workers' papers. Along with some men from the Mexican state of Guanajuato, the Tzintzuntzan men decided they would tackle the field. They woke up at 4 A.M. every day, leaving nothing but full boxes by 8 A.M. when the officials came looking. In a week they had finished harvesting the field and had caught the attention of a man with extensive lands in Tacoma. He hired the men, giving them a house and a good hourly wage for the next ten years. During that time, more migrant workers from Tzintzuntzan arrived in Tacoma to stay with the men. I had a running joke with my landlady, Estela, that everyone in Tzintzuntzan was related to one another since every person she introduced me to was her cousin, her in-law, or her godchild. This high degree of interrelatedness helps Tzintzuntzeños upon arriving in the United States. They nearly always live with relatives in Tacoma at first, relying on them for connections to find job openings. Relatives also regularly advance migrants the fee smugglers charge for guiding them across the border. Moreover, the weather is not as cold in Tacoma as in other parts of the Pacific Northwest. In this way, Tacoma and its suburbs have become a destination point for people leaving Tzintzuntzan. The original migrants were all male, but as their lives in Washington became more permanent, they brought their wives to join them. When I lived in Tzintzuntzan, entire families shuttled between Mexico and the United States.

Migration to the United States has allowed many Tzintzuntzeños to achieve a level of material comfort their parents never imagined. It has not, however, given Tzintzuntzan a stronger voice in defending its interests. To the contrary, migrants in the United States are prohibited from voting in domestic Mexican elections, and their long periods abroad make participation in local activities impossible. In addition, migration has made Tzintzuntzeños dependent on other, larger powers that determine how long a worker can earn money and where he can find employment. Recently, Mexican migrant men in Tacoma have been taking jobs on fish-processing boats off the Alaska coast (Cahn 2000; Sarmiento 1999). Some men claim that the pay for three months of labor offsets the seasickness, chill, claustrophobia, boredom, and stench of packing and freezing fish. I met another who suffered dementia because of it and had to be airlifted off the boat.

Tzintzuntzeños have little capacity to generate sustainable livelihoods themselves. Arable agricultural land around the community is scarce, and they cannot turn to the lake. In recent years the state government has banned fishing in Lake Pátzcuaro during the spring months to allow the fish population to replenish. Unfortunately, the animals' reproductive cycle coincides with the time of Lent, when fish consumption, and thus sales, is highest. Enraged, fishermen have organized protests, but the prohibition has remained in effect. In Mexico, Tzintzuntzeños must rely on state-promoted tourism, remittances from relatives abroad, and precarious profits from local small-scale businesses. In the United States, they must take advantage of whatever opportunity presents itself and promises not to check documents. Some families

have benefited from the increased access to education and markets for selling artisanry that increased interaction with external agents brings, but many
others have little recourse but to defy the state ban on leaded glaze. It has become increasingly clear that in Tzintzuntzan, people are not all equal. Even
the one unifying constant for the past four centuries—the Catholic Church—
has lost its monopoly on local spiritual life.

CHANGING MEXICAN CATHOLICISM

Communities in many parts of Mexico echo the transformation that Tzintzuntzan underwent in the second half of the twentieth century from self-
sufficiency to dependence on larger economic markets (see Reck 1978). What
distinguishes Tzintzuntzan is the near-constant ethnographic surveillance
that has accompanied those changes. With a few gaps, the involvement of
researchers from the University of California, Berkeley, in Tzintzuntzan has
continued uninterrupted for fifty-eight years. In that period, anthropologists
have conducted six communitywide censuses (1945, 1960, 1970, 1980, 1990,
2000) that, together with qualitative data gathered by about a dozen researchers, give Tzintzuntzan one of the most complete ethnographic records
of any single community in the world. Census questions are exhaustive. When
I participated in 2000, I collected the following information on each resi-
dent of the household: age, birthplace, schooling, literacy, occupation, travel
experience, languages spoken, and access to social security. I also noted
whether the household contained any of forty-one different material items,
from glass windows to raised mattresses. But in none of the six censuses did
the investigators ever ask what religion the family professes.

By the time of the first census Tzintzuntzan was mostly a Spanish-speaking
mestizo community, but it once served as the administrative and ceremonial capital of the pre-Hispanic Purépecha Empire. The Purépecha people,
or Tarascans, as the Spanish would call them, maintained dominion over
large swaths of the contemporary states of Michoacán, Jalisco, and Guerrero.
They managed to defend themselves against the military incursions of the
Aztecs, but fell to the Spanish conquerors in 1522 (Alcala 1981 [1541]; Beals
1969). Shortly afterward, Tzintzuntzan became a center of Catholic evangelization. Using stones from the round pyramids called "yácatas" where the
Purépecha priests had ministered to their followers, Franciscan friars con-
structed a parish church and convent dedicated to Saint Francis. Some forty
gnarled olive trees ring the churchyard today, the legacy of the first bishop
of Michoacán, Don Vasco de Quiroga.

Don Vasco moved the seat of the diocese from Tzintzuntzan to Pátzcuaro and then to its current home, Morelia. Even so, he is remembered around Lake Pátzcuaro as a benevolent leader, a follower of Thomas More's *Utopia* who encouraged each community around the lake to specialize in a certain type of artisanry (Gómez 2001; Verástique 2000). Along with the Catholic faith and olive trees, many Tzintzuntzeños claimed Don Vasco left Tzintzuntzan with the craft of pottery. The fondness for this Spanish lawyer-turned-cleric in Michoacán remains strong centuries after his death. While I was in Michoacán, one former parish priest in Tzintzuntzan began an effort to canonize Don Vasco by documenting miracles he performed during his time as bishop.

The Catholic religion that Don Vasco inculcated in the indigenous populations came to be the dominant approach to spirituality in Michoacán.[3] Along with the adjacent heartland states of Aguascalientes, Querétaro, Guanajuato, Zacatecas, and Jalisco, Michoacán consistently ranks as one of the most Catholic states in Mexican census data on religious affiliation. Catholicism touches every life in Tzintzuntzan, from baptism to burial. Since, in the eyes of Tzintzuntzeños, no one can be without religion, Catholicism becomes the default religion for the anthropologists who live there as well. The family that hosts the Fosters told me with great admiration how devoutly Catholic George and Mary Foster are, attending Mass and praying the rosary. Though not Catholic or even practicing Christians, the Fosters participate in the religious life of the community as part of their ethnographic fieldwork. Their hosts choose to interpret their actions as evidence of their Catholicism. When I told the family who hosted me (and any others who asked) that I had been raised Jewish, they immediately thought of the bearded figures in the Easter passion play. I had to explain modern Jewish worship, eliciting some surprise when I mentioned that Jews celebrate similar festivals and follow some of the same sacred scriptures (the Old Testament) that Catholics do. On a few occasions I heard disparaging comments about Jews who had assisted in the murder of Jesus Christ, but this did not translate into contemporary animus. To the contrary, since most adults were familiar with the biblical designation of Jews as God's chosen people, being Jewish conferred on me a kind of celebrity.

My Jewish background offered the additional advantage of justifying my ignorance about many Catholic customs. At many religious rituals, fellow worshippers patiently explained symbolic traditions, waiting for me to record the information in my notebook. Older Catholic women in particular took interest in my religious education, presenting me with rosaries and leading one-on-one tutorials on the proper recitation of the Lord's Prayer. My Catholic neighbors in Tzintzuntzan accepted my Jewish background, but still praised me when I attended Mass every Sunday. My Judaism opened me to relentless proselytizing as many Catholics encouraged me to join their church, even offering to serve as godparents at my hoped-for baptism and confirmation.

Identifying publicly as Jewish for the first time since my bar mitzvah did not eliminate my discomfort with that religion. For me, Orthodox Judaism, with its arcane rules of kosher foods and agricultural holidays, seems designed for a specific group of people in a particular geographic and historical place. While its teachings have contributed immeasurably to present-day society, a life based on strict adherence to Jewish texts is, in my mind, an anachronism. Similarly, I began my research of Christianity suspicious of its contemporary relevance to Mexican lives. In religious imagery, Jesus Christ is always depicted as fair-skinned, long-haired, and toga-clad, more part of European heritage than any indigenous New World tradition. His elevation to Messiah for all Christians struck me as an imperialist imposition. However, in the course of fieldwork, I came to appreciate how Catholics and other Christians in Mexico have infused this spiritual legacy of colonialism with their own understandings.

With a single priest to oversee a flock of three thousand members, most expressions of Catholic religiosity in Tzintzuntzan take place outside the parish church. The home of my host, Estela, is typical in its display of devotional material. On the back of the front door, she hangs palm fronds that the priest blessed and sprinkled with holy water before the Palm Sunday Mass. In the front hall, she displays a butcher shop's promotional calendar dominated by a fanciful illustration of Saint James astride a horse. All the bedrooms, which open onto a central uncovered patio, feature posters or placards of Catholic figures. In my room, a celestial Virgin of Guadalupe, purchased by Estela's son when he completed the fourteen-day pilgrimage to her shrine in Mexico City, looms over the bed. Estela always keeps a candle burning in the kitchen beneath a picture of the Holy Trinity that shows the Holy Spirit as a white dove between two ethereal men with flowing beards. By praying to them, Estela assures me, she has never lacked for food, shelter, or clothing. A moving altar dedicated to the Divine Providence circulates through the town, spending each night of the year in a different house. When our turn came, I accompanied Estela and her children to the house next door. We lit candles from the flickering flames of the neighbor's shrine, then carried the painting, flowers, and collection box to our living room, where Estela had prepared a spot on top of the television.

Her Catholic faith also guides Estela during her daily routine. Every morning, upon waking, the first thing she does is make the sign of the cross to thank God for another day. Next, she walks across the open-air living room to the kitchen. Grabbing two plastic buckets, she fills one with oranges and the other with carrots. She hefts these to the front door, followed by a second trip for an electric juicer that has been placed in a basin of drying dishes. By 7:30 A.M., Estela swings open the wooden door flecked with red paint and sets up her juice stand. When the youngest of her seven children was twelve years old, Estela's husband died suddenly as he returned from tending his fields. Fortunately, four of her children already had begun to earn money, but she still needed income to pay for books and tuition for the others. Taking advantage of her home's conspicuous location across from the main plaza and bus stop, Estela opened her juice stand. After the first sale of each day, she slips the coins under the metal base of the juice extractor and makes the sign of the cross.

Around 11 A.M., after the schoolchildren and commuting adults have passed by for their breakfasts, Estela brings the equipment back into the kitchen. Some afternoons, she takes a taxi to Pátzcuaro to purchase yogurt, cereal, or toilet paper, items that are found cheaper in bulk than in the local stores. Estela always carries rosary beads with her so she can pray during the thirty-minute ride. In the evenings, Estela cross-stitches napkins while minding the wine shop she opened in the front room of her house. Usually around 9:30 or 10 P.M., when I was in Tzintzuntzan, we would eat dinner together — sweet bread and hot chocolate. Her three-year-old granddaughter, who lived with her, liked to show how grown up she was by helping in the kitchen and eating with us. Before bedtime, Estela led us in singing, "Good Night, Jesus," and then guided her granddaughter's right hand to form a cross with her thumb and index finger. The young girl first gave her grandmother the benediction and then turned to me to do the same, pausing at the end to allow me to kiss her crooked fingers.

FINANCING THE FIESTAS

Catholic devotion in Tzintzuntzan reaches a climax during the numerous fiestas throughout the year. After hearing firecrackers going off, indicating a fiesta somewhere in the community, Estela remarked to me:

> There is not a month here without a fiesta. In January, it's the Day of the Three Kings. In February there is the February Fiesta; in March, the first day of spring; in April, Easter; in May, the Holy Crosses;

in June, Corpus Christi; in July, school graduation; in August, the Marias are celebrated; in September, Independence Day; in October, the day of San Francisco; in November, Night of the Dead; in December, the Virgin of Guadalupe, Christmas, and New Year's.

Each religious event calls for a Mass, followed by an elaborate meal and music. I asked Estela why she thought fiestas had come to dominate the calendar. She did not have to think long before answering, "We have no bar here, no movie theater or disco. This is our distraction. At least we're not spending our money on drugs." To her and many other Tzintzuntzeños, fiesta time disrupts the tedium of eking out a life on the margins. It provides a colorful "distraction" requiring special foods, wardrobe, and behavior. I interpret Estela's comment about drugs as tacit acknowledgment that fiestas, like controlled substances, offer only temporary escape from life's problems or make them worse in the long run, but at least fiestas are a healthy way to spend money.

For the weeks prior to a Catholic liturgical celebration, people of all ages in Tzintzuntzan talk about and prepare for the fiesta. In the last days of October 1999 before the Day of the Dead fiesta, Estela set up a table next to the television in her living room and began to arrange orange marigolds, called *simplasuche*, in an arc (see Figure 1.3). With the help of her visiting grandson, she arrayed fruit, bread, and candles on the table. On a trip to Pátzcuaro, I purchased several chocolate skulls etched with family members' names in colorful icing, which Estela added to the display along with a cross made of flower petals. Everything looked so tempting that I commented sarcastically I'd like to take some of the offering. Estela assured me that on November 2 I could eat from the altar after reciting the Paternoster. On November 1, Estela visited the graves of her husband and her parents, clearing them of weeds and lining them with candles. That night I joined her in the cemetery to sing and shiver by the bonfire. At sunrise, the priest led a Mass among the tombs.

Although it draws the most tourist attention, Day of the Dead is not Tzintzuntzan's largest religious celebration of the year. Both February Fiesta, honoring a miraculous representation of Christ in the community, and the Easter week festivities demand more time and energy from participants and deliver more spiritual intensity. During these principal fiestas, the population of Tzintzuntzan doubles or even triples with the influx of migrants returning from other parts of Mexico and abroad.

In addition to the robust cycle of communitywide fiestas, every life passage of every person merits religious attention and celebration. Before Es-

1 . 3 Estela and her grandson prepare their home altar for Day of the Dead, 1999.

tela's son married, his godparents and family accompanied him to the young woman's house to ask for her parents' permission. When they had agreed on the conditions for marriage, the godparents gave the future in-laws a bottle of Dom Pedro brandy to seal the arrangement. All the guests drank brandy or soft drinks and ate snacks in a convivial party. Later, on the day when the son and his fiancée visited the parish priest to register their intentions to wed and met with a judge for the civil ceremony, Estela hosted another party for the two families. She set up long tables in the patio of her house, topping them with beer, brandy, and roasted chicken. After the religious ceremony itself a month later, Estela and her son's godparents sponsored another celebration, filling her sister's backyard orchard with rows of rented tables and chairs and a lively band. Baptism, first communion, and fifteenth birthdays for girls receive the same festive attention. Even seemingly secular events like Estela's youngest son's graduation from public secondary school involve a Mass, the naming of godparents, and a feast afterward.

Organizing and participating in so many fiestas cost Tzintzuntzeños significant amounts of money. Under the old mentality of "Here we are all equal," the large number of fiestas and excessive expenses associated with them ensured a redistribution of income within the community. In the past, a religious hierarchy governed the celebration of community fiestas in a way that concealed the development of wealth differences. The hierarchy, found throughout Mesoamerica, consisted of a ranked ladder of offices called *cargos,* or "burdens," ascending in both prestige and obligations for financial sponsorship of a religious fiesta. Typically, community members would encourage—or coerce—powerful men to assume charge of sponsoring the music, fireworks, food, and decorations for a fiesta, thereby transferring their wealth back into the general pool (Wolf 1959).[4] A hierarchy of eleven cargos used to govern religious celebrations in Tzintzuntzan. Starting with the minor cargos, a man could pass through the hierarchy, taking on increasingly burdensome responsibilities until he fulfilled the most prestigious cargos.

The system of cargos succeeded in redistributing surpluses but did not necessarily militate against the formation of class differences. Participation in the cargo system corresponded to and reinforced officeholders' economic and social rank, yet allowed for the appearance of equilibrium by reducing the envy of the poor (Cancian 1965). As respected elders, men who had completed their cargo service (called *cargueros*) occupied the most powerful positions of authority in the community. Although women helped their male relatives with the responsibilities of the cargo, only men held the title.

In Tzintzuntzan, a former cargo holder traditionally commanded deference. Whenever he attended a fiesta meal, he could sit at the head of the table, and when he died, his body would be placed in the church during mourning without charge. By contrast, men who had not served as a cargo holder could never be highly respected (Foster 2000:279).

Foster (1967) analyzed the cargo system in the context of a world vision marked by limited good. Since "prestige and status were the only commodities the community could permit a man to accumulate in large amounts," completion of the cargos rewarded the wealthy while diminishing any threats to Tzintzuntzan's perceived ideal of financial equality (205). Nader (1990) identifies a similar effort to promote local solidarity, which she calls "harmony ideology," in the southern Mexican community of Talea. There, the heavy use of litigation resists the state's political and cultural hegemony by preventing social cleavages. In the same way, the cargo system limits outside intervention in community life through the local resolution of internal differences (Cohen 1999; Greenberg 1981).

An example from the Purépecha community of Ihuatzio best illustrates the insulating power of a functioning cargo system. During the 1960s, Dutch anthropologist van Zantwijk worked for a nongovernmental organization in Pátzcuaro which had attempted unsuccessfully to introduce community development projects in Ihuatzio. Through several years of fieldwork, van Zantwijk (1967) determined that the major obstacle was the distrust of outsiders on the part of Ihuatzio's entrenched leadership. To be a community leader in Ihuatzio, a man had to have risen through the entire hierarchy of religious cargos. Even the nominal civil leader was chosen by and beholden to the cabal of traditional village chiefs. The parish priest delivered sermons opposing the cargo system, but the community rejected his authority. When one non–cargo holder nominated himself for a position of leadership, the traditional chiefs humiliated him at a public meeting by asserting that he had not demonstrated the sacrifice for the community that they had. Shamed, the challenger relocated to Pátzcuaro.

The residents of Ihuatzio so rejected secular authority that only thirty-seven of nine hundred registered voters participated in municipal elections in 1962; they saw the religious cargueros as the only true leaders of the community (van Zantwijk 1967:191). As effective as the cargo system was in maintaining internal consensus, it faced a crisis when the expenses for fiesta sponsorship soared. In Ihuatzio, the elders estimated that passing through all stages of the hierarchy required thirty-two hundred dollars at a time when hardly any man earned more than four dollars a week. Facing the prospect of financial ruin, men began declining offers to assume a cargo. Leaders in Ihuatzio responded by lessening the demands placed on cargueros, which managed to mute dissent (van Zantwijk 1967:128).

In a survey of several ethnographies of Mesoamerica, DeWalt (1975) shows how, as communities come into increasing contact with the larger world, the cargo system tends to decay and give way to a system of shared community giving. Concerted state efforts to reach previously closed communities and new forms of generating income through international migration undermine the ability of local leaders to enforce their authority. Cancian (1992) observes that in Zinacantán, in the southern Mexican state of Chiapas, the number of cargos has dropped dramatically since the 1960s due to political and social decentralization. In Tzintzuntzan the decline in individual financial sponsorship of fiestas received impetus from a forceful parish priest in the 1940s who eliminated several of the many cargos. A reduction in cargo duties, as in neighboring Ihuatzio, also hastened the dismantling of the cargo system. In its place, a system of sharing the costs of fiestas across the community has emerged over the past fifty years as the primary form of financing fiestas (Brandes 1988:44–46). For the major religious fiestas of the annual cycle, the parish priest, along with his secretary, names commissioners who are responsible for asking their neighbors for financial contributions. The priest then pools these contributions, or *cooperaciones,* to pay for the decorations, bands, and fireworks that accompany all the fiestas.

Unlike cargueros, commissioners neither receive spiritual compensation for their duties nor play a role after the event has concluded. Importantly, the commissioners bear relatively little personal economic risk and do not earn any significant prestige. Although no formal punishment exists for refusing to serve, commissioners rarely turn down their appointment.

During the 1999–2000 fiesta cycle, commissioners asked Tzintzuntzan households four times to make monetary offerings. The suggested donations depended on the commissioner as well as the person asked. Commissioners requested higher amounts from store owners. For February Fiesta, commissioners asked for between 300 and 400 pesos, at Corpus Christi they requested between 20 and 50 pesos, at the fiesta of San Francisco they requested up to 150 pesos, and for the Posadas[5] at Christmastime they requested between 40 and 100 pesos. If the suggested donation exceeds the family's ability or desire to pay, the household head may contribute a smaller amount or an appropriate quantity of food. In addition, family members and friends of commissioners devote time to helping coordinate the fiesta activities.

Paying the cooperaciones is both voluntary and negotiable, yet nearly every household gives something; on occasion they give more than requested. Theoretically, a family can be asked to donate the equivalent of seventy dollars a year for religious celebrations. That does not include contributions for civic ceremonies and life-cycle rituals that a household incurs during the year or the collection of alms during every Mass. Shortly before the Posadas began, I followed a pair of commissioners on their rounds soliciting contributions. Not a single family refused, though some gave more willingly than others. In most cases, the household head asked how much they were requesting, then gave it to them. The commissioners emphasized that the festivities belonged to everyone in the neighborhood and that all were welcome to participate regardless of their donation.

Cargos still exist in Tzintzuntzan, but they are no longer part of a ladder of leadership, nor are they limited to men. Vestiges of the old system remain in place to care for two chapels that belong to the community, not the parish. La Soledad, adjacent to the parish church, and the chapel of the Virgin of Guadalupe, in the settlement called Ojo de Agua, play central roles in the communitywide celebrations of Good Friday and December 12, respectively. Since the two buildings do not receive money from donations to the parish church for maintenance or utilities, teams of twelve cargueros take responsibility for their upkeep. Usually a married couple holds the cargo, one for each month of the year. During the month assigned to the couple, they clean the sanctuary, pay the parish priest to celebrate Mass there, and host a day-long feast which marks the end of their service and the handover to the next couple.

Even though having several cargo holders distributes the ritual expenses, the costs are still considerable. The proprietor of Tzintzuntzan's taco stand and his wife accepted the cargo of the Virgin of Guadalupe's chapel for May 2000. On the day of the monthly celebration, they decorated the chapel with flowers, paid for the priest and a band, and then served breakfast and lunch to all the cargueros and their guests. They killed a calf and two pigs for the occasion. The taco seller told me afterward, "We spent twenty-five thousand pesos [nearly twenty-five hundred dollars]. I don't know where it came from, but we did it." Cargueros from decades ago remember that the feasts used to be limited to the midday meal and the guests just the families of the cargueros. In recent years, the cargueros must serve breakfast as well, and the roster of invited guests has ballooned to three hundred or more. So elaborate is the celebration that cargueros liken their responsibility to putting on a wedding. In the case of La Soledad, which was undergoing renovation in

2000, the twelve cargueros could not find any successors willing to take on the burden of paying for the restoration, so they had to extend their commitment for another year until the project was completed.

In addition to the expenses associated with maintaining the church building, the cargueros also give up time during their assigned month. One carguero of La Soledad slept in the building every night while his wife and children stood guard during the day. Instead of accepting cargos as a way to gain authority in the community, most cargueros in Tzintzuntzan are motivated by religious vows. The taco seller's story is typical. "My wife and I didn't have a house. We made a vow to the Virgin that we would receive the cargo if she helped us build our house. We built it in three months and paid it off in a year, so we accepted the cargo." For him and his family, serving as cargueros repaid the Virgin for the blessings she had conferred on them. Rather than constituting a hierarchy of powerful offices, cargos in Tzintzuntzan have come to further a relationship of reciprocity with the divine.[6]

EXPANDING FIESTAS

In spite of the changes that migration and cost-sharing mechanisms have brought to Tzintzuntzan, Catholic fiestas have prospered and even expanded. The elaboration of the fiesta of the Holy Cross, which extends into every neighborhood, shows the importance locals continue to place on celebrations of community cohesion. Traditionally, Mexicans mark May 3 as the Day of the Holy Cross and a chance to honor bricklayers. On that day in 1945, when Foster began his fieldwork in Tzintzuntzan, local Catholics decorated eight stone crosses that usually stood unadorned, scattered through different neighborhoods. The festivities began at dawn with firecrackers, summoning the faithful to recite a rosary at the crosses. At night, the four people in charge of each cross offered food to those who had come to pray (Foster 2000:304).

In 2000, the May celebration began on a chilly Saturday night in January. While their wives, children, and extended family waited outside at long tables drinking brandy, four men sat at a table in the patio of a house on the edge of Tzintzuntzan to plan the celebration for their neighborhood. These four cargueros had volunteered at last year's fiesta to take responsibility for decorating the cross, praying at it, and sponsoring food and music in its honor. On the table, five candles arranged in a "T" shape pointed to a tall wooden cross painted red and decorated with a rosary and an image of the Virgin of Guadalupe. Behind the table, female relatives of the cargueros stirred simmering pots of *pozole,* a hominy stew. Firecrackers popped as the men began their conversation.

The Purépecha word for this event is *miyukwa,* meaning "count." In the past, the cargueros measured the expenses for the upcoming fiesta using maize kernels, each one representing one hundred pesos they were assigned to spend. This year, the bowl of kernels stood nearby for tradition's sake, but the men tallied their contributions on a calculator. First, the men discussed what day to hold their fiesta. No longer was there just a handful of crosses to honor on a single day. The crosses throughout the streets of Tzintzuntzan had multiplied to more than twenty, each with its own complement of cargueros. In 2000, celebrations began the evening of May 1 and continued every night until May 7.

After selecting May 2 for their celebration, the men debated the relative merits of an acoustic band versus an electric one. They set a limit of seven thousand pesos ($740) for the music and agreed to solicit demo tapes from a few bands. The deliberations went quickly. Two would provide breakfast for all the worshippers on the day of the celebration and two would provide the midday meal. All would bring firecrackers, candles, flowers, streamers, a three-tiered cake, and a bottle of alcohol. One man transcribed the agreed-upon duties and later distributed copies to his companions. After an hour, the men disbanded to the sounds of more firecrackers and joined their hungry families outside for pozole.

For the next few months, I regularly heard the pop of firecrackers in the evenings, indicating the convening of another miyukwa. On May 1, the cargueros of the cross in the adjacent community of Ojo de Agua sponsored an all-night bash accompanied by a ten-piece band and pozole and alcohol for all. Tzintzuntzeños feted at least two other crosses that night and three more on May 2. During the day on the second, the cargueros I had met in January, their wives, and close relatives sat vigil by their neighborhood cross, praying the rosary in its honor. The cargueros had cordoned off a street block and placed the cross in the center. A long table holding the cakes and bottles of brandy stood in front of the cross. Around 10 P.M. a crowd of one hundred people converged. The band set up a stage and played ranchera music at high volume while couples danced giddily in front of the cross. I asked one of the cargueros how long the party would last. "Until we find new cargueros," he replied. "Do you want to do it?" When I demurred, he said that if they waited someone would get drunk enough to take on the cargo; that was how he had accepted the job the previous year.

On the morning of May 3, the priest celebrated a Mass in the parish church. During the day, cargueros prayed the rosary at their respective crosses, feeding any worshippers who accompanied them. That night, Estela and I decided to visit as many crosses as we could. Usually she stayed at a cross where her friend or relative served as carguero, whereas teenagers tended to flit from cross to cross deciding which had the best music. We arrived at one cross just as four new cargueros had volunteered for duty. They performed a line dance in which the previous year's cargueros paraded with the cakes and bottles before handing them to their replacements. We walked on, listening for the next band. In two hours, we managed to receive servings of pozole from seven different crosses. The next night, four more bands arrived in Tzintzuntzan to celebrate four more crosses. Only one block separated two of them so that the electrified, amplified music of each band drowned out the other.

After four consecutive nights of daily praying and late-night partying, I went to bed early for the remaining three nights of the crosses. No one seemed to know exactly how many crosses existed in Tzintzuntzan, but most adults celebrated far more than the half-dozen or so they remembered from their childhood. Even as the celebration expanded, the role of the priest remained peripheral. Aside from a single Mass, the parish priest did not participate in the worship of the crosses. He did not determine which crosses merited cargueros. As Estela explained to me, "Tomorrow you, my two sons, and I will erect a cross outside the house. We'll sponsor a band and give out pozole. We'll hand over the cargo to whomever accepts that cake." Taking charge of a cross has become so customary that even local children have their own petite cross. Four children (sponsored by their parents) accept responsibility for putting on the fiesta each year. They hire a keyboardist, who plays music while the children eat pozole and cake.

A young woman studying to be a nun was as curious as I was about the development of the fiestas for the cross, so she asked her grandmother how the crosses used to be honored. When there was just a handful of crosses, the parties all fell on May 3, the grandmother recalled. Instead of fancy cakes worthy of a wedding, the cargueros offered a simple pastry ring. The priest celebrated a Mass at every cross. In 1995, before the young woman left for the convent, the cross celebrations had spread to May 1 in Ojo de Agua, May 2 in a neighborhood called Yaguaro, and May 3 in the churchyard. Soon after, the fiestas extended to May 4. "Now it's from Sunday to Sunday. They pray, look for new cargueros, and dance all night. It's such an expense now. I don't know why someone would want to receive the cargo." Other Catholic Tzintzuntzeños also questioned the validity of spending so much money on a lavish series of parties. Still, every year more crosses receive cargueros, and the cakes add more tiers, offering a joyous contrast to the solemn celebration of Lent and Easter in the prior months. The distribution of ritual costs across many households continues a trend away from the once popular civil-religious hierarchies.

To finance community fiestas, Catholics also have to take into account the substantial number of Tzintzuntzeños who spend most of the year in the United States. Contrary to the assumptions of many Tzintzuntzan Catholics, moving to a non-Catholic majority country does not tempt many migrants to lessen their faith. In fact, through the exporting of fiesta traditions, the making of vows, and the infusion of United States currency, migration actually fortifies Catholic faith. In Tacoma, Washington, Tzintzuntzeños have spread out to live in areas too dispersed to allow daily interaction. In addition, intense work schedules in "the North" make informal hanging out difficult. Regular church attendance is equally difficult since Sunday is often the only rest day in the week.

But they make time for fiestas. Two parish churches serve the Mexican population in Tacoma, both with Spanish-speaking North American priests who have visited Tzintzuntzan. One church marks December 12, the day of the Virgin of Guadalupe, with a procession and feast. The other church celebrates February Fiesta, Tzintzuntzan's largest fiesta of the year. On a Tuesday in February the week before Ash Wednesday, Tzintzuntzeños in Michoacán honor El Señor del Rescate (the Lord of Redemption), a painting of Jesus deemed responsible for saving the community from a smallpox epidemic a century ago. Tacoma's celebration falls on a Sunday to accommodate work schedules, but is no less festive. Estela's nephew painted a duplicate image which heads a procession around the neighborhood of the Tacoma church. Just as in Tzintzuntzan, all members of the migrant community contribute to the event. They rent a party hall, where after the Mass they serve beef to large crowds and watch traditional dances. In the future, the churches in Washington also plan to replicate the colorful celebrations of Corpus Christi and Easter.

Many migrants time their returns to Mexico to coincide with a major fiesta.[7] Even when they cannot attend in person, they contribute monetarily to the Tzintzuntzan celebrations. During February Fiesta, I spotted two handwritten posters next to the door outside the parish church in Tzintzuntzan. One listed the contributions made for the evening's pyrotechnic display. Only ten families in Tzintzuntzan gave donations above the minimum contribution asked from each household, totaling 3,450 pesos ($360). The second poster listed thirty-three families from Tacoma who had contributed to the fireworks. Their donations totaled $2,575.

The families in Chicago remain in contact with Tzintzuntzan even after years of living in the United States. Since the migrant community in Chicago is smaller than the one in Washington, they do not celebrate holidays on a large scale. Instead, when they attend Mass, they go to a parish with a Spanish-speaking "gringo" priest. The only times they all converge is for a life-cycle ritual. When one young woman in Chicago turned fifteen, her parents sponsored a *quinceañera* birthday party in true Tzintzuntzan style: hundreds of guests, a dozen godparents, four male escorts, two five-tiered cakes, a mariachi band, and a Mass. Only during these special occasions are migrants able to block out the cold weather, the long work hours, and the homesickness.

Another way that migration reinforces Catholic faith is through the offering of vows to saints. To lessen the peril of border crossing, many migrants turn to their Catholic faith. Traditional saint worship, in which a devotee promises sacrifice in return for a divinely assisted favor, fits the circumstances. In Tzintzuntzan, the most common manifestation of this devotion involves vows to the Santo Entierro, or Sacred Sepulcher, a waxy figure of the crucified Christ. He spends most of the year reclining in a glass coffin in La Soledad, but plays a central role in the parish's Easter re-creation of the events of Jesus' death when he stands on a crucifix between two criminals on Good Friday. In recent years, the wax figure has been growing miraculously. The caretakers of La Soledad added a glass extension to the Santo Entierro's case to accommodate his longer form. This inexplicable growth further reinforces belief in the image's supernatural powers.

For men, who are the majority of undocumented migrants, making a vow to the Santo Entierro is the most common way to tap into this power. In exchange for divine assistance in crossing the border, a man vows to go out as a penitent in gratitude to the Santo Entierro on a future Good Friday evening when he has returned from the United States. When Foster first saw the procession of Easter penitents in 1945, he doubted their sincerity. Hooded men with only a cloth covering their waists take off running while dragging a wooden cross over their shoulders. At several stations throughout the town, they kneel, recite prayers, and lash themselves with a nail-studded whip. The supposed gore of the spectacle did not impress Foster. He suspected that the penitents "cheated" on the more remote blocks, where no one would see them (Foster 2000:302).

Since the 1940s, adoration of the Santo Entierro has increased. Returning migrants attribute their successful crossing of the northern border to the image's holy intercession. A neighbor of mine reported that she saw several men at the parish church signing up to be penitents when she went to the priest to confess a few weeks before Easter. Each man made a voluntary contribution. Some gave fifty to one hundred pesos, she noticed, but the men who had returned from the United States paid up to one hundred dollars! Her four sons and two sons-in-law lived part of the year in Washington. On some visits to the United States, usually when they had prearranged work in Alaskan fishing boats, they carried the legal documents. Other times, they relied on a coyote to lead them across. She described how her sons left candles lit in front of the Santo Entierro just before their departure so that the saintly figure would guide them safely across the border.

While in the United States, migrants continue to rely on the munificence of the Santo Entierro. My neighbor recounted how a migrant from another Mexican community ended up imprisoned in Washington for a murder he had not committed. A Tzintzuntzeño he knew told him to pray to the Santo Entierro and promise that, if released, he would visit the image in Tzintzuntzan. A few days after the prisoner had prayed to the Santo Entierro, a mysterious lawyer from Mexico came to secure his release. The lawyer did not leave his name, but as he walked away, the prisoner could see a tall man with a beard. When he later came to Tzintzuntzan to offer thanks, he realized that the lawyer who had saved him was the Santo Entierro himself.

In exchange for a successful crossing, male migrants return to Tzintzuntzan to fulfill their vows to the Santo Entierro as penitents. As a Catholic friend explained to me, a vow must be something that constitutes a sacrifice. For instance, when she had chest pains, she made a vow to the Virgin of Health in Pátzcuaro. In return for healing her illness, she would not cut her hair for a year. "I'm bothered by long hair, so not cutting my hair is something that costs me. It wouldn't be effective to vow to go to Ixtapa [a beach resort] every weekend. You have to give up something." This sounded to me like a contradiction of the benevolent God image. So I asked her, "Does this mean the Virgin and saints want you to suffer?" "Yes," she replied.

Not until I saw the penitents myself did I understand how much the devoted made themselves suffer to please the divine. Around 9:30 P.M. on Good Friday in 2000 the first penitent left the churchyard wearing a white hood and a swath of white fabric around his waist. In one hand he held a rosary and a whip. Two helpers, called "cirineos," assisted the penitent in lifting a heavy wooden cross onto his bare shoulder. Then, they took off running. Less than five minutes later another penitent received a cross and began the procession. At 6 A.M., Estela's sixteen-year-old son served as cirineo to one of the last penitents to leave. He was number 320.

Starting at a stone cross in the middle of the churchyard, the penitent gives the cross to his helpers while he kneels in front of a makeshift altar. Using his rosary, he recites a silent prayer, then stands. Hopping from one foot to the other, he flays his bare back four to six times with a whip. Then, he immediately hefts the cross again, sprinting to the next altar. Depending on their vow, some men make a loop of the whole community, others just the churchyard, and some carry the cross all the way to the outlying settlement of Ojo de Agua. The penitents who pass through the streets make several stops along the way at curbside shrines where caretakers have set up flowers, candles, and religious images. When their penitent stops to pray, the cirineos remove shards of glass and pebbles from his bare feet. The entire penance takes from thirty minutes to an hour. By the time the penitents pass along the highway returning to the churchyard, their backs are streaming with blood.

The performance of penance follows certain unwritten rules that heighten the sacrifice. Penitents are not permitted to talk. If they fall or drop the cross, they must begin the route over again or go out as a penitent another year. When the last penitent completes his tour of the community, all the men form two lines to pass by the Santo Entierro, giving thanks for his aid. Most men vow to be penitents for more than two years. In their last year, they run the course in the opposite direction. But in further testament to the Santo Entierro's supernatural abilities, men claim that no whip wounds ever scar, and that all injuries heal within days.

Late on the night of Good Friday, I sat on the front stoop of Estela's house watching the silent parade. As soon as one man passed by, knelt to pray, and flagellated himself, another came into view. By then, the tourists had returned to their hotels, and the merchants had packed up their wares. I went inside at 3 A.M., still listening to the near constant sound of wooden crosses dragging across the asphalt outside my house. Contrary to Foster's interpretation, I saw real and unflinching self-castigation. Even when no one was watching but a sleepy anthropologist, the penitents vigorously lashed themselves with the nails tied to the end of the whip. The increase in migration fuels Catholic worship in Tzintzuntzan by giving men and their families a new source of uncertainty for which to seek saintly intervention. In their far-flung receiving communities, migrants also call on traditional religious practices to maintain their connections to Tzintzuntzan, which they see as integral to their identities.

TWO	DRINKING AND
	THE DIVINE IN
	CHIAPAS AND
	TZINTZUNTZAN

BEFORE getting settled in Tzintzuntzan, I made a pilgrimage to the National Museum of Anthropology in Mexico City, whose overwhelming two floors of exhibit halls illustrate the pre-Hispanic and contemporary lifeways of dozens of indigenous groups. I focused on the displays related to religion. In the hall devoted to present-day Maya peoples, I admired the life-sized dioramas depicting Catholic fiestas and the colorful attire of cargo holders. Given that the southern states boast the highest concentration of evangelical churches in Mexico, I found it curious that the wall labels made no mention of the Maya who have opted out of the Catholic fiesta system.

Then, in a corner partially obscured by a potted plant, I saw two dry-mounted color photographs. Each one showed a simple, fenced-in church with its name stenciled above the entrance. Both were Presbyterian churches in the state of Chiapas. Next to the photos, an explanatory label read in Spanish and English, "Since the 1960s outside religious beliefs and different churches, opposed to the old cargo system, have made inroads in the native communities in an ongoing search for supporters." The English translation stopped there, but the Spanish continued: "The presence of these churches has unleashed divisions in the communities, although in reality they only conceal the political and economic motives that are at the root of the conflicts" (my translation).[1] En route to study religious change in Michoacán, I was grateful that the curators had included this reference to new churches. However, their reluctance to make the knowledge of religious conflicts available to an English-reading audience made me feel as if I possessed a state secret.

CAUSING CONFLICT IN CHIAPAS

Where traditional religious hierarchies persist, the presence of evangelical converts has sparked bloody confrontations. Reports of religious violence by scholars and journalists in Chiapas indicate that local configurations of power help stoke conflict between members of different churches. As the museum label suggests, these conflicts between faiths often mask political and economic divisions. Municipal leaders, or *caciques,* in many indigenous Chiapas communities still derive their power from membership in a religious hierarchy that accords prestige to the men who shoulder expensive cargos. Evangelical nonparticipation in the fiesta system undercuts the financial and symbolic bases of cacique authority. In Tzintzuntzan, where cost-sharing mechanisms spread the costs of religious fiestas across the whole community, the absence of a cargo hierarchy permits the peaceful coexistence of several faiths.

San Juan Chamula, a municipality of eighty-two communities with nearly sixty thousand people in the highlands of Chiapas, illustrates how a tight cadre of leaders, backed by the state and federal governments, defends its position of power against challenges to the cargo system. Upon taking office in 1936 as the director of Chiapas's Department of Indigenous Protection (known by its Spanish initials as DPI), Erasto Urbina recruited bilingual, literate young men from Chamula and other indigenous communities to serve as liaisons rather than working through the older, more traditional, local leaders. In 1944, the DPI rescinded a previous ban on the sale of alcohol in indigenous municipalities and permitted religious officeholders to sell liquor to defray the costs of the cargos. In the subsequent rush of volunteers for cargo service, many of Urbina's handpicked young men entered the religious hierarchy and gained wider community acceptance (Rus 1994).

As the young men rose in local authority, state officials and nonindigenous elites helped augment their power in return for ensuring the control of their communities. By the 1950s, the bilingual liaisons had formed a ruling oligarchy in Chamula with a monopoly on the sale of alcohol (Crump 1987). Wealthy patrons lavished community leaders with gifts and perks. In 1976, one Chamula leader boasted two stores, five trucks, over two thousand hectares of land, a thriving money-lending business, and control of the sale of Pepsi, Coca-Cola, and beer for fifty thousand Chamulas. By way of gratitude, he blocked petitions from Chamula for agrarian reform, guaranteed certain wholesalers access to Chamula stores, and allowed merchants to underweigh produce bought from Chamula growers. Other community leaders around Chiapas silenced landowners who objected to road building and allowed the state oil company to drill on indigenous land.

When enterprising young Mayas challenged the authority of the entrenched leaders, the older men incorporated them into the religious cargo system. In the name of tradition and community unity, they made cargo service a prerequisite for selling alcohol or buying a truck. Unfortunately for the younger generation, fiestas have grown more elaborate and expensive from the time that the current leaders served their cargos in the 1940s.[2] An ethnographic film of one fiesta in Chamula depicts how the elaborate rituals and consumption of alcohol dominated the community for several days. The fiesta required one young cargo holder to spend his entire savings of ten thousand dollars, leaving him financially ruined, but affirming the power of the caciques (Anderson 1988). Without fear of government reprisal, caciques have summarily expelled from the community anyone who opposes the cargo system. Under these authoritarian conditions, many Mayas have sought alternate means of social organization. Some have turned to opposition political parties. Others have opted out of the Catholic faith altogether to join an evangelical church.

When Miguel Kaxlan, a Tzotzil Maya from Chamula, left the Catholic Church to become a leader in the Presbyterian Church, the Chamula caciques acted brutally to reassert their power. In 1982, he was kidnapped and hacked to pieces with machetes. No suspects were ever apprehended nor was any investigation opened. Gossen (1989) characterizes the story of Kaxlan's life as a microcosm for the struggle between traditionalist and modernizing forces in indigenous Chiapas communities. As Kaxlan's demise illustrates, the guardians of tradition have enough at stake in preserving their power base that they are willing to resort to violence when they feel their positions threatened.

Before Kaxlan became a Presbyterian, Gossen relates, he was a troublemaker. He grew up an orphan and as an adult became an alcoholic. His reputation in the community suffered even further when he abused his wife and let his children wander outside unclothed. Eventually, he left Chamula in shame as a result of accusations of burglary and his continued drinking. During the period that followed in the nearby city of San Cristóbal de las Casas, Kaxlan relied on his brother, an evangelical convert, for help finding a job. Through his brother, Kaxlan met a North American missionary couple, accepted a job translating the New Testament, and became a Presbyterian himself. He returned to Chamula a teetotaler to preach his religion to others. Although he had conquered his shameful behaviors, he was even less welcome in Chamula than before. The growing number of followers he converted attracted the negative attention of Catholics in the community, who in 1967 burned the homes of converts, forcing them to flee to San Cristóbal.

The resulting negative publicity from the unlawful expulsions forced the state government to intervene. The parties negotiated an arrangement that allowed converts to work their agricultural lands but not to live in the community of Chamula. However, this truce lasted only until 1974, when Chamula leaders declared the converts forever unwelcome. Since the municipal leaders belonged to the same political party that ruled the state and federal governments, the PRI, officials had little incentive to enforce constitutional guarantees to the freedom of religion. Still, Kaxlan persisted in bringing his complaints to government authorities and aligned himself with an opposition party called PAN. Some converts favored abandoning their property claims to establish a new community on the outskirts of San Cristóbal. Kaxlan led a faction of Presbyterians that sought the return of ancestral lands. Then, in 1982, on the pretense of speaking to him about the expropriation of land in Chamula, kidnappers captured and murdered Kaxlan. The government has made no attempt to investigate the crime; Gossen speculates that local authorities may even have orchestrated his murder.

Kaxlan would not be the last convert to lose his land or his life in Chiapas. The reaction of Chamula to evangelicals has been especially notorious. One local judge defended the policy of expelling non-Catholics: "Foreign religions are the disease of the Chamula, our number one enemy here. We expel families who no longer believe in the saints, who no longer want to use candles or incense" (McGreal 1989:10). The judge neglected to say that families who convert also tend to stop buying the ritual alcohol called *posh*, funds from which directly benefit local leaders. The growing number of non-Catholics also threatens the authority of the religious hierarchy, which, in the name of tradition, legitimizes caciques' power.

Calculations vary, but the most common figure for the number of Chamulas expelled from the municipality since the 1970s for their religion is thirty thousand (Bonner 1999; Limón and Clemente 1996; Sandoval 2000; Thompson 2000). Ramshackle settlements of displaced evangelicals with optimistic names like "New Hope" ring the city of San Cristóbal. The former Catholic bishop of San Cristóbal, a champion of indigenous peoples named Samuel Ruíz García, welcomed the refugees and even blessed their new homes (De

Witt 1998). Still, other converts faced with expulsion have chosen to fight to retain their property. In 1992, the expulsion of forty-four evangelicals from Chamula sparked a riot that left fifty-three people injured (Darling 1992). More recently, evangelicals and Catholics brawled over a proposed evangelical church in the Chiapas community of Plan de Ayala (Flores 2000). Some months later, I heard a Mexico City news report that Catholics in Plan de Ayala had destroyed nineteen homes belonging to evangelicals and expelled them from the community. Dismayed, the radio announcer paused after reading the news item to ask, "Who puts this in the heads of the Catholics?"

Several commentators have likened the intractable religious violence in Chiapas to the situation in Northern Ireland.[3] While the clear divisions between Catholics and Protestants may resemble fighting in Belfast, the conflict in Chamula and other indigenous communities is only incidentally about religion. Mexican anthropologist Stavenhagen puts it succinctly: "It is a conflict about power in a community where the actors are identified by their religion. Clearly [conversion] pulls the rug out from under traditional community controls and power" (quoted in Darling 1992). In Chamula, large numbers of evangelical converts threaten to undermine the authority of local power holders, many of whom benefit monetarily from Catholic traditions.

Chamula caciques themselves place the preservation of community traditions over affiliation with any specific religion. Since the 1970s, the parish church in Chamula has maintained only a tenuous link with the Catholic hierarchy. Objecting to the violent expulsions of converts, Bishop Ruíz withdrew the priest assigned to Chamula, so for many years Chamula had no official Catholic presence. More recently, the caciques have arranged for a Tzotzil-speaking priest to perform the basic sacraments, though they will not let him do much else. To enter the whitewashed church with blue and green trim in the center of Chamula, guests must purchase tickets from a municipal office. Inside, instead of the usual array of pews, worshippers sit on straw-strewn floors in front of any of dozens of glass-enclosed saint figures, decorated with multicolored ribbons and dangling mirrors. In front of each glass case, believers leave candles and bottles of Pepsi as offerings. The collective smoke from the hundreds of burning candles completely obscures the paintings of the main altar. A nearby ethnographic museum run by the community proudly states that they have mixed Catholic saints with pre-Hispanic gods. They believe the world is a cube supported by pillars surrounded by water. As the bishop of a neighboring diocese reports, there is no "authentic evangelization" in Chamula (Jeffrey 1997).

A Chamula cacique expressed no embarrassment about placing indigenous tradition over Catholic faith in the expulsion of religious converts: "To stay in their villages, they must follow our traditions. I told them life comes before religion. All they have to do is respect the old ways [and] say, 'I will accept my religious offices.' We will forgive them and accept them. For me there is no pure religion. There are only our customs" (Darling 1992). In the perspective of Chamula leaders, evangelical converts represent not a religious challenge, but a secular one, bent on destroying the customs that sustain local structures of authority. Given the political alliance between state and local caciques, Bastian (1996:306) believes that the act of religious conversion in Chiapas constitutes a "strike against a system of exploitation linked to the fiesta system" more than any spiritual statement. It is this battle for power, not the Catholic versus convert division, that underlies the explosions of violence in Chiapas.

Like Kaxlan, who came to support the PAN, many evangelicals in Chiapas have aligned themselves with opposition parties and even the Zapatista rebels to challenge the control exercised by local officials (Collier 1997; García Méndez 1997; Limón and Clemente 1996). Their religious conversion forms just part of a larger backlash against a political system that denies them power in the name of tradition. Sullivan (1998) offers an example of how, in opting out of a corrupt fiesta system, converts recuperate a traditional identity untainted by cacique greed. Her research in Chamula finds that most of the religious refugees in Chiapas originate in communities like Chamula where the cargo system is still strong and local caciques exercise tight control over dissenters (56). The converts she interviewed assume the role of "moral overseers" in Chamula, sifting through evangelical tenets to select the principles that best affirm an indigenous spirituality (3). Though their conversions may have triggered discord, evangelicals in Chamula aim to restore a more profound sense of balance to a community that has lost its equilibrium.

Recent elections in Chiapas have dislodged the PRI from national and state office, further weakening the authority of local caciques who deliver PRI votes in exchange for autonomy. Pablo Salazar, the opposition leader elected governor of Chiapas in 2000, is an evangelical Christian. In one of his first acts as governor, Salazar teamed with President Vicente Fox to address the Zapatista rebels and paramilitary groups fomenting violence in Chiapas (J. Smith 2000). He denounced the militarization of Chiapas under its former PRI governors and vowed to end bloodshed. And there have been reports from Chamula that expelled evangelicals have returned and even begun construction of a church there called "Prince of Peace" (Thompson 2000).

DOING ECUMENICAL RESEARCH

According to the 2000 national census, no Mexican state has a larger percentage of non-Catholics than Chiapas. Considering all denominations together, more than 22 percent of the state professes an evangelical faith. Some observers call these numbers conservative, suggesting the proportion of non-Catholics in the state may be as much as 40 percent (Giménez 1988). In contrast to the large numbers of evangelicals in the southern Mexican states, converts remain a distinct minority in Michoacán—fewer than ninety-five thousand of three and a half million people in the state and eleven families in Tzintzuntzan—but the numbers have risen rapidly since the 1980s. Another significant difference between Chiapas and Michoacán is the extent of each state's integration into the world economy. Chiapas's wealth of natural resources attracts foreign investment, but little of the profits extend to the largely uneducated and impoverished indigenous population. The cargo system there enriches the caciques while offering Indians only "a palliative [that] lessens the pain of subordination while doing nothing to eliminate its causes" (W. Smith 1977:40). By contrast, extensive migration to the United States has transformed both Michoacán's economy and the system of fiesta sponsorship. The system of spreading the cost of fiestas across the entire population neutralizes leaders who would otherwise derive power from coercing others' participation in communal events.

In the 1980s, families in and around Tzintzuntzan began to leave the Catholic Church to join one of a range of Christian churches that proselytize around Lake Pátzcuaro. Since there is no evangelical church building in Tzintzuntzan, converts meet in private homes for worship or travel to nearby communities. As part of my research, I too traveled to religious services in Santa Fe, Quiroga, Tzurumútaro, and Pátzcuaro. Twice I joined the peripatetic converts for worship in Morelia and once in Guadalajara, the capital of the adjacent state of Jalisco. Although the converts in Tzintzuntzan remain few, they connect to a larger network in the area of thousands of believers, many of whom spoke to me about their experiences.

During my research, I visited fourteen different congregations around Lake Pátzcuaro, including the Catholic Church in Tzintzuntzan (see Map 1). Since observing and participating at each church required a significant outlay of time, I focused on five evangelical groups and the Catholic parish. I attended services and spoke with leaders and laity at all the churches, and participated more fully at the five churches geographically closest to Tzintzuntzan and the single largest evangelical congregation in the region. Choosing

M a p 1   The state of Michoacán and the Lake Pátzcuaro region. From *Power and Persuasion: Fiestas and Social Control in Rural Mexico*, by Stanley Brandes. Copyright © 1988 University of Pennsylvania Press. Reprinted with permission.

the churches by geography was not just a matter of convenience. A church's location largely determined who would attend. One Tzintzuntzan convert family began as members of a large evangelical congregation in Pátzcuaro, but eventually stopped going because it was thirty minutes away by bus and on the side of a busy highway. In another case, a convert family from Pátzcuaro worshipped at a church in Tzurumútaro, a small town on the way to Tzintzuntzan. They preferred that church to others in their own city since the wife's family resided in Tzurumútaro, and they could have Sunday lunch with them after services.

Before attending my first service at a given church, I would introduce myself to the pastor and conduct a semistructured interview about the church's history, doctrine, and administration. I explained to all the pastors that I was attending several denominations as part of a study on the religious diversity of Lake Pátzcuaro. In every case, they introduced me to the congregation (sometimes asking me to speak) and explained why I was there. On a typical Sunday during my yearlong fieldwork, I attended a Jehovah's Witness meeting in the morning in Quiroga, a Pentecostal service in La Colonia at midday, and a Catholic Mass in the evening. Other Sundays, I would start with a morning worship service in Ichupio, midday Mass in Tzintzuntzan, and an evening prayer meeting in Pátzcuaro. During the week, I participated in Bible studies or arranged interviews with converts and Catholics in their homes.

I spent the most concentrated time in the following six churches:

1. The Roman Catholic Church in Tzintzuntzan: Led by Father Rogelio and part of the Archdiocese of Morelia, this congregation meets in the parish church in Tzintzuntzan. The church serves more than three thousand members with Masses daily. Franciscan monks founded the parish in the 1520s. Other members of the Catholic Church who appear in the following chapters are Father Huacuz, Father Gilberto, Estela, Miguel, Yunuen, Diana, Marta, Barbara, and Luz.

2. Nueva Vida en Cristo (New Life in Christ) in Santa Fe de la Laguna: Dr. John Cook founded this group in 1998 as part of his chain of evangelical missions. He installed an indigenous pastor in the community to lead services twice a week for forty-five people. The doctor himself travels throughout Michoacán supporting his pastors and offering free medical consultations. Members of his ministry include Alejandra and Rodrigo (who is also a Catholic).

3. Jehovah's Witnesses in Quiroga: This congregation of eighty people forms part of a larger religious network based in Brooklyn, New York. Since the late 1980s, the group has been meeting three times a week in an unmarked rented room. The Tzintzuntzan members hold a Bible study session each week in a private home there. A Jehovah's Witness family from Tzintzuntzan, who live most of the year in Fort Worth, Texas, lend their house to a church leader. Two additional Jehovah's Witness congregations meet in Pátzcuaro. Norma and Ricardo attend Jehovah's Witness meetings in Quiroga, Tzintzuntzan, and Pátzcuaro.

4. The family of Odilón Sánchez in Ichupio: Odilón and his wife Antonia were the first people in the immediate area of Tzintzuntzan to leave the Catholic Church, doing so in 1983. He began a congregation in his home, preaching four times a week for his family and an elderly woman who comes from Tzintzuntzan to attend the services.

5. The family of Nestor Ocampo in La Colonia: He is a cousin of Odilón's and became an evangelical in the Ichupio church. After meeting

Pastor Orozco, a preacher from a town near Pátzcuaro, in 1992, Nestor allowed him to hold services in his home. Every Sunday fifty people from La Colonia, Pátzcuaro, and small communities in between congregate in Nestor's home for worship. They meet once a week without the pastor as well. Sara and Sergio from Tarerio worship regularly with Nestor and sometimes with Odilón.

6. Centro Cristiano Emanuel (Emanuel Christian Center, or CCE) in Pátzcuaro: A missionary couple from Seattle founded this church in 1994, and it grew to become the largest non-Catholic congregation on Lake Pátzcuaro. The founders began a mission in Uruguay in 1998, leaving a Mexican pastor in charge of CCE. He and his family live behind the church in its prominent location along the highway to Morelia. The 250 members attend services twice a week plus another meeting with a smaller Bible study group. Some Tzintzuntzan converts attended the services under the original pastors.

There were eight other congregations that I visited occasionally throughout the year. These did not have any Tzintzuntzeños as members, but they illustrate the diversity of spiritual organizations in the area:

1. Assemblies of God in Pátzcuaro: Since 1997 they have met in a plain building on the outskirts of the city, led by a pastor from Morelia. He conducts services five times a week for about twenty-five people.

2. Baptist Church in Pátzcuaro: This church dates from 1945, making it the oldest non-Catholic church and one of two mainline denominations in the area. Its forty members meet four times a week in a large hall near the center of the city. A full-time pastor and his family live next to the church. Gloria and her sister belong to the Baptist Church.

3. Torre Fuerte (Strong Tower) in Pátzcuaro: In 1995, members of the Baptist Church, frustrated in their attempts to introduce ecstatic forms of worship, split off to found this church. They have grown to ninety members, meeting twice a week. Their success has enabled them to purchase land for building a permanent home and to begin searching for a full-time leader.

4. Puerta de Salvación (Door of Salvation) in Pátzcuaro: In 2000, three members of Torre Fuerte left to found this small mission to bring their message of healing by faith to a neighborhood not previously served by an evangelical church. They meet twice a week in the home of their

pastor, a roving missionary originally from the Michoacán coast. In their first two months as a church, they claimed fifteen members.

5. Luz del Mundo (Light of the World) in Pátzcuaro: This church holds services for its 120 members eight times a week in a modern building in a residential area. The pastor, who lives above the church, comes from Guadalajara, where this organization has its world headquarters. I spoke with Juan, a church member in Guadalajara.

6. Iglesia Apostólica Manantial (Fountain Apostolic Church) in Pátzcuaro: The Mexican pastor founded this church in 1994 after having lived in California. The forty members meet in a large room adjacent to his house near the lakeshore three times a week.

7. Presbyterian Church in Pátzcuaro: This mainline denomination has met in its rented hall since 1970, but membership totals only fifteen people, at least four of whom are the pastor and his family, from Morelia. They hold services once a week.

8. Nueva Vida en Cristo in Tzurumútaro: This community lies between Tzintzuntzan and Pátzcuaro. Missionaries from the United States founded the congregation in 1972, but in 1995 an indigenous member of the Presbyterian Church in Pátzcuaro took over as pastor. In 1999 the pastor met Dr. Cook and agreed to fold his church into Cook's chain. The twenty-five members meet once a week.

In addition, one church closed in 1999 before I could visit. Una Voz Que Clama en el Desierto (A Voice That Cries Out in the Desert) splintered from Centro Cristiano Emanuel in Pátzcuaro, establishing itself in a member's courtyard. After a year, the pastor borrowed money from the wife of the man who lent the space and disappeared. The members returned to worshipping at Centro Cristiano Emanuel.

The litany of churches suggests both the vitality and tenuousness of the conversion movement. The region sustains a full range of Christian churches, with the congregations most rigid in their prohibition of alcohol and emphatic in the imminence of the Apocalypse attracting the most members. Still, most evangelical churches have fewer than fifty members, compared to the several thousand parishioners who worship in the Catholic Church. In terms of longevity, the evangelical churches also lag far behind the Catholic Church; most of the evangelical congregations trace their origins back less than a decade.

By emphasizing the relative quantitative insignificance of evangelicals in Michoacán, I do not mean to underestimate their perceived presence. The evangelical nature of the new churches calls them to the attention of the majority. Every week Jehovah's Witnesses from Quiroga pass door-to-door offering magazines and invitations to services, and Odilón and Nestor, both of whom drive pickup trucks through Tzintzuntzan regularly on personal errands, encourage acquaintances to attend their meetings. In response to proselytizing, the Catholic Church issues publications to educate parishioners about evangelical groups who may approach them. A weekly diocesan newsletter sold door-to-door in Tzintzuntzan regularly features question-and-answer columns in which readers write in for more information about other religions. At Catholic bookstores in Morelia, I found pamphlets with such suggestive titles as "I Was a Jehovah's Witness" and "100 Questions to Ask a Mormon."

In Tzintzuntzan, evangelical faiths coexist peacefully with the majority Catholic Church, with members of both faiths living on the same blocks and shopping at the same stores. In fact, Catholics around Lake Pátzcuaro frequently impressed on me the importance of mutual tolerance. One Catholic potter worried about his young son, who suffered from epilepsy. When he told me he and his wife were praying for the boy's recovery, I asked if he had tried attending services at any evangelical churches, many of which claimed powers of healing. He mused:

> All religions have their gods—maybe one will help my boy. But, no, I haven't tried a new religion. We've had the same religion for hundreds of years. The new religions are okay as long as they don't try to change our traditions. I know they expel religious converts in Chiapas, but one has to respect all religions. We all arrive at the same place.

I found this father better informed than most people who live around the lake—at another point he quoted me Marx's maxim that religion is the opiate of the masses—but still representative of the acceptance Catholics in Michoacán feel for evangelicals. Even the most disparaging critics end their reproach of evangelicals with a resigned, "To each his own."

Several times during my fieldwork in and around Tzintzuntzan, I heard people say, "All religions are good." For me, this phrase came to replace the mantra Foster had heard until the 1960s and came to encapsulate the lack of animosity between evangelicals and Catholics in Michoacán. This ecumenical outlook differs sharply from interfaith relations in other regions of Mexico, as the potter's comments suggest. Had I conducted fieldwork in Chiapas, I likely would not have found the same willingness among my neighbors to speak so thoughtfully and even self-critically about religion. I attribute the comfort Tzintzuntzeños felt in expressing their opinions partly to a familiarity with ethnographers, but I found the same tolerant spirit in nearby communities that have never hosted an anthropologist. By replacing the hierarchy of cargos with fiesta cost-sharing, Catholics in Tzintzuntzan have prevented Chamula-style caciques from rising to power. No cadre of leaders gains prestige or income from the observance of Catholic festivals. Unlike the political protest that religious conversion in Chiapas registers, leaving the Catholic Church in Michoacán does not undermine the structures of community organization since participants in traditional celebrations do not rely on a select few individuals to shoulder the burden of fiesta sponsorship. For evangelicals in Tzintzuntzan, the decision to convert is not framed in opposition to a domineering majority, but rather in relation to personal or familial crises. In particular, the affliction of alcoholism motivates men and women to seek alternative spiritual spaces where they can repair their lives.

BATTLING THE BOTTLE

In the evangelical churches around Lake Pátzcuaro, religious leaders encourage their followers to see themselves as enlightened minorities besieged by a sinful majority. Sermons and hymns prepare converts for the contest against Satan's minions that they must endure before achieving the ultimate reward. However, converts perceive this struggle as an internal battle between temptation and self-discipline, not as a call to attack nonbelievers. In Tzintzuntzan and elsewhere, men and women take on different roles in this battle, and, significantly, they approach conversion from different perspectives. In Colombia, women convert first and then pressure their husbands to join the church (Brusco 1995). Even secular transformations follow this trend. Frye (1996:34) describes how a Mexican Catholic woman experienced a "conversion" to Amway sales and then persuaded her husband to join her. In Tzintzuntzan, after being proselytized, women nearly always initiate the process of conversion as a way to escape an environment made intolerable by an alcoholic husband. Men, on the other hand, tend to convert later, in response to their wives' subtle pressure and encouragement. In most cases, the husband eventually joins the rest of his family in attending the evangelical church. If not, at least the suffering wife immerses herself and her children in an alcohol-free environment where like-minded women offer her support.

Norma and her husband, Ricardo, typify many evangelical families. As a retired schoolteacher, Ricardo receives a modest pension, which he supplements through selling toys he makes out of wood and playing in a band hired out for fiestas. Their two-story house is more solidly built than many of their neighbors', and they enjoy a modern entertainment center with television and stereo. Still, with four children at home, one of whom is frequently ill, Norma and Ricardo face many expenses. Ricardo's drinking problem was an additional burden.

Women have little recourse to counter the debilitating effects of a husband who drinks. Even in economic straits, Tzintzuntzeño men still insist on their role as primary breadwinner and give their wives the money they deem necessary to run the household. As the wife of an alcoholic, Norma received insufficient funds to carry out her duties and had to contend with all too frequent abuse. Evangelical churches explicitly prohibit the consumption of alcohol, linking it to forces of evil. When Norma, distressed by her husband's drinking, heard from a visitor about a place that forbids alcohol and preaches the importance of healthy families, she found the message appealing.

A Jehovah's Witness superintendent, the man appointed to oversee several regional congregations, told me that often women are the first to convert, and then they convince their husbands to join the new religion. This was the pattern with Norma. "I think it's because women are better listeners," she said by way of explanation. When Jehovah's Witness proselytizers first came to her home, she was skeptical, but listened to them and took some of their literature. As she heard and read more, she came to appreciate the strict biblical base of their teachings. After she started going to services more regularly, she tried to persuade Ricardo to join. She took him to a two-day assembly as an introduction to the Jehovah's Witnesses. Waving a dismissive hand toward the Tzintzuntzan churchyard after one Catholic fiesta, Norma told me, "Unlike the mess left by the Catholic fiestas, the assemblies are spotless. There is no grime. People bring cold lunches, so the vendors know not to come, and no one leaves trash. They have first aid, lost and found, and signs telling parents to silence their children. There is no pushing or jostling. Even the bathrooms smell good!" The organization and strong scriptural emphasis of the event impressed Ricardo, he later told me. "Fiestas in themselves aren't bad, but they have to be *ordered*."[4]

When I met Norma, she was in her living room talking amiably with her sister-in-law. Her niece interrupted to introduce me, explaining that I was doing a project on religion and wanted to learn about all the different churches around Tzintzuntzan. After inviting me to sit down, Norma spoke eagerly and without further prompting. "Since becoming a Jehovah's Witness, my life has changed. Before my husband used to drink, and now he doesn't. Others think we get paid for joining the church, get new clothes and a new car, but I stay with them because I learn. It is God who will pay us someday." During this testimony, Yunuen, her sister-in-law, remained quiet, so I assumed she also worshipped with the Jehovah's Witnesses.

When Norma turned to how she disapproved of the drunkenness at community fiestas, Yunuen spoke up in defense of the Catholic Church. She willingly paid the cooperaciones for the religious holidays, she said. The money raised went to pay for bands, not to the church. Since her family played in a band, she understood how bands needed business. "Besides," she continued,

> I like to dance. God doesn't want us to stay in a corner with no laughing and no dancing. That would be a sad world. I find the traditions of the town beautiful. They are worth preserving. The priest doesn't prohibit anything. He says, "Everything in moderation." Sometimes I go to Mass, sometimes I don't. I have never read the Bible, but I don't need to because I can go to Mass and hear the priest tell me the same themes. I was raised Catholic. My parents inculcated it in me. I won't switch. I respect Norma, but it would be a sad world if we were all of one kind.

Norma responded defensively,

> I was Catholic too, but I never learned what I know now. I'm very grateful. I've seen the benefits. My husband is a better spouse and a better father. What he saves on alcohol, he spends on the house, on the children. Before I used to worry that he was out wandering the streets. This has been the biggest benefit.

Yunuen replied, "I also had a problem with my husband's drinking, but I was just resigned to it. Now we're content. He was just at that age. Now he's stopped drinking."

The first and most important benefit of conversion for Norma is that her husband has stopped drinking alcohol. While she does criticize the Catholic Church, she does not offer this as a reason for conversion. Rather, she compares her years as a Catholic unfavorably to what she experiences with the Jehovah's Witnesses. The most noticeable difference for her and her family has been her husband's sobriety.

In 1999, I attended a Jehovah's Witness assembly in Morelia with Norma and her husband, Ricardo, where church leaders claimed to have representatives in 233 countries and counted nearly 6 million members. Jehovah's Witnesses began evangelizing in Mexico in 1893 (Fortuny Loret de Mola 1995). In the early 1990s, Jehovah's Witness growth reached 6 percent a year, among the highest of any religious group in Mexico (Fortuny Loret de Mola 1996:194). After the United States, Mexico is home to the largest population of Jehovah's Witnesses—half a million "publishers," as they call their baptized members. Although national numbers are difficult to verify, some twelve thousand of their members journeyed to fill the main soccer stadium in Morelia for the three-day assembly. In Tzintzuntzan, five families worship with the Jehovah's Witness congregation in Quiroga.

Their theology is extremely literal. They apply contemporary events to the Book of Revelation, with its fantastic seven-headed beasts and apocalyptic battle scenes, indicating that God will soon destroy creation. By mining allusions to periods of time in chapters of Daniel and Revelation, the church leaders predicted several times in the early twentieth century that the world would come to an end, only to revise their calculations when the expected date passed without calamity. Finally their theologians concluded that Jesus had already begun his reign in heaven and had started preparing for Judgment Day in 1914 since the symbolism of World War I best fit the omens presented in the Bible. This also saves them from the repeated embarrassment of explaining foretold apocalypses that never arrive. Given the imminence of destruction, converting and behaving in an approved manner become imperative because only the faithful will be rewarded with eternal life. Yet, even among the select, just 144,000 souls will be with Jesus in heaven while the remaining Jehovah's Witnesses—the "other flock," as the Bible calls them—will enjoy a terrestrial paradise.

The intricacies and history of Jehovah's Witness doctrine are not revealed succinctly in any of the numerous publications that the organization distributes. It took me months of twice-weekly Bible study meetings in addition to probing questions asked of the congregation elders to sketch the contours of their beliefs. What new members do learn quickly is that the church forbids most "worldly" activities, such as drinking, and it espouses political passivity.[5] At the assemblies and in subsequent meetings, the Jehovah's Witnesses insist that Scripture prohibits drinking alcohol. As confirmation, they point to verses from Proverbs. Proverbs 23:20–21 reads: "Do not be among winebibbers, or among gluttonous eaters of meat; for the drunkard and the glutton will come to poverty, and drowsiness will clothe them with rags."[6] Proverbs 20:1 says: "Wine is a mocker, strong drink a brawler, and whoever is led astray by it is not wise." To me, these passages do not support the vehemence of the Jehovah's Witness sermons in condemning alcohol; further, Proverbs 31:6–7 seems to condone drinking: "Give strong drink to one who is perishing, and wine to those in bitter distress; let them drink and forget their poverty, and remember their misery no more." Given the severity of alcohol consumption among converts in Michoacán, I understand the added emphasis Jehovah's Witness leaders place on abstention.

Ricardo admits that he used to drink heavily. Looking back at his life before converting, he is amazed he survived: "If you put alcohol on meat it will cook. Imagine what drinkers do to their bodies!" A Jehovah's Witness leader talking to Ricardo and me after a Bible study class made explicit how conversion relates to alcoholism: "There are two reasons to change religions: One—you avoid problems like drunkenness, drugs, immorality, sexually transmitted diseases, and fighting with your parents. Two—you please God as He wants to be pleased." I found it revealing that, according to this pastor, pleasing God came second to stopping drinking. Ricardo certainly considers that his sobriety contributes to his strong relationship with God. When I asked him how conversion had changed his life, he said it made him feel more "clean" and "pure." Other Jehovah's Witnesses characterize the move to a new church as a shift from "undisciplined to disciplined." To one woman, joining the church is tantamount to a spiritual housecleaning.

Before he was a Jehovah's Witness, Ricardo attended Mass every week at the Catholic Church, often with his brother's family. He also played in the band his brother managed, earning money by providing entertainment at Catholic celebrations. In retrospect, the decision to leave the faith he was raised in was difficult for Ricardo. "We adored images in the Catholic Church. Holy images were very important to us. It was very difficult to give up the traditions of so many of our ancestors." Conversion becomes such a transformative experience precisely because it requires the abandonment of long-accepted ways of being and believing. Although he continued to play in the band after converting, Ricardo gradually distanced himself from his previous way of life as a Catholic. Norma's family, who live in Pátzcuaro, had also joined the Jehovah's Witnesses, so Ricardo found himself spending less time with his brother and more time with his in-laws. He feared that being around Catholics might tempt him to return to drinking.

There is tremendous pressure to drink alcohol in the Lake Pátzcuaro area because it is a central element of the numerous traditional Catholic fiestas. A medical doctor in Quiroga who treats alcoholics expressed the embarrassment he feels around colleagues at national conferences. When he identifies himself as being from Michoacán, they exclaim, "Oof!" When he proceeds to tell them he is from the Lake Pátzcuaro region, they groan even louder, "Oooof!" Tzintzuntzan, Santa Fe, and Quiroga, communities that retain a full calendar of traditional religious celebrations, form ground zero of the alcohol epidemic in Mexico. The doctor understands why the Lake Pátzcuaro region is so infamous in medical circles. He attributes the constant consumption of alcohol mostly to the frequent community and familial fiestas:

> Every year forty-five people in Quiroga die from alcohol. The majority are between sixteen and twenty-eight years old, but I've seen two cases of nine-year-olds with liver cirrhosis. Most drinkers are on a march to the tomb. At the fiestas of the patron saint, alcohol. At baptisms, alcohol. At first communions, alcohol. At fifteenth birthday parties, alcohol. At weddings, alcohol. At funerals, alcohol. There's alcohol at every event. Many will give up drinking for Lent, but then on Easter Sunday make up for all that they missed. There exists the idea that a party with little alcohol is a small party. However, it's a grand bash if there's lots of alcohol, even if the music, the salon, and the people are the same.

His description matches my own experience as a guest at many Catholic fiestas. When I wanted to avoid drinking so I could observe the event closely, I had to resort to a variety of improbable excuses to placate the hosts.

Expectations for local people to drink at fiestas are even higher than for outsiders. An older Tzintzuntzan man who quit drinking after throat surgery recounted the difficulty he had in attending the fiestas that accompany life passage rituals. "It used to be dangerous to go to a wedding. When I stopped drinking, my friends would say, 'Why did you come to the fiesta if you don't want to drink?'" On one occasion, his peers poured alcohol on his head to provoke a fight. Except for the celebrations of close relatives and friends, he stopped attending fiestas. While typically men drink the most flagrantly, women and children also participate enthusiastically (Figure 2.1). I saw kindergartners tipsy from beer at weddings. A woman suffering from diabetes acknowledged that at fiestas her friends insisted that she drink even after she refused to do so. More than once she gave in, despite knowing that she would suffer later.

The Catholic Church does not condone drinking in excess, but priests seem resigned to accept periodic episodes of widespread inebriation. One retired priest blames endemic drinking on the persistence of tradition among indigenous and mestizo peoples in this part of Mexico. "They are very at-

2 . 1 At the celebration following a Catholic wedding, the godparents form a line and dance with bottles of rum. I asked a private doctor in Morelia for the medical explanation of alcohol consumption. "The people in the villages," he said, "get drunk because there's nothing else to do. It's not the drinking of the urban professionals. It's social and communal."

tached to their traditions," he explained to me. "It is part of the culture; it's almost a ritual to drink." No matter how much authority a priest carried, he could not change drinking patterns permanently. In one instance, he remembered, a priest in a community on the lake asked his parishioners to abstain from drinking in honor of a visit from the bishop. They did, but as soon as the honored guest left, they began drinking again in earnest. In an episode from his tenure as Tzintzuntzan's priest, the father recounted how he traveled to a small settlement to collect the list of volunteer caretakers for the chapel there. Men and women from the community accepted responsibility for maintaining many of the parish chapels that did not come under the direct control of the priest. Before the meeting he had asked the men to limit their drinking, but when he arrived, he found that, without alcohol, no man had mustered the nerve to accept the expensive responsibility. After he left, the men drank heartily and within a day had delivered to him a list of cargueros for the coming year.

Father Huacuz, who once served in the Tzintzuntzan parish, also feels powerless to affect his flock's drinking habits. "All fiestas and the taking on of cargos involve alcohol. And in Tzintzuntzan, there is always a fiesta: baptisms, weddings, and fifteenth birthday parties. They drink in excess. You tell them and warn them, but they don't understand. It goes in one ear and out the other. They find refuge in alcohol." He feels the only natural brake on the amount of drinking is price, and for that reason he is grateful so many of his parishioners are poor. Twenty years ago, when he was ministering in Tzintzuntzan, he used to buy the drunks a bottle of liquor and send them home so that they would not disrupt the fiesta. I asked him if he thought this reliance on alcohol might change.

> No. You see many of the young people starting to drink at fiestas. When they celebrate the Holy Cross, they have to motivate people to receive the cargo by getting them drunk. But fiestas are life. They make everyone a family. Fiestas are the tree that everyone gathers under for shade. The people enjoy a fiesta. Even with computers and new means of communication, you can't get rid of them. Look how now they are using calculators for the miyukwas!

When Father Rogelio took over the Tzintzuntzan parish, one of his goals was to reduce alcohol consumption by stressing that drinking is a sin. However, he implements his work in a weak fashion. In one sermon, he referred to the vice of alcohol as a type of slavery, but made no explicit condemnation. At the end of Mass on fiesta days, he would offer oblique reminders that the celebration should be in a "Christian" manner. He never delivered an unambiguous denouncement of drinking and never sought to minister to those men who did not come to church on Sundays. When an Alcoholics Anonymous group in Tzintzuntzan invited him to speak during its anniversary week, he agreed to participate but then never showed up.

Before Catholic priests can preach abstention from alcohol effectively, they must confront their own relationship to the bottle. Tzintzuntzeños gossip privately about priests so drunk at fiestas that they cannot lead a procession, but the first time I heard the topic addressed publicly was when a Catholic priest spoke at a regional Alcoholics Anonymous outreach event. José Guadalupe introduced himself to the 150 or so AA members and their families in a Quiroga ballroom by saying, "I am an alcoholic and I am a Catholic priest." After a pause, he continued, "It took me a long time to accept that." Father José Guadalupe contended that there were many alcoholic priests, but very few who admitted to their condition. He explained to us the vulnerability of priests to alcoholism: "I felt the consecrated wine would do me no harm. The priest is invited to weddings, baptisms, first communions, and funerals. The first thing they give you is a glass of liquor. I arrived at AA destroyed." Anthropologists also feel the obligation to express their respect for priests through alcohol. Whenever the Fosters arrive in Tzintzuntzan, they always bring a bottle of Jack Daniel's to the priests they have befriended.

Fueled by money from returning migrants, alcohol consumption occurs outside fiestas as well. I heard complaints about men passed out in the streets at midday and some grumbling from Estela when she had to sweep away the broken glass and bottle tops left outside her juice stand. But rarely does the annoyance turn to anger. For instance, the deceased artisan they call respectfully Tata Plácido[7] is known to have been an inveterate drunk. Yet, his talent as a wheat straw weaver and his willingness to share his innovations earn him unanimous praise. After he died, one of the artisanry shops on the main street took the name "Tata Plácido" in his honor. When I asked Estela why people in Tzintzuntzan remember him so fondly if he was a drunkard, she explained to me a subtle difference. "*Borracho*," the word I used for "drunkard," refers to the good-for-nothings who never do any work since they usually are passed out on the sidewalk. *Borrachito*, with the diminutive ending, means "little drunkard" and refers to men like Tata Plácido who mischievously drink too much but usually in approved settings without harming anyone and still managing to provide for their families.

Unknowingly, I already had made the distinction. Every so often, I would be walking to a friend's house when a man would stagger over to me reeking of alcohol. Some were courteous and easy to brush aside; others seemed intent on engaging in a slurred debate about the United States and Mexico. One man physically restrained me when I tried to excuse myself from a conversation. He followed me down the main street, grabbing my arm until I could twist away. Estela told me that one night she was seated on the front step of her house and saw a couple coming back from a party, both drunk. They began to fight playfully until the husband knocked down the wife and kicked her. Estela jumped up and surprised the man with a punch to the mouth. Such men are the borrachos, those who violate social conventions by acting erratically and sometimes violently. They do not fill the role of father and husband properly, thus earning the opprobrium of the community. On the other hand, I knew borrachitos, men who drink to excess at socially sanctioned occasions and without compromising their ability to support a family. The community regards these men with affection.

I came to understand the difference during the weeklong celebration of El Señor del Rescate in February when Tzintzuntzan sponsored two days of *jaripeo,* or rodeo. In a typical year, there would be only one or two jaripeos in Tzintzuntzan, yet they built a special stone arena accommodating hundreds of spectators on the outskirts of town solely for that purpose. The rodeos attract so many people that even though the procession of the holy image (in whose honor the community threw the fiesta) was scheduled for the same time as the first jaripeo, the stands were filled to overflowing to watch the bulls. Unlike rodeos in the United States, jaripeos in Michoacán carry a distinctly Catholic flavor. At the beginning of the event, all the riders line up, kneel, and remove their hats while the announcer leads a prayer to God, the so-called "Rider of Apocalypse." Before rising, the men all make the sign of the cross in the dirt of the bullring floor. When his turn to mount arrives, each rider makes the sign of the cross again and tucks an image of a saint into his hat. Rodeos almost exclusively take place in conjunction with a community's patron saint celebration. Under previous priests, the holy procession followed the rodeo, and the priest would make an announcement at the event.

The rodeo organizers contract out to a professional team that provides ten swaggering riders and ten surly bulls. After assistants corral the animal into a pen, where they cover its horns, the rider drops on top of him as the door of the pen swings open. Most of the riders manage to stay on the bull for the thirty seconds or so until the handlers lasso the creature. Despite the potential for serious harm, the atmosphere of the rodeo is pure circus. Vendors sell cotton candy to children, clowns in drag flirt with boys, and all the men drink alcohol. As some men drink, they gain more courage. By the fifth bull or so during the fiesta, several men had wandered onto the arena floor (see Figure 2.2). The majority of the time, while the bull was being readied in the pen, there was no danger in standing on the dirt floor. However, a six-foot stone wall separated the floor from the seating, so in a moment of danger, a man would have to scramble up the wall quickly to escape. One bull that afternoon put up a particularly fierce fight when the handlers tried to steer

2.2 During February Fiesta, the *jaripeo* arena in Tzintzuntzan fills up with spectators, including some drunk men who stand in the ring with the bulls. The white dome of the parish church is visible in the background.

him into the pen. When he was finally subdued and mounted, he put up little resistance to the rider. After the rider dismounted, the assistants tried to rope in the bull, but missed. Newly enraged, the bull charged a group of drunken men standing along the wall inside the arena. Before the handlers could subdue the bull, the animal picked up one with his horns and tossed him into the air. Although it was gruesome to watch, I found it difficult to have any sympathy for the victim. He was drunk and standing inside a bullring. Before his run-in with this particular bull, he recoiled in mock terror when bulls came near, but always returned to his spot with his fellow drinkers, laughing.

The people I spoke to in Tzintzuntzan did not feel the same way I did. One woman expressed great concern for the victim, who was her *compadre* (i.e., he served as godparent to one of her children). A few months after the incident, she told me that he had been a carguero of La Soledad and the miraculously growing sculpture there for thirteen years. When he saw the bull charging toward him, he invoked the saint he had cared for, "Santo Entierro, take care of me as I took care of you for many years." She reported happily that he had emerged from the hospital with just a fractured rib. Her compadre is a "little drunkard." His drinking does not harm anyone but himself;

it may even serve to strengthen his ties to his male friends. Drinking at a rodeo is an acceptable, almost necessary, behavior given the festive atmosphere. Moreover, this borrachito fulfills his Catholic duties both as a godparent and as a cargo holder for La Soledad. When the man suffered his injury, many people in Tzintzuntzan expressed their concern for his health. No one shared my reaction.

Without any other form of entertainment, Tzintzuntzeños sanction drinking as a hobby for men. Estela realized this after opening several unsuccessful businesses in the rooms of her house that faced the street. She experimented with renting her space to a stationery store, a coffin shop, a florist, and a candle business. By far her most lucrative venture was a liquor store, which competed with the numerous small-scale grocery stores in Tzintzuntzan that also sold alcohol. Her strategy was to sell bottles of Corona beer for five pesos each, making it cheaper to drink alcohol than Coca-Cola or even milk. Suppliers from the Corona distributor in Pátzcuaro came three times a week to restock her shelves. Tzintzuntzan had neither bars nor full-service restaurants, so Estela's shop came to function as a place for men to hang out and drink. In an adjacent smaller room, Estela set up two arcade games where adolescent boys would crowd and play until midnight, surreptitiously smoking cigarettes and drinking. Profiting from the vices of others embarrassed Estela, but she justified her business by saying that few other activities generated as much income. When customers approached inebriation, she would jokingly but firmly refuse to sell them more beer.

Bunzel (1940) traces the centrality of alcohol in Mesoamerican life to pre-Hispanic ceremonies, where the consumption of wine filled an essential role in worship. When the Spanish arrived, they "quickly recognized and took advantage of the use of alcohol as a tool of imperialism" (362). While the colonizers were interested in many of the resources that belonged to the Indians, one of the few Spanish items that the Indians craved was alcohol. So intense was the Indians' desire for alcohol that they would contract debts in exchange for a drink, a willingness that the Spanish exploited to maintain their control. Through the twentieth century, landowners in Chiapas and Guatemala continued to use alcohol to lure indigenous men to work on plantations. By encouraging their laborers to drink, nonindigenous overseers both ensured a steady supply of indentured workers and exacerbated the incidence of alcoholism.

As in Native American communities in the United States, alcohol has damaged indigenous and mestizo peoples throughout Mexico. In one agricultural community in the Mexican state of Morelos, Maccoby (1972) determined that more than a quarter of all adult men were alcoholics or excessive drinkers. For many of the peasant farmers, drinking was their only hobby. With seven cantinas in a town of 850 people, there were few other diversions besides drinking. Sutro (1989) also found that in one Oaxacan Zapotec community drunkenness carried little stigma for the indigenous inhabitants; in fact they considered refusing a drink socially unacceptable. In a survey of the forty-five most deviant activities, Zapotec respondents ranked drinking fortieth (Selby 1974).

Alcohol occupies a dual position in many Mexican communities. Ritual drinking ensures the continuity of local traditions and strengthens connections between religious participants. However, in excess, drinking destroys families and undermines women's and men's ability to perform social obligations. Eber (1995) documents the pervasive and ambiguous presence of alcohol for one indigenous community near Chamula. According to most ethnographic accounts, Mexican men are more prone than women to alcoholism, but its harmful effects damage the entire family. Drinking in moderation facilitates the renewal of the universe according to practitioners of the traditional Maya religion. But having suffered abuse, neglect, and the tragedy of fetal alcohol syndrome when drinking crossed into alcoholism, the Maya women who collaborated with Eber rallied against alcohol in traditional religious ceremonies, replacing rum with soda. In other cases, women left drinking altogether by joining an evangelical church. However, Eber worries that in the long run the prohibition against alcohol will eliminate the integrative functions of drinking and undermine the role women play in balancing the universe.

Alcohol also lubricates religious rituals in Tzintzuntzan, though it has lost its pre-Hispanic association with a pantheon of gods. In the fiestas, alcohol not only adds to the merriment of the revelers but also cements social ties. When Estela's son visited his fiancée's family to ask permission to wed, his godparents brought a bottle of brandy to share with the young woman's godparents. Accepting the bottle indicated that they accepted the marriage. Similarly, at the fiestas marking the handover of the monthly cargo at the chapel of the Virgin of Guadalupe, the incoming cargueros symbolize their new responsibilities by receiving a bottle of brandy from the retiring cargueros. Under these circumstances, refusing to drink is tantamount to rejecting the bond between ritual participants.

In a staunchly Catholic environment that values alcohol consumption as part of community spiritual life, individuals who want to quit drinking have to reorient their relationship to the dominant church. One option is to leave the Catholic Church altogether. Nash (1960:50) suggests that for some Guatemalan Catholics "joining a Protestant sect was analogous to becoming a member of Alcoholics Anonymous." Kearney (1970) also found during his fieldwork in Ixtepeji, Oaxaca, that to control their drinking habits men had to affiliate with an evangelical church. He explains:

> By becoming a member of a sect that specifically forbids drinking
> or even participation in events where drinking occurs, the individual
> wishing to get out of the drinking pattern has a ready-made alter-
> nate mode of behavior that he can assume, backed up by an alternate
> supernatural sanction system and, even more important, by a group of
> sympathetic people who are grappling with the same problems. (151)

Both Kearney and Nash conclude that where the pressure to participate in ritual drinking is strong, Catholics must join an evangelical church to eliminate alcohol from their lives.[8]

I will give examples of conversion experiences from three different evangelical churches that operate around Lake Pátzcuaro. Together, they illustrate how converts from all denominations have suffered from alcohol or related health crises that threatened the stability of their families. These crises, more than any animosity toward the Catholic Church, typically characterize the families who convert. The appeal of the evangelical church is its strict biblical interpretation, which explains illness as the work of evil external forces that can be expelled through the practice of certain divinely sanctioned behaviors. Health and sobriety become marks of spiritual as well as physical rectitude.

Shedding Light on the Light of the World

Luz del Mundo, or Light of the World, is a Guadalajara-based evangelical church that draws nearly a hundred worshippers every week to its sanctuary in Pátzcuaro. It is one of only three non-Catholic churches I attended that count on the services of a full-time pastor who lives on the premises of the church compound. Luz del Mundo preaches a doctrine as idiosyncratic as the Jehovah's Witnesses do, but its members give the same reasons for conversion. A desire to stop drinking, among other reforms, motivates their decisions to convert. Once a part of the new church, Luz del Mundo members change what they consume and how they behave.

When I passed through Guadalajara on my way to the American Anthropological Association meeting, I visited the church's headquarters, established by a Mexican enlisted man named Eusebio Joaquín González. In 1926 he left the military upon meeting two Pentecostal preachers. After being baptized, Eusebio heard God's voice instructing him, "Here's a man whose name will be Aaron." God went on to entrust to him the restoration of the primitive church of Jesus Christ (de la Torre 1995:55–57). Eusebio, now calling himself Aaron, and his wife began a six-month journey across Mexico that ended in Guadalajara, where he began evangelizing. He brought military discipline and charismatic preaching to his ministry, but even more compelling to his poor followers was the way he correlated his own life with biblical events, suggesting that he was an apostle on this earth. Before Aaron died in 1964, he designated his son, Samuel, as his successor on God's mission. Under Samuel's leadership, La Luz del Mundo has grown to include eleven thousand congregations in twenty-two countries, with approximately 1.5 million followers in Mexico alone (de la Torre 1995:149).

In 1952, Aaron established a main church and residential quarters for his followers in the eastern part of Guadalajara. "La Hermosa Provincia" (The Beautiful Province), as he called it, came to function as a full-service, enclosed community while the metropolitan area grew around it. The bus ride took me only thirty minutes from the downtown area, but upon entering the community, I felt I had traveled to another planet. The streets narrow into pedestrian-only zones as the houses become more luxurious. Well-manicured trees in pots labeled "La Luz del Mundo" line the walkways. Similarly labeled trash cans appear every few feet alongside elaborate wrought iron park benches. The houses, as well maintained as the streets, feature opaque reflective windows and Stars of David as decorations. Walking around the several blocks of the colony, I noticed a primary and secondary school, a gymnasium, a market, a post office, a bank, and a roasted chicken store.

The streets, all with Old Testament names like "Jericho," radiate from a central circle that encloses the main building. I recognized the outline of the architecturally striking structure from the logo on church literature I had seen in Pátzcuaro. Shaped like a wedding cake, the cream-colored building consists of seven stacked, tapering layers topped by an abstract bronze sculpture where the figure of the couple would be.[9] Like the neighboring houses, the church does not permit a view inside, its windows covered with a reflective coating. I entered from the rear of the church, under a low ceiling. As I walked down the aisle toward the central altar, the ceiling receded to reveal a soaring, tepee-shaped dome. Gold cylinders outline each of the seven rings of the ceiling, tinted on the bottom with a different color of the rainbow starting with purple on the lowest level and ending with red in the top-most.

Crimson velvet pads the wooden pews, with a gilded menorah decorating the end of each row.

Several young men in somber suits stood at the back of the church clutching Bibles and talking when I entered. One of them, a tall twenty-year-old named Juan, came over to offer me a tour. He explained that the building accommodates several thousand worshippers. During services, married men and women sit on the ground floor, unmarried women in the first balcony, and unmarried men in the second balcony. They face an altar of white marble decorated with white flowers. Flanking the altar are red chairs for the adult and the youth choirs. Above the altar and beneath a row of foreign flags, there is a balcony for the international choir that comes every August for a special Holy Supper ceremony. At the back of the altar, workers have drained a baptismal pool for repairs. Center stage there is a high-backed red plush chair and a few smaller chairs behind a glass-topped table whose base forms a stylized golden tree trunk. At the front of the altar, the leader directs the services from a podium with a microphone.

After the architectural tour, Juan invited me to sit in a pew to answer any questions. I learned that he was relatively new to the church. He was unmarried, but still it was a woman—his mother, in this case—who converted first and talked to him about salvation when he was still a Catholic. Before he converted he worked as a musician, so he attended many Catholic fiestas, a lifestyle that disposed him to vices, he said. He smoked, he drank, he was "wild." Many times he tried to reform his ways by making a vow to the Virgin not to drink, but then he would do so anyway. Within the Catholic Church he could not alter his behavior. Then, one day God manifested himself to Juan while he was in his bedroom. He heard "celestial music, perfect music" for several consecutive days. He knelt to God, making a sincere repentance, and decided he was ready for baptism. He became convinced that the Bible contained the ultimate wisdom. For him, "The Word is perfect. It never fails. Everything else in the world was made by men, but not the Bible." Juan sees the Bible as a manual for living in which God spells out how he wants humans to behave.

Luz del Mundo members share with Jehovah's Witnesses a belief in the imminent end of the world. Pastors point to the fulfillment of scriptural prophecies to warn their followers of the impending Apocalypse. Consequently, sermons impress on the audience the importance of proper behavior to guarantee salvation when the final judgment comes. According to Juan, the modern world abounds in sin; only the members of Luz del Mundo follow God's true wishes. "There are only two paths: heaven or eternal condemnation," Juan told me. Proper Christians signal their disengagement from the vice-ridden world and their readiness for eternal life by avoiding specific behaviors and adopting others.

When I attended a worship service of the Luz del Mundo congregation in Pátzcuaro, I could see the emphasis on a new behavioral regime clearly. The church in Pátzcuaro is a two-story stucco building in a residential neighborhood twenty minutes from the city center. The pastor, sent from Guadalajara, lives with his family upstairs, while the congregation meets in the worship hall on the ground floor. As I entered on one typical Sunday, I faced a raised stage with a wooden pulpit, a decorative menorah, and two rows of chairs on either side. An idyllic scene of a mountain stream decorates the back wall, bordered by two columns on which the names "Aaron" and "Samuel" have been stenciled in gold letters alongside a Star of David. Women, all in floor-length skirts and head coverings, sit in the pews on the right, while men, dressed more casually, sit to the left. Mirroring the gender split in the pews, female members of the choir sit on the right of the stage, male members on the left. The pastor, dressed in a gray suit, took the microphone to begin the service. He directed us to kneel and pray. I heard a cacophony of mutterings with no one voice dominating, as one would hear during a Catholic Mass. Then, we stood to sing a hymn titled "The Predestined Day Approaches."

We sang more songs from the hymnal, knelt, and prayed again before listening to the sermon. The pastor's style was serious, even scolding. He asked many questions, but tended to answer them himself. The audience limited itself to occasional interjections of "Amen!" and quiet note taking. He exhorted us to refashion how we used our bodies:

> Romans 12:1 says we must make a living sacrifice. What kind of sacrifice? A living one. Some people like to go to the movies, dance, drink, play cards, and so many other vices. You have to deny what the body craves. Those who pay a vow to the Basilica and prick themselves with spines, is this a living sacrifice as God orders? Yes, they feel it in their flesh, but it's not holy. The Lord doesn't want you harming your body. Romans 12:2 says not to conform to the world by drinking, playing games, visiting prostitutes. As James 4:4 puts it, being a friend of the world is to be an enemy of God. It costs you to serve the Lord. You have to leave many things.

When he finished, the choir sang, allowing us to come forward (women first) to drop coins in a donation box.

In this representative sermon, their pastor calls for all congregants to resist the temptation to drink alcohol or have sex with prostitutes. Even though the cited passage, Romans 12:2, makes no reference to alcohol or any other specific vices, no one questions the pastor's authoritative interpretation. Much as the Catholics are supposed to do, they are to deny themselves in order to please God. Only, in the case of Luz del Mundo, their sacrifice comes in the denial of sinful behaviors, not in the self-castigation of Catholic pilgrims.[10]

Attending a Church without a Name

Alongside established ministries with an international scope, small, independent congregations have won converts around Lake Pátzcuaro. These churches meet in members' homes and make do with visiting pastors or occasionally male church members to give the sermon. Many times these churches do not even have a proper name. Odilón and Antonia live in the indigenous hamlet of Ichupio, a lakeside outpost of fishermen next to Tzintzuntzan. When they were Catholics, they asked my landlady Estela to be godmother at the baptism of their twin boys. Estela suspects her compadres have received outside funding since they converted, but she still maintains cordial relations with them. After she introduced me to the couple, I visited them for a prayer service at their home overlooking the lake. Attendance was small: Odilón, Antonia, their daughter, and the twin son who had not migrated to the United States. I sat with them in the church sanctuary—the hallway of a newer, concrete part of the house. When the service ended, they invited me to have dinner with them. I explained my project and then asked how they came to leave the Catholic Church.

Antonia, who deftly flipped tortillas on the grill with a prosthetic arm, melodramatically described what her life was like before she converted. She just wanted to die. She wanted to be dropped into the middle of the lake that glinted so invitingly from outside her kitchen window. Her husband used to be an inveterate drunk. He would go away for fiestas and not come back for three days; and when he would get drunk at home, he fought with the neighbors. He played soccer and would drink if his team lost. He would drink if they won. Sometimes his drinking got so severe that he would threaten her or choke her.

Antonia prayed in the Catholic Church for help, and, though she did not realize it at the time, God sent help in the form of a team of biologists who came to study the lake. She and Odilón were suspicious of the outsiders at first, but as they began to talk to the scientists, they became collaborators and friends. When they had completed their project, the researchers repaid Odilón and Antonia's kindness with a month-long trip to the state of Hidalgo, where they set them up as instructors of artisanry. It was there, in 1983, that Odilón and Antonia met a pastor who told them about the Word of God. They had been Catholics all their lives, "very fond of parties," but during the month they spent in the company of evangelicals, they were impressed. "Not one cigarette, not one drop of alcohol," Antonia declared. Soon after they had returned to Ichupio, the pastor from Hidalgo paid them a visit. Antonia received him eagerly, inviting him back to offer them further instruction. Odilón, on the other hand, resisted the preacher's message. He said he could not join a church that did not venerate the Virgin Mary, but Antonia realized he was using that as an excuse. In reality, she knew he was reluctant to give up drinking.

Odilón remembered those years when the pastor from Hidalgo visited them nearly every month. Antonia received the call to accept Jesus in her heart and confirmed her born-again status through baptism, but Odilón could not bring himself to accept the strict limitations on his behavior. In retrospect, he understands his reluctance: "Our customs are very deeply rooted—fiestas, beer. I didn't want to leave them. They would pray with me, but then I'd go back to drinking with my compadres." Odilón resisted the call for five years. Then, Antonia had her accident. Nine months after being baptized, Antonia caught her hand in a mill while it was grinding corn. Her entire forearm had to be amputated. When Odilón saw her recovering in the hospital, he mocked her religion, "See what good your God did you!" But she countered, "Yes, it is because of my God that I am still alive." Odilón considered his wife's accident a test for him, so he went to speak to the pastor who had been teaching them. The pastor counseled Odilón that Antonia had angered Satan by finding God, and so Satan caused her to have the accident. He saw how brave his wife was and realized how much they fought when she had two hands. "The Word entered me through my wife," Odilón admitted. When she left the hospital, he became baptized too.

Even after he was baptized, Odilón continued to drink. But now, with every drink he began to see a hundred faces poking over the fence at him, pointing and chanting, "You did wrong!" Finally, he asked God for forgiveness and gave up drinking altogether. Without alcohol, Odilón said, he no longer swore, no longer fought, and no longer mistreated his wife. Antonia noted the difference in their lives: "Odilón used to hit me, strangle me. But now no one in the family drinks. We're separate from the world." Like other evangelical congregations, they aim to distinguish themselves from the majority by their restrictive behavior.

Odilón or his son (before he too left for the United States) gave the sermons during their thrice-weekly worship services (see Figure 2.3). The emphasis on the imminent end of the world sounded familiar to me after having attended other evangelical congregations. They too argue that the biblical signs of the end time have been evident in recent years: wars, earthquakes, and killings. This makes following God's commandments all the more imperative. The Ichupio congregation places many of the same restrictions on members' behavior as do the Jehovah's Witnesses and Luz del Mundo. "We don't have music, we don't have fiestas, we don't dance, we don't smoke, we don't drink, we don't adore images," Antonia said. The sermons Odilón delivers to his family emphasize how their behavior sets converts apart from nonbelievers: "A song says, 'the world does not know us.' The believer is known by his way of acting and his clamor for God. He is different from the unconverted, who says bad words. A child of God stops his tongue." Though lacking the scriptural proficiency of more extensively trained pastors, Odilón exhorts his listeners to distinguish themselves from the unconverted by exercising restraint in their behavior.

Although Odilón and Antonia have evangelized around Tzintzuntzan for two decades, their congregation remains limited to their immediate family. Antonia attributes their lack of success in winning more members to people's unwillingness to follow the rigorous prohibitions her church requires. Nearly two dozen men and women have prayed with them over the years, but all broke off to attend other, less strict, evangelical churches. One cousin, Nestor, and his family, who live in La Colonia, converted in Odilón's church but then left to worship with another pastor. When Nestor was Catholic, he played in a band and spent all his money on alcohol. Many times he tried to quit drinking by making a vow to local saints, but even after subjecting himself to penitence, he would still have cravings for alcohol. With the help of his cousins and his family, he realized that God did not want him to suffer self-castigation, but to follow the commandments in the Bible. When people asked him how he stopped drinking, Nestor told them he never went to Alcoholics Anonymous, just to the Word. In 1993 he began worshipping at his home in La Colonia with an itinerant preacher named Pastor Orozco.

When I asked Odilón and Antonia how their worship differed from the services Nestor held in La Colonia, they admitted they were identical theologically. To them, the only significant difference comes in Nestor's looser standards of daily practices. Antonia scoffed at his defection, claiming he found the rigid discipline in Ichupio too demanding to follow: "They [Nestor's new church] are almost the same as the worldly Catholics. They dress however they want. We don't allow earrings, necklaces, or long hair on men.

2.3 Before he left to work in the United States, Odilón's son helped lead worship ceremonies in Ichupio.

And women can't wear makeup or long pants. You should be well dressed, simple, honest, and humble." In her mind, physical practices are the most salient markers of religious identity.

Nestor faced his own challenges of defection when his neighbors, who had been attending his services, left his congregation to worship with the Jehovah's Witnesses in Quiroga. As Antonia did to him, Nestor criticized them for not comporting themselves as he felt Christians should. According to him, the supposedly converted neighbors attended dances and bullfights, drank alcohol, and uttered swear words, all of which the Bible prohibits. Evangelicals around Lake Pátzcuaro contrast their own restrained consumption habits with the profligate ways of people from other churches.

Healing Evangelical Style

Not every conversion narrative focuses on a debilitating case of alcoholism. I also occasionally heard accounts of conversion involving the curing of other kinds of illness. While only Dr. Cook accompanies his Bible study sessions with prescription medicines, most evangelical churches devote part of their services to healing the ill. All the churches stress that lasting health demands a decisive shift in personal behavior. Converts who experience healing in evangelical churches often adopt a Manichaean worldview that depicts a "true" Christian community besieged by pernicious forces of evil that cause illness. They see their infirmity as one battle in the larger war between Satan and God. Through upright Christian behavior, the sick can dislodge the demons that cause them pain. Strict adherence to the Bible ensures both health in this world and salvation in the next.

Military metaphors prevailed in all the evangelical churches, presaging an imminent spiritual battle. In Torre Fuerte (its name a reference to fortifications), the imagery of invading enemies and courageous defenders comes through explicitly. Torre Fuerte and its sister mission, Puerta de Salvación (Door of Salvation), have earned a reputation in Pátzcuaro as centers for faith healing. The family that founded Torre Fuerte originally formed part of Pátzcuaro's Baptist church, but in 1995 they split in order to worship in a more ecstatic way. The pastor incorporates a multipiece rock'n'roll band, earsplitting prayers, and the spiritual gift of healing into the worship services. In 2000, the congregation already had outgrown its third temporary meeting place and purchased a lot to build a permanent structure.

Torre Fuerte and Puerta de Salvación link physical illness to spiritual causes. Through special gifts of the Holy Spirit, the pastors expel the demons that weaken members. One pastor developed an entire etiology that attributes all illnesses, be they alcoholism or cancer, to demonic possession. He cites passages from the Gospels where Jesus cures the sick by merely reprehending the evil spirits that inhabit them. In one faith healing I witnessed after a three-hour Sunday morning service, the pastor, his wife, and two other women surrounded an older woman seated in a chair. The pastor positioned himself directly behind the woman, who was suffering from arthritis. He placed both his palms on her head, while the women touched her legs or simply raised their arms around her. Following the pastor's lead, all four addressed the evil spirits in commanding voices with statements like, "In the name of Jesus, I beseech you to leave this woman." Eyes closed, they pleaded and prayed according to their own rhythms for several minutes.

More than causing personal harm, demons can damage society. In these end days, ministers note the omnipresence of evil: "The Devil knows we're here. We need to be awake and alert until Jesus comes for us." Like the Jehovah's Witnesses, Torre Fuerte uses the imminence of Judgment Day to motivate members to proselytize in the streets and to endure embarrassment. Whenever they encounter difficulty, converts turn to prayer. "Prayer is our weapon," one young evangelical woman explained. "As with a gun, you have to practice how to use it." The need to defend against this immediate threat comes through particularly clearly in the infectious songs Torre Fuerte performs. One song—whose lyrics are projected onto the wall of the meeting place—begins:

> God is calling us to war.
> We will take the weapons he prepared for us.
> You and I are a people.
> You and I are preparing to show the greatness of the Lord.
> We are preparing to take the land that he delivered to us.

Another song reinforces the martial message:

> With my God I will assault the walls.
> With my God armies will fall.
> He is in my right hand for the battle.
> He is my liberator.

Like Luz del Mundo, with its tinted-windows and patrolled compound in Guadalajara, the congregation girds itself for a fight.

In the impending battle, the pastors will lead the brigade, and the church members will be the foot soldiers. Every three months in Pátzcuaro, evangelical ministers of all denominations meet to share information and coordinate plans. One Pentecostal pastor explains, "We are generals in the army of Christ. If we are not united, we cannot protect the Body of Christ." These strategy sessions serve both a celestial purpose and the more pragmatic goal of defending the churches against local opposition.

Pastors give sermons and prayers that instruct their "enlisted" men and women to suppress their egos and follow rules. In any effective army, soldiers must act in unison, conforming their behavior to the wishes of superiors. In one Torre Fuerte service, the pastor gave a lesson about the twelve apostles that underscored the importance of following divine will. He emphasized that serving God requires neither intellect nor wealth. It is enough to be like the humble apostles with their open hearts and willingness to be guided. Reinforcing the message, the band followed with a song that called on believers to submit themselves to divine will:

> The more I know you, the more I want to know you.
> Break me. Transform me.
> My God—what a great potter!
> Mold me in your image, Lord.
> I want to be more like you.

Fighting for God requires humble soldiers, steeled for battle through the enforcement of rigid codes of behavior.

By conceiving of the world as a battlefield between the demons of Satan and the will of God, evangelical churches give added importance to the adoption of new behaviors. Eliminating alcohol not only pleases a man's family but also helps his congregation conquer the forces bent on destroying the world. In this sense, faith healing provides only temporary relief from the threat of evil. Believers must remain vigilant against future satanic temptations as they prepare for the Day of Judgment. The evangelical focus on keeping at bay the personal demons of alcohol addiction internalizes the reasons for conversion. Converts tend not to be critical of the Catholic Church until after they have joined a new church and assimilated the doctrinal messages of their pastors. This personal approach to religious conversion presents less of a threat to the dominant Catholic faith and opens a space for mutual tolerance.

THREE

ACCOUNTING FOR MISSIONARIES AND MONEY

I N Latin America, it is a standard refrain of Catholic and civil leaders alike that new churches constitute a foreign imposition, taking root only with the help of North American resources and malevolent chicanery. They blame missionaries for luring men and women away from the Catholic Church with cash, clothing, and the promise of further riches. La Farge raised this concern as early as 1932 on a visit to two Maya communities in Guatemala. While the parish priest evinced little interest in delivering more than the basic sacraments, three evangelicals from the United States operated a health clinic, from which they based their aggressive proselytizing. La Farge foresaw difficulties with the prospect of conversion:

> Nothing could be less well suited to these particular people. . . . They are an introverted people, consumed by internal fires which they cannot or dare not express, eternally chafing under the yoke of conquest, and never for a moment forgetting that they are a conquered people. In occasional drunkenness, in dancing, and in the more elaborate ceremonies with their pageantry they find a much-needed release. A bleaker and stricter religion might result in repressions which would come out eventually in most unpleasant ways. (La Farge 1947:100)

So intense was the local dislike for evangelicals that residents would rush to the parish church to burn a candle when they accidentally came in contact with a missionary. Since Mesoamerican people are not suited to evangelical Christianity, then some powerful force, most likely backed by North American funds, must be responsible for large-scale conversion.

This commonly voiced criticism of evangelicals, which continued throughout the twentieth century, exaggerates both the number and skill of missionaries. More representative of conversion experiences in Mexico is the example of Miguel Kaxlan in Chiapas. Although missionaries play a role in the establishment of non-Catholic churches, native proselytizers like Kaxlan quickly take over in expanding their ministry and responding to local concerns. Attributing the popularity of evangelical faiths to coercive missionary tactics overlooks the significant contributions of Mexican-born leaders in spreading new faiths. The influence of foreign missionaries in supporting evangelical congregations is declining, and the churches' current success is homegrown.

A historical survey of non-Catholic missionaries in Mexico since their arrival in the nineteenth century illustrates how membership in evangelical churches flourished only after the presence of missionaries had diminished. Of the thirteen non-Catholic congregations I included in my fieldwork, missionaries founded seven, Mexican pastors began three, and three more arose through schism from other churches. By 1999, the only church left with its original foreign patron was Dr. John Cook's Nueva Vida en Cristo. Ethnographic evidence from his ministry shows that even with the involvement of the well-financed founder, converts choose to affiliate with his church without coercion. Interviews with members of Dr. Cook's church suggest that conversion must be understood as a personal—not an imposed—choice. Where women and men convert to evangelical churches, they do so according to their own spiritual understandings, which often retain Catholic beliefs and practices.

WANING MISSIONARY INFLUENCE

After winning independence from Spain, the nascent Mexican state battled to forge a viable government without the apparatus of colonial bureaucracy. Protestantism held a certain attraction for Mexican liberals due to its association with their increasingly powerful northern neighbor and with separation from the Spanish Empire. Comparing the thriving economy of the United States with their stagnating one, liberal leaders considered Protestants "more active, more industrious, and more rich than Catholics" (Bastian 1980:49). The challenge for the Mexican nation builders would be to balance the utilitarian spirit of North American Protestant society with the distinctive, Catholic-infused Mexican culture.

When the liberals achieved national power, they established religious freedom in the 1857 Constitution. In subsequent measures, the liberals disestablished the Catholic Church from its status as official state church and further circumscribed its wealth and power (Martin 1990:93). Benito Juárez, Mexico's strong central executive at the time, paved the way for missionary activity. In 1870, he showed interest in spreading Protestantism to Mexico's millions of indigenous peoples, who remained outside federal control. He reasoned, "They need a religion that obligates them to read and not to waste their savings on candles for the saints" (quoted in Bastian 1989:38). The government invited Protestant groups from the United States to begin missionary work in Mexico during the administration of President Lerdo (1872–1876). North American missionaries had been eyeing Mexico since the early nineteenth century, but it was not until 1872 that the General Conference of Methodist Churches declared that "the situation in Mexico was good, because the government had broken the chains of Rome, abolished the convents, established religious freedom and confiscated the properties of the Church not used for worship" (quoted in Bastian 1989:52). With the newly tolerant climate, sixteen missionary societies established congregations in Mexico, which soon attracted a following of seventy thousand believers (Bastian 1989:13). The missionaries represented mainline denominations, churches like Methodists, Presbyterians, and Baptists, which traced their roots to the Protestant Reformation.

Regions like Michoacán remained resolutely Catholic, while in other parts of the country non-Catholic groups began gaining prominence through a network of schools (Bastian 1990:32). Initial adherents came from the textile workers, miners, railroad workers, and rural farmers living in regions with hacienda conflicts (Bastian 1989:62). Few liberals themselves joined the movements, preferring deism or agnosticism, but they offered their support for the missionaries' spread. Until 1877, Protestant churches clustered in the Valley of Mexico. With the aggressive recruitment of foreign investment and development of railroads under Porfirio Díaz, missionaries found expansion easier. They established churches in the regions of the Gulf and Pacific, and in the North, which had seen little Catholic penetration. So eager were representatives from the mainline denominations to missionize in Mexico that they met in Cincinnati in 1914 to divide the country into geographic regions where each would have a sphere of influence (Macín 1983:56).

During the Porfiriato, Protestant missionaries ran 163 schools, educating 11,862 students. This constituted 1.7 percent of all Mexican schools, a small number that belied their disproportionate influence (Bastian 1989:148). Like the congregations, the schools were located in areas with liberal leanings, which reinforced the Protestant identification with progress and responsible citizens. Moreover, many of the schools operated in communities without government- or Catholic-sponsored education. A foreign Anglican bishop recounted in his diary a trip to Toluca in the state of Mexico in 1926. He inspected a school run by the church—one of the few places young women could go in that community for an education. His description of the building underscored the Protestant association with modernity.

> [It is a] huge and well-appointed structure, modern in every detail and containing every facility and equipment for the education of women teachers. The huge dormitories, the comfortable and modern infirmery [*sic*], the well-lighted and well-appointed auditorium, evinced a knowledge of architecture and appointments of the most modern institutions. The Physics Laboratory contained many pieces of apparatus lacking in similar American institutions because of their expensiveness. (Creighton 1926)

Though most of their students did not come from converted families, the schools effectively disseminated the Protestant message and competed with the Catholic network of schools.

In time, Protestants came to feel that Díaz would not offer them protection since he had mitigated the state's hostility toward the Catholic Church and violated the liberal spirit of the 1857 Constitution by extending his term for more than three decades. When Madero presented himself as a challenger to the entrenched officials of the Porfiriato, Protestants seized on the chance to back him, though differences in their expressions of support revealed a growing gulf between Mexican and North American leaders. Native ministers, who rose mostly from the jobs of artisan or educator, were active and even aggressive in their support, while foreign missionaries kept their approval for Madero passive (Baldwin 1990:81). As revolutionary leaders multiplied, Protestants consistently supported the Constitutionalists, including future national leader Venustiano Carranza. Carranza defended Protestant activities, and many members of his governing cohort had been educated in missionary schools (Bastian 1980:58).

Carranza's nationalistic ideology contributed to the growing distance between foreign missionaries and non-Catholic Mexican religious leaders. A 1926 law expelled missionaries from the country and mandated that all foreign priests be deported and replaced with Mexican ones. In protest, the Catholic Church suspended the celebration of Mass. Between 1926 and 1929, rural Mexicans—many from Michoacán—rose up in arms in the Cristero

Rebellion, calling for the reinstatement of the Catholic sacraments (Meyer 1976). Many Protestant missionaries remained in Mexico in spite of the law banning their presence, which involved frequent trips to the border to renew their tourist visas (Bowen 1996:168). The mainline denominations chose not to protest the ban on foreign missionaries and instead focused their energies on identifying promising native leaders. Báez Camargo, an officer of a national Protestant organization, lamented that enrollment in Protestant-run primary schools dropped from 8,704 in 1921 to 2,000 in 1935. The number of evangelical missionaries had also declined in that same period, from 261 to 156. Báez Camargo recommended extending the evangelical net to recruit charismatic Mexican leaders rather than contesting the government's policies (Báez Camargo and Grubb 1935:126).

The formation of a single ruling party with wider state control altered the relationship between the non-Catholic churches and the government. President Lázaro Cárdenas (1934–1940) encouraged Protestant churches to undertake the education of indigenous populations, a project that had concerned Mexican leaders since Juárez. In 1936 the Summer Institute of Linguistics (SIL), a branch of the Protestant organization Wycliffe Bible Translators, received an official welcome from Cárdenas and began work in southern Mexico translating the Bible into indigenous languages (Rus and Wasserstrom 1981). Before then, Protestant missionaries had largely avoided work in the southern states of Mexico because of the strong Catholic commitment of the indigenous communities there and the lack of infrastructure. By the start of the 1940s, Protestant churches had established congregations across all of Mexico and had widened their appeal beyond the base of rural poor. Their membership grew by 86 percent between 1940 and 1950, a period in which the population at large grew by only 31 percent (Martin 1990:95).

The surge in membership coincided with the arrival of a new wave of Protestant churches: the evangelicals. Rather than the cold, literate traditions typical of mainline denominations established in Mexico during the late nineteenth and early twentieth centuries, the new independent churches emphasized ecstatic oral expression. Unlike the historic denominations, which flourished in the northern frontier states, the new churches grew in the southern indigenous states and in the metropolitan suburbs. In contrast to the democratizing doctrine of mainline denominations, the new churches eschewed commitment to social services while splintering into countless divisions and political messages (Bastian 1990:35–38). Pentecostalism, the most successful of the evangelical churches, dominated in the rural and peripheral urban areas and radically withdrew from the structures of local power (Martin

1990:95). In one historian's estimation, the new churches cannot even be called Protestant; they are "new non-Roman Catholic religious movements" (Bastian 1992:346).[1]

Protestants entered their most successful period of growth as foreign control over the churches waned (Bowen 1996:39). The burgeoning applications at this time for legal recognition of new churches signaled their surge in popularity. From 1940 to 1964, only 1,206 evangelical churches requested government registration. From 1968 to 1988, evangelical churches submitted 8,199 requests (Camp 1997:94). Though buoyed by their numerical gains, Protestant missionaries faced new challenges in the 1980s and 1990s. Under increasing suspicion for their persistent proselytizing, SIL translators found themselves no longer welcome in the southern states (Stoll 1982). In 1979, the College of Anthropologists and Ethnologists of Mexico demanded the expulsion of SIL, whom the government had placed in charge of educating some indigenous populations, for perpetrating "ethnocide." Four years later, the Mexican government terminated its contract with SIL and ordered its members to leave the country (Riding 1985:206). However, as one SIL volunteer in Pátzcuaro explained to me, by then most of the missionaries had obtained Mexican citizenship and so were able to stay and continue their work.

The mending of the Mexican government's rift with the Catholic Church also made Mexico less hospitable to Protestant missionaries. In 1992, President Salinas promulgated constitutional changes that gave new legal status to the Catholic Church and renewed diplomatic ties with the Vatican after 130 years. The reforms granted new freedoms to all churches, including the right of clergy to vote, the operation of parochial schools, and the ownership of property. Along with the benefits, the government also imposed the rule that to receive official recognition, a church must show that it has been active in Mexico for five years and possesses sufficient property for its functioning (Metz 1994:76–78). These provisions have made it difficult for most evangelical churches to receive government approval, since many lack the resources or qualifications to complete the application process.

In few Latin American countries has the presence of evangelical believers generated as much public debate as it has in Mexico. Although the number of converts remains statistically small, their presence looms large. Between August 1984 and August 1986 an average of two articles a week appeared in Mexico City newspapers on the topic of non-Catholic religious organizations (Valderrey 1987:13). One alarmist article estimated that the proportion of Protestants (including evangelicals) in the southern states had reached between 50 and 60 percent, a proportion even the churches themselves do not claim. Repeatedly, the articles used words like "penetration," "invasion," and "infiltration" to express their contempt for the certain spread of North American values. According to the mainstream Mexican press, evangelicals bear responsibility for destroying indigenous culture, fomenting community divisions, promoting alienation, rejecting patriotic symbols, and undermining national identity (Valderrey 1987:19).

Despite his efforts toward ecumenism, Pope John Paul II has led the Catholic Church's vociferous opposition to the infiltration of evangelical "sects," as he insists on calling the new churches. In his 1990 pastoral trip to Mexico, he pointedly visited the southern state of Tabasco, where religious conversion has been prevalent. The visit seemed designed to stir up antagonism toward evangelicals; in the months before and after his visit, Mexican cities reported an increase in violence directed at evangelicals (Bonicelli 1993:192). Delivering the opening address at the 1992 Conference of Latin American Bishops, he connected evangelical success in Latin America to United States dollars. "We should not underestimate a particular strategy aimed at weakening the bonds that unite Latin American countries and so undermine the kinds of strength provided by unity. To that end, significant amounts of money are offered to subsidize proselytizing campaigns that try to shatter such Catholic unity." The pope further denounced evangelical sects as "rapacious wolves" who prey on vulnerable Catholics and who are bent on "causing division and discord in our communities" (quoted in Cleary and Stewart-Gambino 1997:10). Neither the pope nor the reporters offered evidence for their allegations, but these nonetheless achieved wide circulation.

The priests in the Lake Pátzcuaro area do not often mention evangelicals in their sermons; however, when I interviewed some clergy about the growing numbers of converts, they echoed the accusations made by the pope. Father Huacuz, parish priest in Santa Fe, on the other side of Lake Pátzcuaro, considers evangelical Christianity to be a foreign faith that lures its members through bribery. "People convert when they go to work in the United States. There they receive help from Protestant groups. Here they receive the same kind of help with clothes and food. They change religions for self-interest. Some people are ignorant and easily deceived." When a group of evangelicals established a congregation in Santa Fe, Father Huacuz opposed the new church out of concern that they would divide the community, reiterating the pope's assertion of "Catholic unity."

Given the animosity toward evangelicals at the highest levels of church and civil opinion, it was no surprise that Catholics in Tzintzuntzan expressed the same suspicions about their converted neighbors. During my first weeks in the community I noticed that several families had placed stickers on their front doors announcing, "This home is Catholic. We reject propaganda from Protestants and other sects." When I asked people why they felt the need to announce their religion on their front doors, I heard explanations reminiscent of the pope's disparaging comments. One mother of three teenagers told me:

> Even though I put the sticker on my door, they still come by to pester me. They're very insistent. If I'm busy they'll say, "What time can I come back?" My grandfather got so upset that he painted "Long Live Christ the King!" over his door so they'd know to leave him alone. But they'd come anyway, and he got into arguments with them. They're always well-dressed. In fact, many of them are only in it for the money and the new clothes. I know a poor potter from La Colonia. She was always going around barefoot. Ever since she joined the evangelicals she's been wearing high heels.

Her mother, who was standing next to her, added, "They do it for convenience, for self-interest. Many don't stay in the religion after they get the initial rewards."

These two Catholic women admit not knowing much about evangelicals —only that they do not believe in the Virgin. That the woman's grandfather thought a sign praising Jesus would turn off the proselytizers demonstrates how little most Catholics in Tzintzuntzan understand about evangelical doctrine. They take it as given that money and the promise of material benefits, not an appealing message, attract converts to the evangelical churches. Although Tzintzuntzeños believe that wealth is not finite and that individual achievement brings rewards, they are still mistrustful of what they see as sudden improvement in the converts' standard of living. Invariably, Tzintzuntzan Catholics depict evangelical churches as originating from outside the community. When I asked the daughter where she thought the funding for all these gifts came from, she answered me dismissively, "From Mexico City, the United States, wherever." Implicit in her response is that outsiders impose evangelical religions on their members, whereas Catholicism arises more organically, or at least consensually. In this framework, her decision to remain with the Catholic Church despite the promise of supposed riches underscores the sincerity of her own faith.

Catholics react with a range of skepticism about evangelical churches, but nearly all conceive of them as originating from outside Tzintzuntzan. Converts join either out of coercion or out of expediency, but never spirituality, in this view. On New Year's Day 2000, Estela's brothers and sisters-in-law gathered at her sister's home in Tzintzuntzan. We ate enchiladas outside in the orchard and talked about the arrival of the new millennium. I had missed dinner the previous night because I had marked New Year's Eve with a prayer session in Centro Cristiano Emanuel in Pátzcuaro. When I explained where I had been, the siblings began a lively debate.

> *Brother #1* (who has lived in Washington State): The converts I know all do it out of self-interest [he makes the gesture for money by holding apart his thumb and index finger]. They don't even know what they're preaching. They're sent out to preach but don't even understand it. They don't have to work. They have all their expenses paid. Their money comes from magazine sales. They're so persistent, so you give them a dollar just to go away. In Washington I've been invited many times to their meetings. They even offer to pick you up, drive you. I went once. Afterward they give you a vegetarian meal.

> *Estela's sister-in-law:* All religions are good because they teach you how to live correctly. But the Jehovah's Witnesses drummed up a lot of fear when they said the world would end in 2000. Look, we're still here. The Bible doesn't say when the world will end.

> *Brother #1:* The Jehovah's Witnesses are all programmed from a headquarters, who knows where—California or New York.

> *Estela's sister-in-law:* They're based in Brooklyn. They even control the number of hours you go out and preach.

> *Brother #1:* Some Protestant leader in the United States raised two hundred million dollars. I saw it on the front page of the newspaper there.

> *Brother #2:* The Summer Institute of Linguistics had a large building in Cherán [a town in the indigenous flatland of Michoacán]. The government supported them until they were removed from the country. They had gringo support. They don't have to work. They get a good house. They just learn a few verses and go out to preach with those.

> *Estela's sister-in-law:* Their Bible is different from ours. Each Bible has its own interpretations.

Estela's brothers and sister-in-law reflect the impressions most local Catholics hold about converts. The brothers fixate on the economic assistance from the United States they assume converts receive. Both believe that evangelicals no longer have to work, a temptation—they note with a touch of self-congratulation—that they have resisted. Even if it means less financial security and more physical toil, they will remain with the Catholic Church, the faith in which they were raised.

Estela's sister-in-law couches her criticism of the Jehovah's Witnesses in general praise for all religions. While she harbors no doubt that evangelicals receive assistance from abroad, she defends their spiritual goals. The majority of Catholics react to evangelical families in Tzintzuntzan with similarly subdued criticism. Even though Estela's brother doubted the evangelical faith was genuine, he agreed to attend an evangelical worship service when he was in Washington. This gentle disapproval and willingness to attend each other's events characterize most evangelicals and Catholics in Tzintzuntzan. The New Year's lunch would not be the only time I heard the pronouncement that "all religions are good."

BUILDING A HOMEGROWN MINISTRY

The aim of my summer in Tzintzuntzan in 1998 was to hone my ethnographic fieldwork skills after having completed my first year of graduate school. To that end I was investigating the marketing of pottery through the use of intermediaries, a topic that was attractive both because it was not controversial and because it could be easily accomplished in one brief visit. However, I soon realized that Tzintzuntzeños, potters and nonpotters alike, had little to say about pottery that Foster had not already recorded. But when a troupe of Florida evangelicals pulled into the central plaza one summer evening with clowns, puppets, and balloon animals, the whole community started talking about this novelty.

My first hint that something out of the ordinary was going to happen had come during Mass the previous Sunday. After giving his sermon and communion, the parish priest announced that a free medical clinic would be held the next day in the town hall. On Monday, after visiting with several potters, I decided to see how the clinic was going. When I arrived, I found a mob of people. A whole section of the upstairs offices had been given over to an optometrist, another municipal office was a gynecologist's consulting room, and the ground floor had been transformed into a bustling pharmacy. Outside, a mobile dental van would end up pulling forty-three teeth that day. I quickly noticed that the nurses and doctors were North Americans, only some with a command of Spanish. One of them, wearing a polo shirt and taking a break from the clinic, noticed me and introduced himself in English. He explained that he was part of a team of physicians and nurses from a West Palm Beach, Florida, church who had been coming to Michoacán in the summer for several years to help a local missionary named John Cook.

During the daylong clinic, there was no overt or even subtle proselytizing. When they packed up the supplies, and the building gradually reverted to its government function, I thought that was the last I would see of my fellow gringos. I went into my room to record the information I had received from the potters that day. Estela, who was used to housing anthropologists and understood my project was to see everything, knocked on the door: "Something's going in the plaza." From the entryway to our house, I saw flashes of movement and heard children's squeals coming from the normally sleepy town square. When I got closer, I saw a school bus unloading blond teenagers and a clown enticing small children with animal-shaped balloons. On the basketball court, they had set up a makeshift puppet theater, microphone stands, and loudspeakers. Members of the medical team I had seen earlier in the day watched from the edge of the plaza. The clown led the kids from the street back toward the basketball court, where other visitors in various sequined costumes were encouraging the children to sit facing the stage. When a ring of kids had formed along with some rows of adults standing on the outskirts, the performance began.

Only a few of the performers spoke Spanish, but that did not matter since they mostly acted their routines to the words of a taped Spanish soundtrack. A group of women singers led the chorus while puppets and magicians entertained. The culmination of the event was the teenagers' allegorical retelling of the Old and New Testaments, in which two young men appeared as a toy maker and his son, who crafted a boy doll and then a girl doll. The couple joined a menagerie of other toys in the workshop with the explicit instructions not to touch one toy. However, a malevolent force (in the form of a young woman wearing a black beret) convinced the girl to touch the forbidden toy, who then told the boy to do the same. Immediately, a barrier of other black-clothed actors appeared, blocking the toys from their creator and his son.

Armed with weapons provided by the original evil beret-topped figure, the toys broke out in choreographed fighting. Soon the discord became so great that the master toy maker decided to destroy the barrier that separated him from the toys he had made. So, he changed his son into a toy and sent him into the workshop to bring happiness to the warring toys. The son mingled with all the other toys, fixing their broken parts and earning high fives of ap-

3 . 1 Young members of the Palm Beach Gardens Christ Fellowship reenact the crucifixion of Jesus on Tzintzuntzan's basketball court.

preciation. However, the figure in the black beret swooped down upon the workshop and persuaded some of the toys to reject this son of the toy maker who had come to live among them. With the dark force and her minions looking on, the angry toys crucified the son (Figure 3.1). Despite their cruel efforts, the son reemerged, tore through the barrier, and reunited with his father in a cheerful embrace. With the barrier destroyed, some of the other toys rushed to give their maker a hug as well. But, as the drama came to an end, some toys remained aloof from the toy maker and his son. The final words of the soundtrack intoned, "This is just the beginning."

For me, this skit encapsulates evangelical theology and emphasizes its contrasts with the Catholic Church. By placing Jesus in the workshop with his father before the creation of Eden, the play recasts the Old Testament book of Genesis in a Christian framework. All of human history since Eve's succumbing to temptation has been a struggle to recover contact with our loving creator and his son. But, as with the evangelical healers who guard against demons, dark, nebulous forces oppose our efforts and foment dissension among us. Even when the toy maker sends his son to live among us and suffer for our freedom from evil, some toys still refuse to accept their true creator. The path to happiness in the workshop has been cleared, but the challenge remains to convince the recalcitrant toys to take it. Conspicuous in the retelling is the absence of the Virgin Mary, who occupies a central role in Catholic rituals reenacting the birth of Jesus at Christmastime. In the play, the mother of Jesus is dressed as a flamenco dancer. She steps out of a group of toys to receive the toy maker's child, then fades back into the chorus of toys for the rest of the play. Nor does the play mention an ecclesiastical hierarchy like the one that mediates Catholic worship. Toys must make the decision themselves to step across the workshop and embrace their creator.

As soon as the play ended, the preaching began. An indigenous man took the microphone. He talked dramatically about the importance of having a personal relationship with Jesus Christ and his own miraculous recovery from drug and alcohol addiction. He ended his sermon by calling forward all those interested in delivering themselves to Jesus tonight. Having read about the hostility evangelical faiths had received in Latin America and having witnessed Tzintzuntzan's own strong Catholic faith, I expected the preacher to have few takers. To my surprise, a woman came forward, then another, and then several more until a group of thirty or so circled the speaker. The Floridians joined hands around them in energetic prayer while the other men and women in the audience watched from their places on the basketball court.

In the days following the visit, I tried to understand why so many people had responded to the preacher's call. As I asked my Catholic friends, it became clear that they did not necessarily distinguish this church from the Catholic Church, which, after all, had announced the Florida missionaries' arrival. In truth, neither the singers nor the puppets had mentioned "conversion" or "evangelicalism." What they had talked about was the redemptive powers of faith and establishing a personal relationship with Jesus. These ideas are not foreign to the regular Mass-goer. The group had sung songs with lyrics such as "Que viva Cristo; que viva el rey," nearly identical to the words of a Catholic song. One Catholic, who did not join the prayer circle but watched the event, told me, "It is a beautiful message that there is one God." Others complimented the "nice" music. The only outright skepticism I heard came from a sixteen-year-old girl who taught catechism. "They don't want us to love the Virgin. She is even greater than Jesus. She is his mother. I just let the message go in one ear and out the other." Although her interpretation of Scripture did not coincide exactly with the teachings of the Catholic Church, it reflected the intensity of Marian devotion in Tzintzuntzan, a devotion that made the decision to accept the new doctrine unappealing for many.

3.2 In the summer of 1998 Dr. Cook led Bible study classes in Tzintzuntzan's plaza. After each session, he wrote prescriptions and gave away medicine to those who had attended.

Dr. Cook returned to Tzintzuntzan without the Florida crew the following Monday for a Bible study and medical consultation. There were sixteen women present on the now-barren basketball court (Figure 3.2). They listened quietly as he read passages from Scripture, then became animated when he closed his Bible and opened his medical kit. He came several more Mondays and even began looking into renting a more permanent location for his consultations, but eventually attendance dwindled. By then I had returned to Berkeley. When I returned a year later for a twelve-month stint in Tzintzuntzan, I asked what had happened to Dr. Cook. A woman who had been among those who went to his Monday sessions regularly told me he was meeting in another community on the lake, twenty minutes away.

John Charles Cook Lawson fancies himself a modern-day Vasco de Quiroga. Like the revered first bishop of Michoacán, Cook arrived here from another country to evangelize and feels special affection for the Purépecha people. While Don Vasco traveled the state on a white mule, Cook prefers a twelve-seat beige van. His personal history plays a central role in his ministry since he himself has experienced the personal transformation that he encourages in his audience. Born a Baptist in West Virginia in the 1940s, Cook became a medical researcher at the University of New Mexico. In Albuquerque he met a Mexican American woman who became his wife and inspired him to convert to Catholicism, though he quickly became disillusioned. He told me about his time as a Catholic:

> I had a flourishing career with NASA evaluating the health of test pilots and astronauts. Then I won a half-million-dollar National Institutes of Health grant to work on kidney modeling. But there was no fulfillment. I was in the Roman Catholic Church and had even gone to seminary. But I didn't know who I worked for. It was a cold experience in the Catholic Church. It was sad to see the examples of Christ as alcoholics, homosexuals, pedophiles. It took me farther away from the Lord. I prayed and asked to know Jesus. I read Scripture. John 3 [verse 3] says you have to be born again. The first letter to the Corinthians 6:17 says you need to be one spirit with Christ.
>
> So, one morning my wife and I were reading the Bible, and we asked to have union with him. It was the most incredible experience. I used to be insecure, but now I have security in him. My life was purchased by his blood. I've had the worst things happen to me, but they're his problems. The second letter to the Corinthians 5:1 says that in Christ you're a new creature. My view of my wife and my children has changed. As Romans 8 says, the old person has to die.

Cook's frequent references to biblical verses give deeper resonance to his intimate reawakening with his wife. It is testament to his deft social skills that he can pepper his talk with citations from Scripture while still presenting himself as a man of the people.

Cook does not fit the profile of a missionary. He arrived in Mexico a Catholic, became an evangelical, and then began his missionary activity without any formal ties to a North American church. Before being born again, Cook and his wife had settled permanently in Mexico. In 1972 he went to Mexico for the first time and fell in love with the children he saw. After several visits, he returned in 1977 to take over an orphanage founded by a Benedictine brother who had died the year before. Not wanting to see the children return to the streets, Cook and his wife adopted the entire orphanage. They all settled outside the town of Ario de Rosales, about two hours west of Lake Pátzcuaro, where the couple experienced their religious rebirth. They named their compound Mano de Ayuda (Helping Hand) and together with their eight biological and thirty-four adopted children, began an evangelical ministry.

They concentrated their initial efforts around Ario de Rosales. Every Sunday morning Cook holds a free health clinic at his ranch for anyone with medical needs. Outside of the cities, health care in Michoacán is underdeveloped. Communities like Tzintzuntzan have a single small government clinic staffed by a nurse and a doctor, both fresh out of school and begrudgingly fulfilling a one-year service requirement. Private doctors are available, but often overcharge patients for advice they are unqualified to give.[2] Dr. Cook will treat any patient regardless of physical condition. He treats skin rashes, broken bones, fevers, diabetes, and even cataracts. One couple came to his clinic with their five deaf-mute children. He travels during the week, lugging a bathtub-size container of medicines to different communities. If he cannot provide the necessary remedy from his overflowing portable pharmacy, he gives the patient money to buy it. He offers free consultations and free medicines, and in the cases of surgery, he provides money for transportation and hospital care. In the past twenty years, Cook claims to have attended to ninety thousand patients of all religions, demanding no loyalty in exchange. I saw him give a consultation to two nuns, who embraced him afterward. "His prescriptions are always right," one nun told me in support of Dr. Cook.

Over the years, he has cultivated a relationship with the doctors at the Civil Hospital in Morelia, who treat his more serious cases. Every Thursday morning the hospital orthopedist clears his schedule to attend to Cook's patients. In exchange, Cook has donated medical equipment to the hospital that in his estimation totals at least one hundred thousand dollars. To raise funds for his programs, Cook loads all his children onto a bus and drives them on a tour of evangelical churches in the southern United States every summer. English-speaking supporters also receive a monthly newsletter with accounts and photos of the people Cook has treated in Mexico along with envelopes for donations. On one of his trips through the United States, Cook began his relationship with the Palm Beach Gardens Christ Fellowship. For the past nine years, a team of doctors from West Palm Beach, Florida, has come to Michoacán to hold one-day clinics like the one I saw in Tzintzuntzan. The same church donates many of the medicines Cook distributes throughout the year. The wife of one of the doctors spoke to me candidly about their strategy in offering medicines to the natives of Michoacán. "We come in with the medical team and win their confidence. They want a piece of what we have. Then Johnny [Cook] follows up slowly with preaching." Neither Cook nor the Florida doctors inflect their consultations with religious overtones, but they invite patients to attend the Bible study sessions that accompany them.

Cook's network of churches grows by founding new congregations and also by adopting existing ones. Federal law requires that religious associations register with the government. In practice most small churches do not comply with the law, but as they expand and become more established, joining a consortium of congregations provides both monetary and legal support. Cook's umbrella group is one of the few organizations in Michoacán available to make links with small congregations. One pastor, who leads her own small church in Michoacán, came to Dr. Cook seeking to become part of his alliance. She had sought help from the Assemblies of God, but they do not allow female preachers. Then she joined another consortium of churches, but she found the group's leadership never visited her congregation or offered her help. So, she went to Cook in hopes of joining his group. Cook does not aggressively court new churches, but, as with his ever-growing number of adopted children, he frequently finds himself unable to say no.

His chain of churches, however, remains independent of any North American evangelical mission and even independent of Cook. His ministry has developed strong local roots, with services led in indigenous languages by pastors from the area. While Cook counts the owner of the state's largest newspaper and the first lady of Michoacán as friends, most church members focus on community concerns and see Dr. Cook infrequently. When they have medical needs, they usually seek his help only after having consulted another medical professional. The visitors from Florida come for a limited amount of time and have little regular contact with the churches. Cook told me that if he were to die today, the religious organization would continue to run without any problems. I witnessed firsthand the degree to which day-to-day church operations occur without him. At the same time, though, I believe his charisma and fund-raising abilities are crucial for the organization's success.

Initially, Cook found success in Santa Fe, where Father Huacuz was the priest. There, using the same strategy of a free one-day medical clinic followed by weekly consultations, he established a regular prayer and healing session. Every Monday his caravan pulled up in front of the house of a local man whose son Cook had helped recover from a car accident. A Mexican doctor and a pastor usually accompanied Cook. Weekly attendance hovered between twenty and thirty people—almost all women—with some coming from Tzintzuntzan and indigenous communities around the lake. Arriving at the Santa Fe consultation, Cook would enter the narrow front hallway in a poncho and sandals, reaching down to hug the women patiently waiting in wooden chairs. When I was there, he flirtatiously ushered us into the bedroom that would later serve as a consulting room, joking to the reticent women, "I won't bite." After we had formed a circle, Cook began to preach in his idiosyncratic Spanish, a Bible in hand. "Let's communicate with the Father. I have forty-two children, eight of my own and the rest adopted. They were left by their parents. We have a father in heaven who will never leave us. Jesus—what a father! He wants the best for you." While Cook spoke, his two assistants called out periodically, "Amen!" and "Hallelujah!"

Another pastor came forward into the circle to deliver a sermon in a combination of Spanish and Purépecha, the first language of most of the audience. Every sermon every week emphasized the ability of the listeners to choose salvation by simply accepting Jesus into their hearts. Cook sat listening with his Bible open, murmuring reverently, "Oh, Jesus," while his assistant spoke:

> The Savior died on the cross, was buried, and on the third day was resurrected. He asks his father for us to live with him. . . . The blessed son is going to come to take us to judgment. Are you sure you'll enter to live with him? Are you forgiven? Salvation is now, here. You may not have the chance tomorrow. We must change our hearts. He offers us eternal life. . . . Jesus came just as Brother John comes here to help you. It's time for salvation. Matthew 24:14 tells us the end will come. Brothers and sisters, listen to me, the end is near. Are you ready to receive him?

In this instance, the audience listened quietly to the standard message of repentance. A few of the women looked up passages in their own Bibles when he cited them.

Cook rose to conclude the forty-five-minute service. "If we're suffering, if we're worrying, it's because we want to. Christ has open arms. Is there anyone who wants to take this true peace? It can do much more than medicines. All those who want to end their suffering, come forward." The assistant repeated the call in Purépecha, then began singing a hymn a cappella. Two women stood and moved into the circle in front of Cook. Then ten more walked into the circle and knelt next to them. While one pastor prayed for them in Purépecha, Cook and the other doctor leaned over each woman lovingly, touching her head and wishing her health. The audience repeated after the pastor that they would accept Jesus into their hearts. I saw one kneeling woman use the edge of her shawl to wipe away tears.

When the women stood up again, Cook returned to his jovial personality as he transitioned to the medical portion of the afternoon. The patients filed into the hallway to wait while he and the other doctor unloaded the case of medicines and set up their consulting spaces. Attending to all the patients, many of whom came with relatives, usually took an hour and a half. Most of these interactions involved more sarcastic joking than mentions of the Bible or any further reminders of the Apocalypse. In a few cases, like that of a seventeen-year-old man who admitted to drinking alcohol, Cook became serious. He invoked God, calling over the other doctor to pray for the boy's health, "I know it's fun to drink with friends," he told the teenager, "but every time you do, you put your foot in a trap. There will come a time when it will grab you, and you won't be able to leave the bottle."

Like the teenagers' skit in Tzintzuntzan, the message Dr. Cook delivered every Monday to the indigenous women of Santa Fe represents well the outlines of evangelical doctrine around Lake Pátzcuaro. Repeated references of the imminent Apocalypse characterize evangelical preaching. With the time of judgment near, only those who adhere to the word of God as recorded in the Bible will enjoy salvation and eternal life. The Catholic Church, with its profusion of saints, ribald fiestas, and clerical hierarchy, does not adhere strictly to the Bible. Although Cook considers himself an evangelical, he does not claim affiliation with any church.[3] Instead, he emphasizes the independent and personal relationship he enjoys with Jesus Christ. On Judgment Day, Christ will not just save the Baptists or the Pentecostals, Cook used to say, but everyone who has accepted him into their hearts.

Since Jesus grants salvation and eternal life only to those believers who welcome him sincerely, adherence to evangelical doctrine cannot be coerced. Cook and his fellow pastors take seriously the biblical command to spread the good news of the gospels, but they realize each convert has to make the choice for herself. In fact, most of his patients have never attended a worship service at one of his churches. Cook's generosity stems from the same biblical principles that led the mainline denominations to sponsor schools and hospitals during the first half of the twentieth century. He does not expect conversion in return for his medical services, yet his method of evangelizing ensures that he meets people during times of suffering, when they are most susceptible to new ideas. By linking health with a particular religious philosophy, Cook makes conversion an attractive choice. However, the converts who join his ministry understand evangelical faith on their own terms. As with the Jehovah's Witnesses Norma and Ricardo, conversion in Santa Fe follows from a personal or familial crisis and not simply aggressive proselytizing. Evangelicals accept a new doctrine of belief and behavior but they integrate it with their existing commitments to community solidarity.

One Monday in Santa Fe, I spoke with a local woman who was waiting for a medical consultation with Dr. Cook. I asked her how she came to know about Dr. Cook. She told me that before converting in February 1999, she was active in the Catholic Church:

> For six years my husband and I participated in Catholic Bible studies with nuns. They read the Bible like Doctor Juan does. But my husband's friends, especially when they were drinking, criticized us. They'd say, "Why are you preaching? Do you think you're a priest?" They criticized my husband for helping to translate Scripture into Purépecha. When they threatened to cut off his hand with a machete, we stopped going to the Catholic Bible studies.
>
> A year ago I went to a doctor in Quiroga, who told me I'd need surgery costing several thousand pesos. I didn't have any money, so I came to see The Doctor. He took me to the Civil Hospital in Morelia. It turns out that they could treat me with just medicine. He paid for everything, even transportation. I didn't pay one dime. He helps a lot of people. I don't know where he gets all the money.
>
> After he helped me, I began attending the services at Hermana Alejandra's [the Santa Fe woman who led Cook's congregation] house. When something is wrong, I read a passage of the Bible, and I feel better. I feel better, but I never really healed. I went to the health clinic here in Santa Fe, and they said I needed surgery. That's why I came today to see what Doctor Juan thinks.

At one level, she converted in gratitude for Cook's generous aid. Yet, her conversion should be understood in the context of a Catholic community that is suspicious of any displays of reading the Bible. She enjoys reading the Bible and quit the Catholic Bible study group reluctantly. When Cook offered her a chance to read the Bible again in a supportive environment, she accepted.

I asked her if she had received any negative reactions since leaving the Catholic Church. I found her response reminiscent of the first time I saw Dr. Cook's ministry in action:

> My husband sometimes asks me why I don't go to Mass or to the Lent talks, but I just use the excuse that I don't have any time. The women in my neighborhood criticize me, say I'm no longer Catholic. To me it's the same. The only difference is that the priest blessed our other Bible, and this one [lifting it from her lap] is not sacred.

Like the Catholic Tzintzuntzan women who answered the call on the basketball court to accept Jesus in their hearts, this woman does not draw significant distinctions between evangelical and Catholic faiths. She stopped attending the parish church, but to her "it's the same."

An older woman with cataracts who visited Dr. Cook every week from Quiroga also saw similarities between the Catholic and evangelical faiths. She sold herbal remedies from a stall in the plaza in Quiroga, but did not earn enough money to pay for the additional medicines she needed. She prayed with Cook and his pastors one day a week and then again in the Catholic church in Quiroga two days a week. Still she considered herself Catholic: "I've been going to a prayer workshop in Quiroga every Monday at four in the afternoon. I like the prayers. It's good because it's Catholic." I asked her if the prayers she heard with Dr. Cook were the same as the ones in Quiroga. "They're not exactly the same," she replied. She paused and looked up at me, "They're evangelicals, aren't they?" I answered, "Yes." She gave a slight nod as if to indicate that I had confirmed her suspicions. Then, instead of criticizing them, she continued, "That's good, because it's the same God. They just don't believe in the Virgin. I would never leave her. We need a mother just like we need a father. I've been to evangelical services before. They praised just the father and not the mother. But they sang some of the same songs we sang in my Catholic prayer group." She understood that the evangelicals downplayed the role of Mary, so she remained committed to the Catholic faith. However, this did not prevent her from seeing that Cook's congregation prayed to the same God, often using the same words and the same songs. As she combined her herbal remedies with prescription medicine, so she combined her Catholic workshop with visits to Dr. Cook's ministry.

It is not surprising that this woman saw more similarities than differences between the two faiths. The minister Cook had placed in charge of the Santa Fe congregation preached in the home of Alejandra, a convert, but when Cook came for consultations they met in the home of Rodrigo, a Catholic. Rodrigo lavished respect on Cook. He opened his house for several hours every week to several dozen potentially contagious strangers. He disrupted his pottery making to help keep track of the patients on a clipboard and to call them into the bedroom one at a time. Though I made it clear I was not Cook's son, I earned some residual respect from Rodrigo and his family, who insisted on giving me personalized samples of their artisanry when I left Michoacán.

Despite his devotion to Dr. Cook, Rodrigo still considers himself a Catholic. He attends Mass once in a while and participates in the community celebrations, and he never goes to the weekly Bible studies held at Alejandra's house just three blocks away. One time Father Huacuz called Rodrigo to his office to urge him not to allow Dr. Cook to meet in his home. But Rodrigo refused. He had to be generous because Cook had done so much to heal his son. Yet he was not so beholden to Cook that he attended the prayer sessions. In the room he lent Cook for sermons and consultations, Rodrigo had a large altar on one wall with images of thirteen saints, a table with candles, incense, and a rosary. During the talks before dispensing medicine, Cook would gesture at the gilded posters, remarking that they were not necessary when you have Jesus in your heart.

Rodrigo, straddling the Catholic and the convert camps, emphasized the volitional nature of religious choice. In a common metaphor, he likened religions to the three dominant Mexican political parties: "The PRI, PAN, and PRD don't obligate you to stay with that party. Father Huacuz didn't want to allow other religions, but he can't obligate us to stay with him. It's not forced. It's personal; a matter of one's own tastes. Just as there can't be one party for everyone, not everyone can have the same religion." Rodrigo's son defended his father's decision to disobey the priest, using language that had become familiar to me: "It's not another religion. It's the same." Just as the converted woman does not see herself as straying far from the Catholic tradition, Rodrigo and his family reconcile participation in evangelical services with their Catholic identity. It is apt that Cook likened himself to Catholic evangelizer Vasco de Quiroga, for he too has to be content with the incomplete conversion of his flock.

KEEPING THE COMMUNITY UNIFIED

In spite of Cook's two years of efforts in Santa Fe, a community with at least a thousand residents, Cook could count only forty-five regular members of his congregation. Far more had passed through his Monday consultations at Rodrigo's house without ever attending a service at Alejandra's. Then, in March 2000, the Santa Fe authorities began a series of maneuvers that resulted in Cook's peaceful expulsion from the community.

In addition to seeing patients at Rodrigo's house in Santa Fe, Cook would bring his medical kit to the homes of the seriously ill (often passing under signs that said, "This household is Catholic. We reject Protestant propaganda"). After one such visit in January 2000, on which I accompanied him, we returned to the narrow street where he had parked his van to find a pickup truck blocking his exit. Alejandra recognized the truck as her cousin Miguel's. Ever since Alejandra had asked Cook to heal her sick son and had changed religions, Miguel had been critical of her. He excluded her from family events, asked her why she had converted, and threatened to burn down her home. Cook, in a hurry to arrive at a consultation in another town, did not pay much attention. Instead, he asked her to find Miguel to have him move his truck. When Miguel finally came out of his house, he walked slowly to the truck. Cook asked his forgiveness, but Miguel replied coldly, "Only God can forgive."

In March, Cook had a second run-in with Miguel. Dr. Cook organized his health clinic activity and religious ministry as separate legal entities. He wanted a letter from the local authorities recognizing his two years of effort in Santa Fe so he could register the Mano de Ayuda program of health clinics as a civil association, unconnected to his network of churches. After a Monday consultation, Alejandra arranged for a meeting between Cook and four of the *jefes de tenencia,* community leaders in charge of landholding, of which Miguel was one. She briefed Cook on what to expect, and then we walked over to the office in the town plaza where the four elected representatives had gathered. Three sat behind a desk while Miguel stood by the door. Fifteen women and two men, Cook supporters, filled the chairs around the edges of the room. A faded portrait of Don Vasco de Quiroga looked down on the proceedings. Most of the initial discussion took place in Purépecha, with the chorus of women defending Cook's presence in the community. Finally Miguel spoke, addressing Dr. Cook directly:

Miguel: Do you understand Spanish, Doctor? [Cook nods.] As authorities, we can't decide for the community. I know you're helping many people. I'm sorry to say your objective is the problem. It can produce divisions in the community. One's free to be whatever you want. Only God has the right to judge. We're not against anyone. The ladies have valid arguments, but we don't have the capacity to decide. If the decision goes to a community assembly, I'm sure they'll say yes. With two years, what's one month more?

Cook [stands]: I'm not asking permission, just a paper recognizing my stay here. If you think I have another objective, we should talk. I've found in this town heart I haven't seen in twenty-four years in Mexican towns. I just love your people; they're so dear. I'm not rich. I'm just an instrument to help people. I have had no motive in twenty-four years. No motive more than to support the neediest folk.

Miguel: We're all poor here. We can't decide for all the people. If you want recognition why don't you collect signatures from your supporters? Paper serves for nothing when you have recognition in their hearts.

Cook: But we have an association registered with the government.

Miguel: I'm not saying you can't come, only what's the urgency? It will be much better in one month.

Cook: Miguel, if I've offended you I want to ask absolution. I sense something in you. I don't want to divide. I have twenty-four years extending a hand to the neediest. I've had seven hundred patients in orthopedic care. I've worked in Colima, Guanajuato, Guerrero, and Michoacán. We've seen young people walk again. Miguel, you're thinking more of me than I have in my heart.

Miguel: This is my role. I'm not against anything.

Cook: All I'm asking for is a letter. The governor and the head of DIF [Infant and Family Development] have recognized us. We need a letter from the authorities. Just a recognition.

Miguel: If you wait until the assembly, there'll be many signatures.

Cook: I need just the authorities' signatures.

Miguel: How come you didn't come to us sooner? How can I sign when I've only heard, not seen, your work?

Cook: Never have authorities opposed us. To the contrary, they've supported us.

Miguel: We're not blocking anything. It won't have validity if we sign it, but it will be bigger if it's backed by the whole community. Now we're talking about your objective. We've had different meetings about community problems, analyzed different religions. The Inquisition is over. They use another method now. We know nothing is free, nothing. I lived in the United States for ten years. I saw that they offer migrants food, housing. It is implicit that the organization wants to gain a member. It's like political parties—they go to the classes they can manipulate. Those here who accept your medicine and your religion are free to do so. Wait one month more until the community assembly meets. You'll win, then you can come to us demanding a signature.

Cook [stands]: I can wait. I know there are people in the United States who manipulate. Miguel, you don't know me. I'm not a manipulator. I don't obligate anyone. You're using a stereotype. And Miguel, I'm at your service. I'm not going back to Gringolandia [slang term for the United States].

Miguel: I don't think the World Bank pays for your medicines.

Cook: I look for donations. The wife of the governor helped us through DIF. This is not an organization with a motive. I'm going to invite you to my house, Miguel. I want you to know me. I don't have a religion. I have a deep love for my Lord, Jesus Christ. [Kneels] I have love for him. I'd give my life for him. [Stands] I don't go house to house. I help the forgotten ones. Sometimes, Miguel, I don't sleep thinking of all the people in ill health.

Miguel: If there's no urgency then there's no problem. We've wasted a lot of words.

Cook: I want you to know me. [Miguel shakes his head.] I have no plan. I didn't ask any of these people here to accompany me.

Miguel: I don't want to offend people.

Cook: I love your people a lot. I'm glad we had this encounter. I'm one-quarter Choctaw, so I feel for the indigenous people.

Miguel: Good. We understand each other finally. We could have avoided all of this.

Cook: Again, I ask absolution. I feel I've offended you. Is it bad to pray to him who has given us life? What's the evil? We're not giving a doctrine. We're praying. We have the doctor of doctors. I'm not saying anything bad about the Catholic Church. I was in seminary for three years.

Miguel: I've tried not to offend. I respect the whole world. I treat all equally. I don't humble myself in front of anyone. Maybe tomorrow I'll need to come to you. Now we understand each other.

The tense meeting ended with an agreement to bring the issue to the community assembly in a month. Dr. Cook offered Miguel a reconciliatory hug, but the local leader demurred. Later, Dr. Cook confided to me that he should not have offered to hug Miguel that night, because he did not do so "with a humble heart." But, he remained optimistic that one day he would hug Miguel.

Cook continued his weekly visits to Santa Fe until one Monday in June. I arrived at Rodrigo's house as usual, but found it unusually quiet. Rodrigo explained to me that he had sent home all the patients. The night before, the community had held an assembly to discuss Cook's presence, deciding "they don't want his religion here." They did not object to the consultations, according to Rodrigo, but rather to his religion. But Rodrigo knew that Cook would not bring his medicine if he were not also allowed to preach. Now I saw that all of Miguel's assurances to Cook that a vote of the community would be inevitably in his favor had been disingenuous. Miguel affirmed the right of each individual to choose her religion, but then orchestrated Cook's ouster to keep the community solidly Catholic. Cook quickly understood that no amount of donated medicine or political connections would make his presence in Santa Fe welcome. As he wrote in a pamphlet to his financial supporters, "I felt the pains of a young man in love when a girlfriend was saying good-bye."

For Alejandra, the setback was spiritual. She interpreted the community opposition in stark Christian terms:

> It's Satan who's driving them. We hope the work of God will go ahead. It's very painful to stop praising the Lord. We'll pray in our homes in the meantime. God has the answer, but we don't know it. This is a test to see if we're really with God. I won't separate myself from God. We'll be orphans for a little while. They can separate me from Doctor Juan, but not from God.

Though she continued to see Dr. Cook at the Morelia hospital and at his main church in Ario, her faith remained independent of him. For a year, Cook had a pastor in Santa Fe direct the worship services and train Alejandra to be a pastor. With Cook's expulsion, the visiting pastor left too, leaving her as the leader of the congregation. Given the danger of meeting as a group, Alejandra coordinated stealth prayer sessions where a few people would come to her home every afternoon at five o'clock, while all the other church members would pray simultaneously from their homes.

In the summer of 2000, Dr. Cook rented a party hall in Quiroga—the scene of many Catholic life ritual celebrations—for the women of Santa Fe to continue their weekly worship. He scheduled the Bible studies for Thursday evenings so he could attend on his way home from the hospital in Morelia. This exile continued until the summer of 2001. When I paid a return visit to

3.3 In 2001, Alejandra and her daughter show me the place of worship that was once her bedroom. Biblical passages and song lyrics line the walls. The device that Dr. Cook uses to accompany their services is on the chair to the left.

Alejandra that August, she led me enthusiastically to the room I remembered as her bedroom, promising to show me "something." Chairs instead of beds lined the perimeter of the room, and a portrait of Jesus decorated the wall (Figure 3.3). She pointed proudly to the posted schedule of services: Thursday at 5:30 P.M. and Sunday at 6 P.M. Cook still has not reappeared in Santa Fe, fearing his presence might cause conflict, but he participates during the Sunday service via speakerphone. Some people in Santa Fe travel to Ario for medical treatment with Dr. Cook, but even without free medicine, the congregation has grown to eighty believers. "They come seeking God, not medicines," Alejandra tells me. After the uncertain months when she thought she would lose both her house and her faith, Alejandra becomes giddy thinking of her good fortune. "The blessings are very high right now. They threatened to take away my land rights, but now I have them back. I have my church back. I'm content. Now we are free." She and her husband opened a small grocery store they call "Tienda de Alfarero," or "The Potter's Store," which is a signal to fellow evangelicals that theirs is a house of God, the divine potter. Alejandra showed me photos of Dr. Cook baptizing her husband, which has also contributed to her happiness. The only stain on her good mood was her son in the United States, who has not joined her religion and continues to drink alcohol.

In the promotional brochure Cook sends to his supporters in the United States, he attributes the positive change of heart among the leaders in Santa Fe to a mixture of divine favor and medical generosity.

> During the next few months, the families of the town authorities began to experience illnesses and require surgery. . . . Four of six families had become afflicted and were in need. Our hearts were opened to them and we blessed them. In June they agreed to allow the Palm Beach Gardens Christ Fellowship Medical-Dental Team to return for a campaign. Again they were blessed and within a month another general assembly was held with a new resolution ratified with not a single vote against us, nullifying the former edict and extending a formal invitation for our return.

However, I heard a contradictory story from Alejandra, who continued to fight the local leaders without Cook. After the first assembly, where she felt the local authorities humiliated her, she called for a meeting with the jefes de tenencia. She described how her willingness to compromise helped soften their opposition to her church.

> They told me that as authorities, religion doesn't matter to them. They are all good because they talk of God. What matters to them is that first, the town is not divided, second, that evangelicals don't pay cooperaciones so the traditions will end, and third, that evangelicals don't participate in politics, and we need everyone to defend our lands.
>
> I replied: First, we won't divide the town. They [Catholics] all like fun, dancing, and drunkenness. In the gospel there is none of this. Even if 1 percent convert, they'll still have the rest. It's very difficult to walk with God. Doctor Juan doesn't say, "I give you a pill so you have to come." It's the same as their church: when the bells ring, those who want to come, come. Those who don't, don't. Second, we'll continue to pay cooperaciones. We know from the Bible that it's not good, but if we don't we'll be harming ourselves. We have to adapt to what the great majority says. Third, everyone knows that I spend a lot of money and effort to defend our lands. We will obey the Law of Agrarian Reform and the authorities. But they have to respect our rights too.

Alejandra made the case for her church without consulting Dr. Cook. Her arguments might even have displeased him. While she seemed content with a small band of evangelicals, Dr. Cook constantly expanded his evangelizing efforts to new communities and new patients. Alejandra also agreed to continue contributing to the Catholic community celebrations, a practice Dr. Cook preached against. After her family converted, Alejandra still displayed images of saints in her bedroom until Dr. Cook saw them and asked her to remove them. Cook condemned the consumption of alcohol and the adoration of images that accompanied fiestas, yet Alejandra understood the importance of unity in a close-knit indigenous community.

To listen to Pope John Paul II and Catholics in Tzintzuntzan, it would seem that evangelical churches owe their success to an unstoppable flow of foreign money and insidious missionary activity. The case of Dr. Cook shows that a well-financed North American leader does not guarantee widespread conversion. His attempt to establish a church in Tzintzuntzan fizzled from lack of interest, and determined resistance from Miguel prevented Cook from establishing a church in Santa Fe. While patently unconstitutional, the expulsion of Dr. Cook carried the weight of the community's wishes. Dr. Cook knew not to challenge the decision, even though he enjoyed access to the governor of the state. Evangelicals succeeded in founding a congregation in Santa Fe only through the courage and persistence of local leaders like Alejandra, who persuaded authorities that she and other converts would continue to participate in the political and ceremonial life of the community. Converts do not accept evangelical doctrine wholesale, nor do they give up their commitments to the larger Catholic community. Individuals who convert, whether to counter the crippling effects of alcoholism or to seek spiritual fulfillment, emphasize the continuity as much as the break from their previous ways of life. They are mindful of maintaining cordial relations with their neighbors. Dr. Cook may be able to retreat to his compound, but Alejandra remains in the community of her birth. The example of Santa Fe illustrates the willingness of evangelicals and Catholics to coexist peacefully and suggests how they can participate in a mutual exchange of beliefs and practices.

FOUR

RESPONDING TO THE MINORITY: CATHOLIC SELF-IMPROVEMENT

ONE Monday afternoon in Santa Fe, I joined a prayer circle with Dr. Cook and a group of two dozen Purépecha women and children. An assistant minister delivered a sermon in the indigenous language. Then Dr. Cook, in sandals and poncho, called in Spanish for those who were suffering to kneel. Approaching each woman, he placed his hands on her head and prayed for her by name. Meanwhile, his partner sang a lilting tune a cappella: "Jesus, I know you are great. Jesus, I know you are strong." When Cook finished, he hugged each woman. I then walked two blocks to the parish church. There, I encountered Father Huacuz celebrating Mass in front of another two dozen Purépecha women and girls. Swathed in a starched white robe embroidered with a wine goblet and grapes traced in gold thread, he stood majestically in front of the altar. He spoke a rapid-fire Spanish into the microphone, eliciting collective responses from the women. During the communion, the parishioners sang a familiar hymn while the priest dispensed the wafers and the wine. As soon as the women returned to the pews, Father Huacuz cleaned the communion chalice, recited the final prayers, and blessed us all.

Compared to the intimacy and personal attention of the evangelical service, Mass seems sedate and routine. This appearance of a changeless and remote Mass, however, belies a very real and active effort on the part of the Catholic Church to make the Church more accessible and relevant to the lives of parishioners around Lake Pátzcuaro. This effort is in part a response to the evangelical churches; as much as Catholic clergy and laity raise suspicions about converts, they have also taken notice of their growing number and success in attracting followers. In Tzintzuntzan, the Catholic Church has not remained static in the face of emerging challenges to its spiritual dominance. At every level of the Church hierarchy, from the Vatican to diocesan leaders to lay members, Catholics have modernized both the liturgy and practice of their faith. In many cases, the reforms incorporate evangelical ideas of a personal relationship with the divine and the reading of Scripture.

CONFRONTING CRISIS IN THE CATHOLIC CHURCH

Minutes after finishing Mass, Father Huacuz greeted me in his office, his robe hanging behind the door. We spoke about the history of the Catholic Church in Mexico and how the seemingly uninspired, rote Mass belies a dynamic and fervently held faith. In the past thirty years alone, Father Huacuz said he has noticed "enormous" differences in the Church, which have caused it to "change completely." In his own case, on Sundays in Santa Fe, he celebrates the Mass half in Spanish and half in Purépecha. He has also established eight Bible study groups, one for each neighborhood. The leaders of each group meet with him weekly to discuss relevant themes. Every Saturday, nearly three dozen children convene for catechism classes.

In the past, Father Huacuz continued, priests administered the sacraments, and parishioners received them. Now the priest involves himself in all aspects of the community, and the parishioners participate more actively in the liturgy. Huacuz learned the indigenous language so he could deliver sermons to his parishioners in their own language. He worked with civic authorities to establish a potable water supply. His reforms aim to make church members become more involved. Children receive religious instruction for three months before taking their first communion. Couples study pamphlets on the religious significance of marriage and must pass a test on their understanding of the material before they can be wed.

These changes are institutionalized throughout the diocese. All the priests around Lake Pátzcuaro meet frequently for conferences and retreats, and once a month they meet with the archbishop's representative for the lake region. Father Huacuz told me these efforts form part of a plan to bring the Church "up to date." The Catholic Church has spent decades responding to criticism that it has failed to adjust to the changing lives of its parishioners. Duncan Green (1991) traces the crisis of the Catholic Church to the period of the 1930s, when it did not move to minister to the growing population on the urban periphery. "Grown fat and lazy through its links to the rich, the Church had only the shallowest roots among the poor majority with which to confront a new era" (174). In the 1960s, the Church distanced itself even further from its traditional base, as evidenced by the diminishing number of baptized Catholics who attended weekly Mass. A Colombian priest called his fellow clergy to act: "If only 20 percent of Latin America's baptized Catholics regularly attend Mass, this doesn't mean that the remaining are not Christians. . . . It means that we priests have not bothered, or known how, to bring these people into the community of the Church" (quoted in Lernoux 1982:380).

With the Vatican's Second Ecumenical Council (1962–1965), the Catholic Church acknowledged the importance of making its canon more accessible to followers. Priests began to offer Mass in Spanish instead of Latin and turned to face their parishioners.[1] In Michoacán, priests also introduced practices into the Mass to foster a sense of goodwill. It is now customary in the region before the priest offers communion to shake hands with other members of the congregation, wishing them peace. When this practice began, one man told me, many people were confused. He thought his neighbor was asking for a donation, so he put some coins in his outstretched palm! In 1968, Latin American bishops met to extend the Church's new emphasis on human rights to liberation theology. Followers of this doctrine formed Christian Base Communities (CEBs in Spanish) in which members applied biblical lessons to contemporary structures of inequality, using religion as a basis for social action. In Brazil and Nicaragua, liberation theology demonstrated the potential to contribute to revolutionary class consciousness (Burdick 1993; Lancaster 1988). However, CEBs never achieved widespread success in Mexico; a more conservative theology remained ascendant in the 1980s and 1990s.

Those at the highest levels of the Catholic Church have continued to recognize the spread of competing religious groups in Latin America as worthy of attention (C. Smith and Prokopy 1999). Several Catholic authors, such as Amatulli (1984) and Galindo (1994), have issued hortatory tracts suggesting reforms to reinvigorate the Church. As part of an ongoing effort at ecumenism, the Vatican Secretariat for Christian Unity began open-ended discussions with the most established Pentecostal churches in 1972 (Cleary 1992). In 1996, the Mexican Council of Bishops released a report on its website detailing challenges to pastoral work in the twenty-first century. The bishops' document blames their own lack of proselytizing activity for the growth in evangelical churches. The bishops conclude that the situation in Mexico "requires that we change our mentality and . . . improve our relationship with other churches and religious groups" (Conferencia del Episcopado Mexicano 2001). The migration of Mexicans to the United States has posed a new challenge to the Catholic Church by further stretching limited resources. Richard Rodriguez (1992), the child of Catholic Mexican immigrants, spoke with Catholic priests in California about the challenges they face in ministering to newly diverse congregations. They told him that without additional bilingual priests and sufficient places of worship in the neighborhoods where migrants settled, the Catholic Church in the United States was not prepared to receive the influx of Mexican Catholics.[2]

The Church in Mexico confronts the same difficulties of recruiting and training young men to be priests, and it is increasingly unlikely that priests will have any connection to the geographic region where they serve. Tzintzuntzan is typical, with a lone priest from another part of the state ministering to three thousand parishioners. Father Rogelio, the parish priest in Tzintzuntzan while I conducted my fieldwork, is one of the community's most sophisticated men, as comfortable working with the Internet as with mourning relatives, but he has few friends and prefers to spend most of his time alone on his laptop computer. The Archbishop of Morelia assigns priests to each parish for six-year stints. When I was in Tzintzuntzan, Father Rogelio had two years left to serve, and parishioners were counting the days. Unlike previous priests, who paid social visits to people's homes and played on sports teams, Father Rogelio remained aloof. He insisted on long-winded and mildly condescending sermons, which sent the audience into either profound concentration or dozing, both of which looked the same to this observer.

Just as Taylor (1996) found in eighteenth-century Mexican parishes, I noticed that Tzintzuntzeño Catholics can be anticlerical without rejecting the validity of the priesthood and that parishioners count on the priest to officiate at life-cycle rituals even if they do not include him in everyday displays of devotion. As the only person in the parish qualified to deliver the sacraments, Father Rogelio maintains a hectic schedule. His blessings do not come free, however. To have a Mass dedicated to the memory of a loved one costs money; so do baptisms, weddings, funerals, first communions, and confirmations. Since he draws his income from the payments and alms he receives, Father Rogelio makes regular trips to the surrounding hamlets to hold as many Masses as possible. Though he lacked the populist streak of Father Huacuz, Father Rogelio committed himself to making the parish church a center of community devotion. When lay members initiated activities relevant to their daily lives as Catholics, he supported them unequivocally, even if he did not participate directly.

LEARNING TO PRAY AND LIVE

During my second week in Tzintzuntzan, I went to visit the parish church. Though I had been there a few times to celebrate Mass, I had not been able to observe the building without worshippers and without worrying that I was not standing up at the appropriate moments in the service. The exterior doors opened into another set of locked wooden doors, forcing me to enter the sanctuary from the side. Before I did, I paused to examine the glass bulletin board on the closed pair of doors beneath a smiling, youthful photograph of Pope John Paul II. I noticed a poster advertising the start of a Prayer and Life Workshop (Taller de Oración y Vida), whose stated goal was "to learn and deepen the art of praying." Classes were open to everyone, with "evangelicals" explicitly invited. A notice on the board directed the curious to see a woman named Diana, who lived in the plaza.

Estela took me to Diana's house and introduced me to a careworn older woman. Though I had passed her door many times, I had assumed from the boarded-up windows that the house was abandoned. Walking with evident pain, Diana invited me into her courtyard, where we sat down. After explaining who I was and the aims of my research, I asked her how she had become involved in the workshops. She spoke deliberately and without much eye contact, telling me how she had been a wife for forty-three years, the mother of fourteen, and the grandmother of eighty before she became a widow. She grew solemn: "When my husband died, I was disconsolate. I was incapable of doing anything. I didn't want to leave the house, and I began to drink." Wiping away tears, she continued:

> A friend encouraged me to come to the Prayer and Life Workshops. My parents raised me Catholic, but at first I didn't understand what they were saying at the workshops. I felt useless. But then, I understood. It made me another person. After finding God, I became a guide myself. I went to a three-day training course in Morelia. Now, I go to Mass every day and don't commit mortal sins. I also teach catechism classes to children. This week we are starting a new cycle of the workshop. No matter how many people attend, I'm committed to teaching the whole course.

She spoke with the zeal of a convert. Indeed, her story of transformation closely paralleled many of the life narratives evangelicals told me. For Diana, it *was* a type of conversion since her previous devotion to Catholicism had been superficial and did not prevent her from committing sins.

She went on to explain that the workshops meet once a week from five to seven in the evening for fifteen weeks. Diana and Marta, the other leader, try to offer two sessions a year. In the fall of 1999, they began by holding a workshop Monday evenings in the parish church, then repeating the lesson Tuesdays at the small chapel in La Colonia. Since both Diana and Marta also teach catechism classes to children, they meet with the priest and other instructors once a week. Although Father Rogelio gives his permission for the workshops, he does not participate in them directly. In fact, the workshops cater exclusively to women. They receive the imprimatur of a Chilean priest, Father Ignacio Larrañaga, who writes the materials for the course, but women comprise both the leaders and the students. Later, Marta admitted to me that she had a difficult time recruiting students for the workshops. Despite announcements in the parish church and pamphlets passed door-to-door, she managed to convince only six women (and one anthropologist) to attend the fall series. After a few weeks with only one woman attending the workshop on Monday nights, Marta merged the two groups so that we all met Tuesdays in La Colonia. In October, halfway through the workshop, Diana closed her house for good and moved to Tacoma, Washington, to live with one of her sons.

Marta vented her frustration about the lack of enthusiasm for the course. "People here have Bibles they receive as gifts at their wedding, but they keep them locked up like souvenirs. They think going to Mass on Sundays is enough. They're too busy to join the workshops, they say. But what better way is there to spend your time?" In reality, I found that the situation was not so dire. Over the past eight years many women in Tzintzuntzan have taken the course, so they did not feel the need to sign up again. Other women would have liked to take the course, but clashed with Diana and Marta. One woman told me that she once had borrowed money from Diana, who charged her exorbitant interest, so she no longer associated with her. Marta alienated many women because she was an outsider to Tzintzuntzan who had separated from her Tzintzuntzeño husband but continued to live in the community.

At the first session I attended, the students and leaders sat in pews in a side chapel of the parish church. I was the only man, and Diana was the only other person I knew. Even so, no one made me feel uncomfortable. Marta asked my name and remarked kindly that Saint Peter formed the rock on which the Church was built. Throughout the two hours, she would call on me by name, asking for my thoughts. Similarly, the other students present did not go silent in embarrassment of my presence. At the end, Marta handed me an assignment sheet for the following week just as she did to the others.

We began by standing and reading from a booklet called "Encounter: A Prayer Manual." It contained prayers, meditations, and poems on several themes. This day's theme was "God of tenderness," which Marta emphasized as she led us from one activity to the next. We stood to recite together the ninth prayer in the book, entitled "Invocation of the Holy Spirit":

> Come, divine spirit
> Send your light from heaven
> Loving father of the poor
> In your splendid gifts
> Your light penetrates the souls,
> Source of the greatest comfort.

Then we sat facing Marta, who spoke with the authority cultivated in years of teaching elementary school. "Just like when you iron you have a goal to press your clothes, so does this workshop have a goal: to know that you are a child of God, a beloved child of the father. He is not a punishing God. Jesus said God is a father who loves us without conditions." Following Marta's instructions, we rose again to read another meditation from the prayer book, this time "with great devotion." Reading together aloud, I could hear the cadences of my companions' voices and tried to modulate my own to match theirs. Though I did not know these women very well, we rapidly gained a shared set of experiences that would spill over into camaraderie outside the classes.

After reading aloud, we sat in silent meditation for two minutes. Then Marta distributed a double-sided card with suggestions for how to read the Bible. As she had told me, most of the participants in the workshops had never read the Bible before. I thought of Yunuen, the Catholic woman who defended her disinclination to read the Bible to her Jehovah's Witness sister-in-law by saying, "I don't need to [read it] because I can go to Mass and hear the priest tell me the same themes." The instruction card outlined the reading process step by step, taking into account Catholics' lack of experience in reading the Bible. Marta read us the suggestions on the card, repeating the points she found most crucial. We should read slowly, without anxiety or haste. We should not get discouraged if we failed to understand a passage. We should underline phrases, scribble in the margins, and ruminate on what we had read. The instructions explicitly undermined the monopoly of the priest in interpreting Scripture. They invited us to substitute our own names for Jacob, Moses, and others, imagining that the Lord had addressed us directly. They also counseled patience. If the meaning of a passage did not reveal itself immediately, we should remain calm and keep meditating on the words, "letting the vibrations and emotions inundate you." Nowhere did the course suggest that biblical verses had a single, correct reading. To the contrary, it encouraged us to engage with the text, arriving at an interpretation with personal resonance.

Next, Marta asked a woman to read aloud from the Book of Hosea in the Old Testament. Of the three female students, only one had brought a Bible, and she had difficulty locating the particular passage. At Jehovah's Witness services, the quantity of biblical passages cited and the speed with which the congregants located them had impressed me. There are more than sixty books in the Old and New Testaments, arranged in a particular order and organized in a varying number of chapters and verses. I empathized with the flustered student who was unable to find Hosea, since until I became familiar with the constant flipping between books of the Bible I had had to rely on Post-it notes or the table of contents. After the woman had read the verses, Marta asked what the passage meant to us. Silence. This might have been the first time anyone had ever asked these women for their impressions of a biblical verse. Parishioners in Mass displayed ritualistic deference to the Holy Bible, standing during a reading from the gospels and marking the end of a reading with the solemn recitation, "Glory and honor to you, Lord Jesus." Then, the audience would listen impassively as the priest offered his exegesis.

I decided to respond. I mentioned that God was so compassionate to his people that, even when they disobeyed him, he offered them aid. Marta seemed pleased, and then asked the woman who had read for her reaction. She remained silent, so Marta asked another student. The woman said simply, "We should show our children the right path." Marta turned to a fourth student, who replied only that she agreed with the previous woman. Marta offered her own lesson: "That's how much God loves us—without conditions. He doesn't love us only if we bring a candle to the church. This is just a building; the Church is all who are baptized. You can pray anywhere and be with God." Her message about the unimportance of the place of worship sharply contradicts what many of the women had been taught as children.

We sang a song, then practiced another meditative silence. The final segment of the two-hour session focused on a "modality" for reading the Bible. During each week of the workshop, we learned a new way of reading the Bible: meditative, auditory, written, visual, collective, and out-of-doors, for example. The first modality asked us to pray while reading. As Marta explained it, we were to read slowly, "with all our souls, making the sentences ours." The prayer manual explained further, "Think of God as the other shore; to connect with that shore we do not need many bridges; a single bridge is sufficient, a single sentence is enough to keep us linked." These strategies privilege literacy as the most effective way to communicate with God. Significantly, this message allows each individual believer to construct her own bridge to the divine without mediation. Once again, we stood for a prayer from the prayer manual, and once again Marta asked us for our thoughts. As with the first time, no one took the floor, even after Marta's friendly prodding. Either my presence inhibited the women's free flow of ideas, or they were unaccustomed to expressing original opinions about religious literature. In future meetings, the women grew more comfortable with both novelties, and they shared their thoughts more openly.

To end the session, Marta passed out a sheet summarizing the modality and assigning us biblical passages to read as homework, with which we could implement our newly learned "prayed reading." During the weeks of the workshop, we were supposed to spend thirty minutes a day reading the Bible. Finally we stood, formed a circle, and held hands while reciting the Paternoster. Before disbanding, Marta led us in a blessing. In later sessions, we began by reviewing the homework. Marta remained the leader, guiding us from song to prayer, but she also came to function as therapist, asking us our impressions of the reading exercises. She played some cassette tapes that retold biblical parables and others that taught us relaxation techniques. At times, I had to suppress laughter as a very serious male voice, presumably Father Larrañaga's, intoned such fatuous phrases as, "Your stomach is peace. Your throat is peace." We would even listen to New Age instrumental music while reading the Psalms. Other times I had the sense of being in a yoga class as we practiced praying in different positions: recumbent, prostrate, a modified lotus position. Marta's probing of our reactions to each passage or prayer remained a constant. She accepted every answer as valid and would often restate it to show she understood.

By the time we consolidated the classes in La Colonia and Diana had left for an indefinite stay in Tacoma, attendance had stabilized at six women who came every week to participate. Although the students never became truly garrulous in the sessions, they did share their thoughts more freely. Most commonly, they would talk about how the meditative silences and unhurried readings helped them relieve tension. One woman remarked that, after practicing one of the modalities for ten minutes, the "stone" that had been rattling in her brain left. Other women spoke of overcoming anxiety, particularly through their strong identification with the Virgin Mary, whose motherly toil and suffering God rewarded in heaven. The participants in the workshop came to see that the Bible did not belong sealed on a shelf. They learned systematic ways of reading a complicated text and placed value on their own interpretations of Scripture. Later I spoke with a woman who had attended the workshop. I asked her if she liked going to the sessions.

> Yes, I try to live my life as a good Christian. Only there's not always time to attend. I'm not perfect. Nestor [her neighbor] has insisted that we come to his sect, but that would make me another Judas. I'm Catholic by conviction, not by inheritance. I take care of my relationship with God. They take care of theirs. I won't judge them.

Her identification as Catholic went beyond Yunuen's, who said she was Catholic because her parents raised her that way. Instead of attacking the evangelical presence in La Colonia as a threat, this woman deepened her own faith.

Despite her unfavorable reputation in the community, Marta remained an effective workshop leader and confidante of the priest. I often stopped to talk to Marta in the evenings when she would hang out chatting at a small grocery store across from my house. Spending time at a store where many men bought and consumed alcohol as well as leaving her house unattended earned Marta the scorn of several women in Tzintzuntzan. I, however, admired her bravado and wondered if her Catholic devotion contributed to her independence. After the workshop I attended had ended, I talked to Marta about the goals of the course. She told me that there was a lot of misunderstanding among Catholics about their faith. Once she tried to begin a workshop in a small community close to Tzintzuntzan, but the Catholics were suspicious and ran her out of town, much as evangelicals have been expelled from Chamula. As the women in Tzintzuntzan became more involved in the workshop, their tolerance for other religions grew. During a round of sharing thoughts that began every session, one woman told us how she had been having trouble with a friend who had joined a "sect." "But thanks to this week's lesson, I've come to peace with her." Marta applauded her maturity: "Everyone has a different way to get to Pátzcuaro; some go by bus, some by taxi, some by foot, but they all arrive at the same place. So it is with faiths." Significantly, the materials accompanying the workshop did not denigrate evangelical churches and promoted tolerance of other beliefs.

The workshop taught a brand of personal faith that deviated sharply from typical Catholic devotion in Tzintzuntzan. Marta commented that many Catholics in Tzintzuntzan tried to outdo each other with false piety, but she followed the example of Jesus: "I have friends of all religions. My sister is a

Jehovah's Witness. But there's no tension in our family. Each of us will have to account to God in the end. The Prayer and Life Workshops are not designed to stop the growth of sects, just to teach prayer. They are open to all. Jesus used to spend time with the sinners and the prostitutes. He came to save the sick, not the healthy." For Marta, participation in the workshops increased her tolerance for other religions and intensified her commitment to her own. She behaved according to her understanding of Scripture, dismissing her detractors as ignorant of their own faith. Over the years, many women in Tzintzuntzan have heard the message of the workshops encouraging them to seek religious guidance from holy texts, not simply from what they learned as children. With the renewed devotion to practicing and improving their own Catholicism, women became less critical of their evangelical neighbors.

REPAIRING MARRIAGES

While the Workshops of Prayer and Life reached a core group of women in the community, another program sponsored by the parish church had a much wider impact. It too exemplifies how the Catholic Church incorporates evangelical elements in an effort to educate its parishioners. In November 1999, a couple from a small community near Tzintzuntzan persuaded the parish priest to allow them to hold a weekend retreat for married couples. The priest sponsored the event and offered use of the convent, but only five couples signed up for the first retreat. A man who attended the first retreat admitted to me that initially he was embarrassed to go for fear that people would think he was an evangelical. After the community accepted that the Catholic Church was adopting uncharacteristic programs, it embraced the workshops. Meeting the overwhelming demand for the event required three subsequent retreats in the following year, with more promised in the future. These have proved extremely popular with women, the usual participants in religious events, and also with men. As a single man, I was not allowed to attend any of the sessions during the two-day workshops, but I heard from participants that the talks concentrate on conquering alcohol to improve family relations and encourage the emotional release associated with evangelical churches.

About thirty couples sign up for each retreat, which take place in the Franciscan convent next to the parish church. Couples from other parts of Mexico who are veterans of the retreat organize each event, which lasts from 7 A.M. to 8 P.M. over a Saturday and a Sunday. They provide food and child care at no cost so the couples can focus on the half-dozen themes addressed each day. Some themes are explicitly religious, including a chat from the parish priest about the role of faith in a family. Other topics address communication, family crises, children's education, and parenting, all presented so as to elicit audience involvement.

On the final day of the second retreat, the priest dedicated the 6 P.M. Mass to the couples. They lined up at the entrance to the church, where the priest greeted them with sprinkles of holy water. He conveyed his congratulations and hopes that they would live differently now. The double column of couples followed him into the church, where they filled the first several rows of pews. All the participants wore heart-shaped nametags, while the women carried small bouquets. At the end of the service, the priest instructed the couples to stand and hold hands. They renewed their marital vows with the men repeating after the priest, "I promise to love you and respect you all the days of my life." The women, in turn, repeated, "I accept you. I keep on offering you my love and fidelity." Then, the priest called each couple forward to hand them a diploma. The rest of the parishioners clapped jubilantly. The couples exited the church into a shower of confetti and the music of a quartet playing and singing a rhythmic tune, "I have faith that everything will change." The couples, their families, and other well-wishers followed the band to a courtyard in the convent, singing and clapping along. Amid hugs and more music, helpers distributed coffee, tea, and bread (but no alcohol) to everyone assembled.

After such a retreat, couples continue their involvement by leading retreats in other communities or by inviting friends to participate in future retreats. All participants take turns caring for a tabletop figure of Christ on the cross that passes from house to house each week. Several couples also serve as godparents for a communal wedding held periodically in the parish church. Father Rogelio revived the custom of offering a free ceremony for couples who want to get married but cannot afford the expense of a Mass and a fiesta. On the first Sunday he celebrated the communal wedding, he married eight couples at once and hosted a party with eight cakes and no alcohol. This too proved so popular that Father Rogelio planned several more with the help of alumni from the marriage retreats.

The participants use the language of conversion to describe the effects of the weekend. The wife of an Alcoholics Anonymous member spoke glowingly about her experience: "I have seen a change in the couples who took part. They have more dialogue, understand their children better, and live better with their spouses. But you have to be disposed to change. If not, you can hear a thousand workshops and they won't do you any good." Because her heart was open to change, as the evangelicals would say, the retreat trans-formed her life. The man who overcame his prejudices to attend the first retreat with his wife told me that during the weekend many women asked how they could help end their husbands' drinking. The organizers prohibited alcohol during the retreat and encouraged the participants to see that alcohol was not a necessary part of Catholic life. He continued, "I used to think that if there weren't fights and drunkenness it wasn't a good party. Now I don't need liquor to have a good time at a party. Most people worry too much about the festivities and forget about the spiritual side. They taught us to respect our partners and our children."

The marriage retreats offer a chance to restore harmony to family relations without couples having to leave the Catholic Church. In much the same way evangelical churches operate, the dominant Catholic Church has adapted its message to reflect the concerns of its parishioners. New programs like the Workshop of Prayer and Life and marriage retreats aim to improve partici-pants' lives using the established resources of the Catholic Church. To convey their message, however, these activities borrow freely from evangelical beliefs and practices.

CONVERTING INVISIBLY

Although most Catholics remain in the Catholic Church and value tradi-tional fiesta celebrations, the prayer workshops and marriage retreats dem-onstrate their respect for ideas prominent in other belief systems. In a ques-tionnaire of Catholics in Almolonga, Guatemala, Goldin and Metz (1991) found evidence that Catholics praised their converted evangelical neighbors. Without changing their religious affiliations, many Catholics accepted evan-gelical criticisms of the wasteful fiesta system. The entire town—not just the self-identified converts—experienced a shift toward an evangelical idea of improvement through individual effort. They call these Catholics who have adopted many evangelical beliefs without public acknowledgment "invisible converts." A similar phenomenon is occurring around Lake Pátzcuaro, but Catholic response to evangelical presence goes beyond a passive mimicry of certain traits. Catholics reserve far more skepticism for their own religious traditions than for the evangelical ones. They sympathize with the evangelical rejection of excessive fiestas and the doctrine of papal infallibility. This self-critique does not predispose Catholics to convert, but rather allows them to deepen their own Catholic faith.

Unlike the evangelicals, who talk incessantly and with great introspection about their faith, Catholics tend to be more reticent when asked about what religion means to them. For many, nothing as dramatic as a conversion event has forced them to consider how they relate to the divine. Even in the Prayer and Life Workshops, where faith is the central theme, Catholics do not articulate their convictions well. They stick to bland generalities, telling me that the Scripture they read and the fiestas they celebrate are "very beautiful." Another factor that may make some Catholics reluctant to express their personal feelings about religion could be their formal relationship with me. Among Catholics who became close friends, I was able to elicit less guarded opinions about their religion.

In some cases, self-criticism emerged through humor. A family that had served as key informants to the Fosters since their arrival in Tzintzuntzan quickly adopted me as well. They asked me to take part in their son's wedding as a godparent and included me in all their family celebrations. During fiesta time, the family took pride in explaining to me the roles of all the cargo holders and the meanings of each ritual. Their experience with anthropologists had made them comfortable around me, and they always punctuated our conversations with jokes. One afternoon as I was leaving Norma and Ricardo's house with a stash of Jehovah's Witness magazines in my shoulder bag, I stopped to chat with my godchildren, who were sitting outside with family members. They spotted the literature I was carrying and asked me what I felt about the Jehovah's Witnesses. Not wanting to disrespect either faith, I decided to tell a joke I had learned:

> There's a long line at the gates to enter heaven. Saint Peter greets each of the new residents and asks them what religion they are. The first man says he's a Jehovah's Witness. Saint Peter says, "Okay, you're in room twelve. Just walk quietly when you pass room number eight." The next man says he is a Buddhist. Saint Peter directs him to room fifteen with the same instructions to step quietly past room number eight. When it's the third man's turn, he says, "I understand putting people with others of their own religion, but why do we have to be quiet when we pass room number eight?" Saint Peter responds, "Oh, those are the Catholics. They think they're the only ones here."

It was a risk. Still, I figured that our relationship had matured to a level of mutual affection. Moreover, the joke drew on an image familiar to Catholics: Saint Peter at the gates of heaven. To my relief, they laughed and laughed. From then on, "room number eight" became our code word for Catholics. Waving hello to them, I would call out, "How are you?" They would reply, "Everything is fine in room number eight!" Their ability to mock their own exclusive claims to salvation showed me how open they were to other ideas.

Catholics express forceful opinions, both positive and negative, about the fiestas. In many cases, they defend the preservation of traditions, but other times they just as vehemently oppose the profligate spending involved. The celebrations of the cross in May elicit particularly disapproving statements from Catholics. One middle-aged man who runs a sandwich stand near the town hall told me he would never receive the cargo for a cross:

> Don Vasco de Quiroga left us with many fiestas. They grow every
> year. Thirty years ago it wasn't like this. There were just six crosses
> celebrated, and it wasn't so elaborate. Each year there are more
> crosses and bigger fiestas. I estimate that in all the crosses they spend
> 350,000 pesos. The Ojo de Agua cargueros spend three thousand
> pesos each. That money would be better spent on fixing my house.
> For that I could buy thirty meters of mosaic tile for the house. If I
> really wanted cake, it would be cheaper to buy it myself. There is so
> much poverty here; how do they afford it?

His objections to wasting his money on the cakes, decorations, and music necessary for a celebration of the cross (see Figure 4.1) sound similar to the complaints of Tzintzuntzan's evangelicals, but they do not prevent him from attending the nightly festivities or from considering himself a devout Catholic.

Many other Catholics consider the elaborate display of the May crosses obscene. They condemn the celebration using language that would be appropriate in any evangelical pastor's sermon. During the first week of May 2000, a neighbor of mine was grieving the death of his grandmother, a custom called the "*novenario*," which involves nine consecutive nights of ritual group mourning. After attending the nightly rosaries and prayers, several of his guests left to participate in the parties at the crosses. He spoke bitterly of his family and friends:

> You can't go dance and receive the cargo of the cross when you're
> in mourning. You should pray, have discipline. It's good to remem-
> ber the sacred sign of the cross, but not with alcohol, fighting, and
> dancing. You shouldn't dance in front of the cross. When Moses came
> down the mountain and then found people dancing around a golden
> calf, he scolded them. It's pagan. There should be respect for the

4.1 The Day of the Holy Cross, May 3, has extended to include a week of celebrations. Each of more than twenty neighborhood crosses receive ritual attention from cargueros, who provide decorations, cakes, and alcohol.

cross where Jesus Christ died. It's valid to dance with the cake to show you've received the cargo, so people know who the cargueros are. But just that bit. Many stay to drink. There are places to dance, but not in a religious cargo. When we drink a lot, we fall in error. It's offensive to drink in front of the holy cross. That's disorder, not Christian faith.

For him, being a proper Catholic means "discipline" and the preservation of order, the same words Ricardo uses to describe his life as a Jehovah's Witness. Like Ricardo, my neighbor does not denounce all forms of partying, only the fiestas where drinking and disrespect detract from the religious message. In particular, the incongruous mixture of mourning and celebrating earns his displeasure.

Other times, I detected openness to heterodox ideas when I revealed how I felt about my own religion. Except for the biblical caricatures during the Easter Week passion play, Judaism remains a mystery to most Tzintzuntzeños. Although my own involvement in Judaism ended in early adolescence, I called myself Jewish when people asked me. The novenario provided an unusually contemplative space to talk about religion. When Micaela González, the matriarch of the family that hosts the Fosters, died, her novenario attracted one hundred mourners nightly. In each one-hour session, a man led us in chanting a rosary and singing melancholy songs. Then, the family served hot drinks and snacks in gratitude for our assistance in praying for the deceased's soul.

While we ate, the mood turned from somber to social. I spoke with Estela's *comadre,* who had come from Morelia to pray in the novenario. Barbara asked me about Judaism. I tried to explain the faith I remembered from my childhood in relation to Catholicism. I described how Jewish festivals also feature mourning for the dead, banquets, drinking, and dancing and how Jewish services resemble Catholic Mass, only on Saturdays. In terms of belief, Jews also follow the Bible, but consider only the books of the Old Testament to be God's word. Consequently, whereas Catholics are waiting for the Second Coming of the Messiah, Jews are waiting for the first. Estela joined us as Barbara began to respond:

Barbara: I'm Catholic, but I've been going to chats at another church in Morelia. I don't remember what it's called. They also say Jesus was a teacher, not the Messiah. We don't use the Bible, but they ask us about religion. There are open themes, and they teach us to talk in public.

Estela: You're convinced so easily, comadre. I won't change my religion. I have a friend who is a Jehovah's Witness. I've been to his church, but I won't change.

Barbara: Who wrote the gospels? How do we know they're true? I'm still Catholic, but I like to be open to all.

Estela: If Jesus didn't exist, why are there so many testimonies about him?

Barbara: The Bible isn't literal. Hell is not the pictures you see with fire. It's how you live. What I like about the Bible are the commandments. They are laws, barriers between good and bad—like the laws of the government. It's the same with religion.

Estela: One tries to do what God says is good, but then it's easy to start to gossip about so-and-so.

Barbara: Each according to her point of view.

Estela: All you need is faith.

Barbara had just participated in a Catholic ritual of prayer, asking the Lord to have mercy on Micaela's soul, yet she expressed doubts about the literal truth of the gospels. Estela tried to defend the Catholic Church, but ended up agreeing with Barbara that the ideals they taught in catechism were difficult to implement. They concluded with an affirmation of each person's right to believe what she wanted.

On the last night of the mourning, I made a point to talk to Barbara, who had come faithfully all nine days. According to the lessons the leader read after the rosaries, it was our responsibility to pray for the redemption of Micaela's soul. I asked Barbara if Micaela was finally out of purgatory now and in heaven. She remained skeptical, "That's what they say, but who knows? The indigenous people had it right. They worshipped the sun, the rain—things you can see." Barbara did not accept blindly the tenets of Christian faith; she wanted empirical evidence before believing. Yet, she still took on the role of godmother to Estela's children and still prayed dutifully at the novenario. She even called herself Catholic, but her idea of Catholicism encompassed more than what the priest preached.

In addition to criticizing their own church, Catholics like Barbara demonstrate a willingness to assimilate the ideas and participate in the rituals of other churches. In the mid-1990s, a team of researchers at the University of Guadalajara administered a survey to city residents about their religious practices and beliefs (Fortuny Loret de Mola 1999). Ninety percent of the 490 people surveyed identified themselves as Catholic, giving an indication of the overwhelming Catholic majority in the state of Jalisco, just north of Michoacán. As it turns out, many Catholics who strayed from the Church orthodoxy in their thinking were not even aware of it. When asked about their image of God, a plurality (42.4 percent) of self-identifying Catholics described him as the Holy Trinity, the belief taught by the Catholic Church. Yet, another 36.9 percent of Catholics characterized God as a "vital force or energy." De la Torre (1999:112) associates this definition of God with the New Age movement, an influence deemed so pernicious by the Catholic hierarchy that no less than the cardinal of Mexico himself issued a pastoral condemning the idea of God as a vital force. In a further contradiction with Catholic doctrine, 15.1 percent of Catholics expressed belief in the Eastern idea of reincarnation.

I encountered several Catholics around Lake Pátzcuaro who shared this willingness to listen to and incorporate ideas from other faiths so that they could strengthen their own Catholic faith. One evening, I found Estela in the kitchen conversing intimately with a young couple. She invited me to join them for some hot chocolate. The man, a veterinarian, used to rent the space in the front of Estela's house for his practice. Since moving his office to Pátzcuaro, he had not been back to visit Estela and her family. I had heard her praise him in the past, but I had never met him. After her husband passed away when he was in his forties, Estela was glad to have the veterinarian around the house as a male role model for her young sons. In conversation, I soon realized he and his new wife were Jehovah's Witnesses. They were talking theology, with the veterinarian quoting biblical passages fluently. After one of his long disquisitions on the afterlife, Estela shook her head solemnly, saying, "But what I don't understand is why my husband died so young." The veterinarian consoled her with more passages from Scripture, assuring her that his was "a God of the living, not the dead. He gives eternal life." Estela seemed unmoved by these words. "I know it's a sin," she said, "but I'm still angry at him for leaving me when we were so happy together." To me, this sounded like confession, only instead of confiding it to the parish priest, she admitted her feelings to a Jehovah's Witness veterinarian.

Although she never considered leaving her faith, Estela did begin to assimilate some ideas from her evangelical friend. She attended his wedding in a Jehovah's Witness Kingdom Hall and pronounced it "very nice." He supplied her with regular Jehovah's Witness publications for her perusal. Estela likes to read, so she simply adds the Jehovah's Witness literature to her personal library. She purchases the Catholic newspapers and magazines when they come to her door, keeping them near her sewing table. At night before going to bed, she reads books on herbal remedies or self-improvement. Once she showed me a Jehovah's Witness book written to encourage moral behavior in adolescents. She announced proudly that she had made all seven of her children read it in their teenage years. With so few magazines available and limited television reception, Catholic Tzintzuntzeños commonly glance at Jehovah's Witness literature. Many people politely refuse the magazines and books, but others accept them and, like Estela, flip through them occasionally. This exposure to other religions does not necessarily encourage Catholics to abandon their traditional faith, but it does contribute to a growing worldliness about religion that no longer views the Catholic Church as the only religious option.

Diana's son, a cofounder of Alcoholics Anonymous in Tzintzuntzan, considers himself a Catholic, though he does not attend Mass regularly. He participates in the community fiestas, but he mixes his Catholic faith with ideas from other belief systems. "All religions are good. I met some members of Luz del Mundo who talked to me about the Bible. I read the Jehovah's Witness literature. They have some interesting, high-quality articles. For the first day of spring, Estela's brother took me to the yácatas for a special ceremony. I felt like I was sweating, but when I wiped my brow, there was nothing. It was energy." At pre-Hispanic pyramid sites all over Mexico, New Age believers gather to absorb the auspicious energy on the solstice. In 2000, a few Tzintzuntzan locals joined a small group of outsiders dressed all in white, who performed a circle dance at dawn. In almost all the major Catholic fiestas, the street vendors sell such New Age items as a bird that selects your fortune, a game tossing coins on tarot cards, and holistic medicine. Diana's son would not call himself an invisible convert, but he sees no contradiction between his Catholicism and learning from Jehovah's Witnesses, Luz del Mundo members, and New Age enthusiasts.

Lastly, I caught up with Luz, a Catholic woman who had accompanied Nestor and me to an afternoon of baptisms conducted by Pastor Orozco. She had just celebrated her saint's day with a lively fiesta when I visited her. It turned out that this was not her first visit to an evangelical baptism. Her husband was a cousin of both Nestor and Odilón, so Luz had been to services at both churches. Already several Catholic women had told me about her involvement with the evangelicals. A friend of hers told me that once, when Luz had broken her arm, she sought help from Odilón's church in Ichupio. Her friend was confused why Luz continued to come to Mass at the same time she worshipped with other churches, so she asked Luz why she remained with the evangelicals. Luz allegedly answered that she felt obliged to attend services with Odilón and Nestor out of appreciation for their help when she was injured. I suspected this explanation really came from the Catholic friend herself, who believed evangelical churches bribed and blackmailed members to keep them loyal. So I decided to ask Luz about her multiple religious associations.

Despite her willingness to participate in the baptisms, she did not intend to leave the Catholic Church: "I like to go to a dance, to the fiestas, to drink a beer once in a while. But they [the evangelicals] don't drink anymore. For my saint's day, we had pozole and many guests. They don't have parties."

"But," I persisted, "what did you think of the baptism?"

"The baptism scared you, didn't it?" she replied with a grin. "You thought they would drown! In the Catholic Church we baptize as babies. It was funny. And it took so long to eat. I didn't eat breakfast, so I was dying of hunger when I finally ate."

I asked her what she saw as the main differences between the faiths.

"They [the evangelicals] sell Bibles to their members."

I pointed out that the Catholic Church also had Bibles for sale in the parish office.

She relented and stopped trying to distinguish the two faiths. "Listen, Pedro, only the foolish believe everything. When we die it's all the same. We're buried in the same cemetery." She captured well the sentiment of many Catholics and converts: only the foolish believe everything in a church's doctrine. It was acceptable, almost preferable, to be critical of your own faith.

GAUGING YOUR FAITH THESE DAYS

Summer months mean daily downpours in Tzintzuntzan. School is out and there are no major holidays until Independence Day in September, so the pace of life slows. During my first fieldwork season in 1998, the relaxed pace helped me collect information on pottery manufacture and marketing. Potters allowed me to sit in their workshops for hours, learning about their craft. Weekends I would spend sitting with sellers in the marketplace, chatting during the downtime between customers. In the middle of this tranquility, an MGM film crew arrived. They parked a trailer truck in the lot outside the churchyard and began intense construction in the open chapel outside La Soledad (Figure 4.2). Immediately rumors began traveling around about the upcoming filming. Someone said they would need a hundred extras, so I made sure my rounds each day included a trip past the wardrobe truck in hopes that I might be "discovered." It worked. The costume designer spotted me and asked if I wanted to participate in a scene as a tourist. I could start tomorrow, and I would not even have to change my clothes.

Along with nearly one hundred other extras, I reported to work at 5 A.M. A team of handlers shepherded us from the wardrobe tent to the breakfast tent set up in the main churchyard. When the sun came out, the first scene we shot took place in the Capilla Abierta, an open-air chapel that served as a space for mass baptisms in the sixteenth century. Located next to La Soledad, the stone chapel was chipped and worn, but it provided just the decadent look the director wanted.

The crew had converted the usually open grassy space into a bustling Brazilian market. Wooden stalls displayed all sorts of religious paraphernalia, food, and jewelry. The majority of the extras, drawn from Tzintzuntzan and Pátzcuaro, played the part of Catholics on pilgrimage to a Brazilian church, represented by La Soledad. Wrapped in white fabric and holding candles, the women and men formed a solemn procession from one end of the chapel to the door of the church. To give the illusion of Brazil, all the signs in the

4.2 For a week during July 1998, an MGM film crew turned the outdoor chapel and La Soledad into a Brazilian marketplace and shrine. The movie they shot there, *Stigmata,* employed about a hundred extras from Tzintzuntzan.

marketplace were written in Portuguese, while the extras with the darkest skin stood closest to the cameras. Some light-skinned extras and I played the part of tourists who had come to watch the spectacle.

All the handlers explained to us about the plot was that this Brazilian church housed a miraculous sculpture of Mary, who cried blood. Gabriel Byrne, the protagonist, played an emissary from the Vatican sent to inspect the potentially miraculous phenomenon. The director wanted to cultivate an artistic look, which meant that numerous fog machines blew at us from off camera. Through a translator, he implored the extras to express awe for the holiness of the pilgrimage site. As inspiration, he had them sing Catholic hymns. The first day they performed endless takes of the procession past the market vendors into the church. Although the heat from the relentless sun, the dripping candles, the heavy costumes, and the fog machines became unbearable, the extras dutifully repeated their parts. Byrne appeared for a few of the scenes before retiring to his air-conditioned trailer and letting his double stand in for him. My job was almost as easy. I had to act like a tourist, fingering rosaries and snapping photographs.

For the next two days of filming, we moved inside La Soledad. With its paint-chipped, barrel-vaulted ceiling and gilded altar, it too fit the part of mysterious religious shrine. The crew had placed hundreds of flickering candles around the altar to heighten the aura of holiness. All the extras sat in the pews facing a life-size marble statue of Mary (the bloody tears would be added later digitally). Byrne, stoic-faced, approached the image to take photographs. With every flash, the pilgrims made the sign of the cross. An actor, planted in the crowd of extras, rose to shout out in Portuguese: "They are tears of blood. What more proof do you need?" In the final scene shot in the church, the director instructed us to look awed, as if a miracle had taken place. Then, a fan propelled several pigeons from their cage on the floor toward the ceiling. From the side windows, crew members shook open bags of feathers until the entire sanctuary was covered in a layer of snowy down.

The men and women who had served as extras complained of the "abuse" they had endured at the hands of the urban Mexicans hired to support the North American crew. As expatriates, my fellow tourists and I were immune, but the workers treated the local extras with condescension. They spoke to elderly participants in the familiar form of address and prohibited workers from leaving the set even when they were not needed. Worst of all, some extras who failed to follow the appropriate bureaucratic procedures ended up without pay and were too timid to demand their rightful wages. One woman wanted to take home her costume to wash it before the next day's shooting, but the crew told her that poor people were supposed to be dirty. Offenses like these generated grumbling among the extras. However, no one objected to the transformation of the community's chapel into a film set full of feathers. We all made the sign of the cross and sang in honor of a statue that came from the props department. The filmmakers gave us no indication that the finished product would criticize the Catholic Church in any way.

The filming lasted only a week, after which they removed the Portuguese signage, returning the open chapel and La Soledad to their normal states. Some of the North American workers had told me that the film would be called *Stigmata* and would open in theaters a year later, in time to capitalize on millennium hype. When I returned to Tzintzuntzan in the summer of 1999, most locals had forgotten about the week the studio crew came to town. Though the extras earned between ten and fifteen dollars a day, the employment was too brief to have any lasting economic impact. Nor had I heard anything about the film before I left the United States, so I asked my parents to alert me to any mention of the film *Stigmata*. In October 1999, a letter arrived from California with news clippings enclosed. In the box office top ten for the first week of September, *Stigmata* claimed the number one spot with nearly $20 million in ticket sales.

By December 1999, the subtitled version had arrived in Morelia. I invited a woman from Pátzcuaro I had met during the shooting to accompany me to the theater. We agreed to go on a Sunday after attending Mass in the Pátzcuaro Basilica. Getting to Morelia took only about an hour, but the cineplex was located another forty-five minutes away on the suburban outskirts of the city. The theater was crowded, though not overflowing, when the show began. The opening shot frames a boy from Tzintzuntzan ringing a bell above the open chapel. Then the camera descends on a bustling marketplace swirling with pilgrims and vendors. Neither my friend nor I identified ourselves in the scene, but we recognized other people and recalled the suffocating fog machines that had made us cough, though now they gave everything a mystical appearance. Byrne's character, dressed in his clerical clothes and sunglasses, stands at the end of the procession leading into the church, impervious to the merchants hawking items around him. We do see, however, a female tourist purchasing a wooden rosary from one of the stands. Byrne enters the church, where the congregants are in mourning for their recently deceased priest. Since his death, a statue of the Virgin has been crying blood. Clinically, Byrne takes photographs and shrugs off the mysterious arrival of birds.

Tzintzuntzan (doubling as Brazil) does not reappear until the final scene, when Byrne, now defrocked, returns to the church in search of a lost gospel that the deceased priest had been translating. The camera approaches Tzintzuntzan dramatically from across the lake at sunset before narrowing in on La Soledad. My friend and I both gasped at the serene beauty of the sight. However, between the first appearance of Tzintzuntzan and the last, I watched horrified. I worried that my friend, already humiliated once by the film workers, would be offended again by the film. *Stigmata,* or *Estigma,* as it was called when released in Mexico, accuses the Catholic Church of a murderous conspiracy to hide the true teachings of Jesus Christ contained in the missing gospel. For, if found, the text in Jesus' own words would undermine the authority of Rome by preaching that believers do not need a building to be part of the Church. "Split a piece of wood and I am there; lift a rock and you will find me," a fragment from the so-called missing gospel reads. In these words, Jesus advocates a theology more in line with the Protestant Reformation than with Vatican dictates. Though part supernatural thriller and part horror flick, the film solemnly informs viewers in an epilogue before the final credits roll that indeed a purported gospel of Jesus was found in caves near the Dead Sea and that the Catholic hierarchy has refused to acknowledge it.

The priest character played by Byrne uncovers a plot by his Vatican superiors to suppress the gospel and kill anyone who might publish it. His experience with a young Pittsburgh hair stylist, played by Patricia Arquette, further clarifies the mystery. Arquette's mother is the tourist in Brazil who purchases the rosary from the shrine where the statue is crying blood. Receiving it in Pittsburgh, Arquette, whose character is an atheist, mistakes it for jewelry. Soon after wearing the rosary, she begins to suffer from stigmata, the wounds of Christ. But instead of being a sign of piety and proximity to God, stigmata in her case became an unwanted and potentially fatal affliction. Again, the Vatican dispatches Byrne to investigate and disprove the case. Instead of finding her claims unfounded, Byrne sees that she is indeed afflicted by the spirit of the deceased Brazilian priest who had been secretly translating the lost gospel. In the course of helping her contend with violent episodes, Byrne falls in love. In the film's climax, an enraged cardinal attempts to suffocate Arquette for fear that she will reveal Christ's true words. Byrne and a roomful of special effects intervene just in time to save her.

The film, which cost $32 million to make, earned $50 million in revenues during its cinematic release in the United States alone. When it appeared in video form, it again topped the charts for rentals. MGM and United Artists distributed *Stigmata* to Europe and Latin America, where it attracted increasingly negative reaction. First, the film critics unleashed their venom. One critic opined that "*Stigmata* is so bad, it ultimately leaves you with the age-old question: If there is a God, why would He permit a film like this to be made?" And Roger Ebert called it "possibly the funniest movie ever made about Catholicism" (*Ottawa Citizen* 1999).

While critics made light of the film's overwrought direction and plot absurdities, Catholics expressed outrage. The head of the Catholic League in the United States denounced the film as "a vehicle for making a political attack on the Catholic Church." A spokeswoman for the Catholic Church concurred. "Not only is the film an attack on Christianity," she said soon after it was released, "it is a very bad movie and it's going to be a flop" (Miller 1999). The film's promotional material provoked special ire with its glib taglines, "How's your faith these days?" and "It will scare the Hell into you." Indeed, the film seemed designed to offend. The director defended his depiction of the Catholic Church amid criticism before the film even opened. "The Vatican will be upset for sure," he said to a syndicated entertainment columnist. "This movie is going to be to the Vatican what the movie *JFK* was for the Warren Commission. I'm not saying we're right, but I know that they're lying" (Beck and Smith 1999). Knowing that the controversy would only help the film in the box office, the director deliberately impugned the Catholic hierarchy.

When *Stigmata* reached Latin America, the controversy followed it. In February 2000, government censors in El Salvador banned showings of the film on the grounds that it constituted "an attack on public order." Though they soon rescinded the ban, they insisted that it be screened only to adults and at limited times. According to an Internet source, the government also required that advertising for the film be curtailed (Internet Movie Database 2000).

In Mexico, the Catholic Church also reacted vehemently. Every week Estela would purchase *Comunidad Cristiana* (Christian community), the diocesan newsletter sold door-to-door around Lake Pátzcuaro. As I sat to eat breakfast, a photo of Patricia Arquette caught my eye on the cover of the December 12, 1999, issue. Inside, a priest lambasted the film's take on theology without seeing any of the humor that Roger Ebert had enjoyed. The review accused the film of contributing to fear-mongering in the run-up to the millennium and advancing a "postmodern relativism" with its use of disjointed scenes and camera angle montages. The writer saved his most scathing comments for the religious message. He considered the idea that Jesus could be found in a rock or a log, not in a church, a mockery of the Bible. "We cannot have a relationship with God subject to our egoism and whims," he wrote. Implied is the assumption that priestly intermediaries are free of such personal bias. He did not mention that a parish in his own diocese offered use of its church for the film.

I waited until we had exited the theater to ask my companion what she thought of the film. When the film crew had treated her and other extras disrespectfully, my friend had been one of the few women to complain, so I expected to hear how angry the movie made her. To my surprise, she remarked that it was a well-made film and that she had enjoyed it. Did she notice any anti-Catholic sentiment? Not really. She was more interested in talking about the scenes we participated in.

Two months passed before I heard about *Stigmata* again. Most Catholics in Tzintzuntzan are familiar with the religious concept of stigmata since the patron saint of the parish is Saint Francis of Assisi. Every October during the saint's celebration, the priest explains how Saint Francis was so close to the Lord that he had suffered the wounds of Christ. Also, most Tzintzuntzeños enjoy films. They watch them mostly on television, but some families take special trips to Morelia on the weekends, and others check out videos from a small rental store near the plaza. One afternoon I was waiting in Pátzcuaro for the bus to take me back to Tzintzuntzan for the main meal of the day. While I waited, Marta, the leader of the Catholic prayer workshop, came up to greet me. I asked if she was also returning to Tzintzuntzan, but she said she had just finished teaching and was on her way to Morelia. Her daughter was already there, and they were hoping to catch a matinee showing of *Stigmata*. This would be the first film Marta had seen in a theater in twenty-two years.

A few days later, I talked to her again over dinner at a taco stand in Tzintzuntzan. Like my friend from Pátzcuaro, she also thought it was a well-crafted movie and had enjoyed watching it. This time I protested, "What did you think about the suggestion that the Vatican is withholding a gospel?" She replied calmly, "Maybe they are." Her willingness to believe the nasty portrayal of the Catholic Church fit the reaction my friend had leaving the theater, but it did not fit my image of Marta. Marta directed the prayer workshops, taught catechism classes, attended Mass faithfully, and defended the parish priest from criticism. She went on to quote me the line, "Split a piece of wood and I am there; lift a rock and you will find me." Then she added, "I agree that God is in nature."

"Then why go to Mass?" I responded.

"You still need to go to Mass. It's like a school. Jesus left behind institutions. I'll have to ask Father Rogelio about stigmata." Marta reconciled easily the idea that the Catholic Church could be misleading its followers with the custom of paying respect to its institutions.

In total, I located a dozen Tzintzuntzeños who had seen *Stigmata*, including five members of the Catholic family who would joke with me about room number eight. Significantly, they also quoted with approval the line about splitting a piece of wood. "All this luxury in the churches is for man's benefit, not God's," one commented. Another person complained that Tzintzuntzan did not receive any on-screen credit. However, none of them considered the film offensive to Catholics.

A young woman who was attending middle school in Tacoma in 2000 brought the video to her English as a Second Language class. Her mother, the daughter of Diana and a practicing Catholic, called the film "fabulous." She particularly liked its message. "Don't you think it accused the Catholic Church of wrongdoing?" I asked. "It accused all religions," she replied. "People get so involved in religion that they don't think. You shouldn't follow just what they tell you, but what you believe." Like the Catholic woman who had attended the evangelical baptisms, she questioned the wisdom of unexamined obedience.

Stigmata even made its way into Tzintzuntzan's video rental store. One student in my English class wanted me to teach her the words to the "split a log" refrain. Although she tutored Catholic children before their first communion and attended Mass every Sunday, she liked the film's "beautiful message." I asked her the question I had asked Marta about the anti-Catholic tendencies of the plot. While she saw my point, her approval did not waver. "I wonder," she responded, "if it's true that a gospel in Jesus' own words exists." Then, she and a friend who also had seen the movie compared notes about which extras they recognized.

The label "invisible converts" captures how the Tzintzuntzan women and men who had seen *Stigmata* appreciated its anti-Vatican message. However, conversion, even an unacknowledged one, implies that these Catholics have turned against their natal church. To the contrary, my interlocutors remain committed Catholics. Their reactions to the film indicate that Catholics can incorporate evangelical beliefs about having a direct personal relationship with God without renouncing their Catholic faith. Believers hold seemingly contradictory ideas at the same time by asserting the folly of believing any one faith blindly. They acknowledge differences between the faiths, but agree that no single faith holds a monopoly on divine truth. In the end all Tzintzuntzeños will come to rest in the cemetery on the edge of town. As long as they promote a belief in God to reward followers in the afterlife, all religions have their merits.

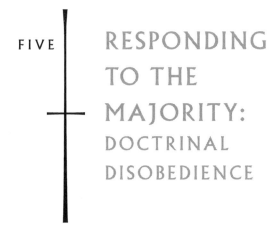

FIVE | RESPONDING
TO THE
MAJORITY:
DOCTRINAL
DISOBEDIENCE

ARLY on the morning of the Jehovah's Witness District Assembly,
I took a taxi with Norma, Ricardo, and their children to Quiroga,
where a chartered bus waited to take members of the congregation
to Morelia. Along the way, Ricardo chatted amiably with the driver, who
had agreed to squeeze seven people in his compact sedan. When we arrived
in Quiroga and hurried out to board the bus, I happened to look back at
the taxi. The driver stashed the fare under his dashboard cover, then made
the sign of the cross. Many Catholics make the sign of the cross after their
first sale of the day. One forlorn salesman I heard the afternoon of a fiesta
even used the phrase, "I haven't made the sign of the cross yet" to indicate he
had not sold any goods all day. The taxi driver that morning, with a Virgin
of Guadalupe icon dangling from his rearview mirror, professed his Catholic faith openly. Norma and Ricardo, for their part, made their conversion
known to the community by distributing Jehovah's Witness literature and inviting neighbors to church events. Despite their religious disagreements, the
driver and Ricardo had much in common for conversation. They respected
each other's customs.

Evangelical leaders establish seemingly unbreachable walls between those
who receive Jesus, who will be saved, and those who have not made the decision to accept him, who will be condemned. However, evangelicals frame
their conversion in more personal terms that aim to expel personal demons
and conquer illness. In defiance of their leaders' rhetoric of separation from
the worldly, evangelicals endeavor to minimize their differences with the

Catholic majority.[1] They do not engage in the same probing self-critique as Catholics do, but they frequently question the wisdom of their pastors' directives. In daily life, evangelical believers do not separate themselves from the rest of the community. They send their children to the same schools, buy meat at the same butcher shops, sell pottery at the same market, and some even attend the same fiestas as Catholics. Converts are more aware than their pastors of the benefits of cultivating positive relations with their neighbors, so, although they respect their leaders, they feel justified in occasional disobedience.

To various degrees, evangelicals around Lake Pátzcuaro continue to participate in Catholic rituals and disavow the strictness of the doctrine preached to them. Even though elaborate fiestas have come to define Catholic excess for evangelical congregations, many of their members participate in the fiestas in some way. Similarly, although their pastors urge them to undergo baptism and confirm their exclusive devotion, many converts choose to postpone making such a public commitment. In Chiapas, ethnographers also encountered a significant number of converts to evangelical churches who held off on the decision to be baptized (Hernández Castillo 1989). Conversion tends to expand rather than narrow the range of religious influences a believer expresses. Converts neither praise the Catholic Church nor follow evangelical doctrine to the letter. Similarly, Catholics mingle their respect for the parish priest with a willingness to disobey his stated wishes when they threaten to undermine community traditions. This selective application of evangelical teachings does not indicate a poorly understood faith or a strictly instrumental approach to religion. Rather, it demonstrates the currency of the phrase "All religions are good" for Tzintzuntzeños who temper the rigid rhetoric of their leaders with inclusive behavior.

CONVERTING AND CONVERGING

The very appearance and structure of evangelical services undermine the pastors' attempts to disassociate their churches from the Catholic Church. Spaces of evangelical worship without exception feature less decoration than Catholic sanctuaries, but the fundamental elements remain. Members of the congregation always sit in rows of chairs or benches facing a table or pulpit, which is often raised. While they never approach the ostentation of Catholic images, evangelicals adorn their walls, too. Instead of saints' portraits, evangelicals hang biblical quotations on their walls. Pastor Orozco decorates his main chapel with pages from a religious calendar, spaced out along the side walls in a manner reminiscent of the fourteen stations of the cross displayed in Catholic churches. A few evangelical churches have no paintings or framed words whatsoever, but even those sanctuaries give prominent place to flowers. Floral arrangements and plants go mostly uncommented on in churches, yet they are always present. The Tzintzuntzan parish church rotates floral displays according to the season, often taking up a special collection just for flowers. Despite their criticism of Catholics for offering flowers to the saints, evangelicals also use flowers or plants to mark their ceremonial spaces as out of the ordinary.

In the structure of their worship, Catholics and evangelicals also resemble each other. Evangelicals tend to go to church meetings more often than Catholics, but every church reserves its longest and most significant service for Sunday. Every church asks for alms from its members. A large sign listing the prices for various religious sacraments greets visitors to Father Rogelio's office. During February Fiesta, he places a display case of religious memorabilia at the front doors of the church with volunteer staffers selling rosaries and stamps. Though only Centro Cristiano Emanuel is large enough to support its own gift shop, all evangelical congregations make explicit requests for donations and tithes.

All the religious organizations rely on music — a cappella, recorded, or live instrumental — to accompany worship services. The act of singing in unison not only elevates church time above the level of the everyday but also connects members of the congregation with one another. Moreover, music serves as a bridge across churches. Once while I was traveling with Dr. Cook, he hosted a family from an Assemblies of God congregation who were thinking of leaving that group and affiliating with his. I observed how the visiting pastor interacted with members of Dr. Cook's church by sharing songs. Some they knew in common and sang together; others they taught each other. Excited to continue the exchange, they turned to me for songs from my church and were disappointed when I responded that I did not know any in Spanish.

Each church also emphasizes some form of movement. In the course of a typical one-hour Mass, parishioners rise from the pews seven times. If they choose to take communion, they walk to the altar to receive it, and, at the moment of consecration, the entire audience kneels. Fiesta days and the period of Lent include processions around the churchyard or through the community, or pilgrimages to other sites. There is the same physical mobility in evangelical congregations. Technically, evangelicals do not permit dancing; nevertheless, the energetic music encourages rhythmic movement. Centro Cristiano Emanuel plays rock'n'roll Christian-themed music that motivates church members to enter ecstatic states of prayer. A popular tune in their repertoire even has its own choreography and playful call and response. The men sing, "Christ is not dead." Then the women reply, "He is alive." Then everyone sings, "I feel him in my hands" while waving their hands in the air; "I feel him in my feet" while stomping the ground; and "I feel him in my entire being" while spinning around.

Outside of musical interludes, evangelical worship requires additional standing and sitting, kneeling and lying prone. Just as Catholics approach the altar to take communion, so many evangelical services end with a call to come forward. "Brothers" and "sisters" uncertain about their faith, suffering from illness, harboring resentment against their neighbors, or in need of holy unction enter the well in front of the pulpit for blessing. Not every Catholic accepts communion every time, nor does every evangelical heed the call to come forward. Many kneel at their place in the pews or stand to watch. Evangelicals do not duplicate the Catholic processions, but they do undertake pilgrimages to holy sites. Dr. Cook's followers described to me with pride the times they had been invited to his ranch and the children, animals, and amenities they saw there. For members of Luz del Mundo in Pátzcuaro, the Guadalajara mother church serves a role akin to the Vatican for Catholics. As a small, autonomous community carved out of a larger city, the Beautiful Province draws thousands of church members from many countries during annual holidays. Converging on a single site, like rising and sitting together in a Sunday service, stresses the common connections between members of a church.

Evangelical churches frequently use the word "saint" even though the rejection of saints forms a principal tenet of Protestant theology. The Catholic Church confers designations of sainthood based on its own formulas and investigations of miracles. In rejecting the adoration of images and accepting Jesus as a personal savior, converts disavow the concept of sainthood. Yet, in the majority of evangelical churches, I heard pastors and laypeople alike give biblical figures the title of "saint." They do not use "saint" consistently or in all cases. Most commonly, I heard pastors instruct their congregations to turn to a passage in the book of "*Saint* John," for example. Dr. Cook was fond of the more elaborate, "The gospel according to Saint John," which is exactly how Father Rogelio refers to the Book of John in Mass. From what I could tell, many of the Bible translations evangelicals use also contain the word "Saint" in the titles of the books written by the apostles.

Most pastors are not aware of these verbal slips. When I confronted Dr. Cook with the question, he denied he was condoning belief in the saints:

"The Catholics have intercessors, saints who have passed certain tests of miracles. In the evangelical church we use the word 'saint' to apply to someone who lives in Christ; someone who's alive. There is no biblical basis for the Catholic saints. The only intercessor between you and God, the father, is Jesus Christ." That explanation perplexed me more. I never heard him or other ministers use the word "saint" in relation to someone "alive." If he meant it in a spiritual sense, then I wondered why only the same men designated saints by the Catholic Church received the appellation, and not others.

Converts generally stay connected to Catholic rituals. Gloria, a Baptist from Pátzcuaro, recognized the growing overlap between different churches. I asked her what distinguishes her religion from the Catholics'. She began by listing some key differences:

> The main difference is that Catholics adore the saints a lot. We don't adore the Virgin like they do, but recognize her as the mother of Jesus. We don't believe in the saints. We pray to Jesus; we need only his forgiveness. They confess, do penitence, kneel, make the sign of the cross. We don't. The form of adoration, liturgy, is different.

In the next sentence, her tone switched as she grew reflective:

> But now there are renovated Catholics who sing the same songs and pray the same prayers that we do.[2] Some go crazy like the Pentecostals. Many priests now say it's not necessary to do penitence or make confession. Pátzcuaro used to be more fanatical. In school, I was embarrassed to say I was evangelical. Friends would tell me their priest said not to talk to evangelicals. Now people respect me. They say, "You're not a Catholic, right? You don't smoke, you don't drink, you don't go to dances." Now people are curious. They say it's good that I don't drink.

In her own lifetime, she has seen Catholics grow more accepting, even appreciative of her faith. She observes how some of their ceremonies and values reflect her own and proudly discusses her religion with neighbors. As Gloria introduced me to her family and invited me to services at the Baptist church, I observed how this interfaith understanding occurs in both directions: Catholics have adopted important elements from the evangelicals, and the evangelicals continue their Catholic customs.

When I met Gloria's sister, she was worshipping at a Baptist church in the city of Zacapu, an hour's bus ride from Pátzcuaro. Although there is a Baptist church within walking distance of her house in Pátzcuaro, she chooses to incur the added expense and time of travel because she feels God wants her to be there. On one visit with her to Zacapu, I asked her if her entire family had converted. She said they were not all "Christians," by which she meant evangelicals. In fact, her nephew was getting married in a Catholic church in Zacapu that very day. I wanted to know if she planned on going since she had already traveled to the city to attend her church. "I don't know. I'm torn. As the aunt, I should go, but as a Christian, it's not my environment."

In the end, she did go. The Mass was swift and sparsely attended. I watched her stand up at the appropriate moments during the service and listen attentively during the sermon. Neither she nor I walked to the altar to take communion with the rest of the family. At the end, she greeted her relatives cordially, but hurried back to her church before they had a chance to include her in a photograph. How did she feel at a Catholic Mass? "I was uncomfortable. I didn't know what was going on. But it was a bridge between my family and me. They didn't expect me to come, knowing I'm a Christian. I've invited them many times to my church. Maybe now they'll come to mine." For practical considerations of maintaining healthy family ties, she had agreed to participate.

Gloria and her sister live across from a Catholic chapel dedicated to the Virgin of Guadalupe. They affixed a decal on their front door that gently mocks their neighbors' signs rejecting evangelical "propaganda": "In this household we are Christian. Everyone is welcome." When I went to her house, Gloria showed me the photo album from her wedding. She met her husband after he had finished the Baptist seminary and accepted a post in Michoacán as a preacher. Gloria described the wedding to me, emphasizing how Baptists do not have godparents or several of the symbolic gifts that Catholic couples receive. I expected that the event would be austere and focused on prayer, yet, when I saw the photos, I recognized the scenes instantly from the jubilant Catholic weddings I had attended in Tzintzuntzan.

The couple, dressed in formalwear and kneeling, listened to a sermon that Gloria admitted she found boring. At Catholic weddings, godparents—usually married couples themselves—bestow items like coins, rings, and pillows on the bride and groom during the Mass. Gloria and her husband received a Bible from a pair of friends, who took the role of godparents but without the title. After the ceremony, all the guests dined on entrees of chicken with mole sauce, and then the couple cut a multi-tiered frosted cake. The absence of alcohol from the party hall was the only sign this was not a Catholic wedding. In other photos, the bride tossed her bouquet to a group of single women, just as they do at Catholic weddings. I pointed out a photo of the couple dancing the "viper" with their guests, a seeming violation of the Baptist prohibition on nonreligious music and dancing. With the couple standing on chairs and forming a bridge, a train of female guests wind through them, trying to knock over the bride. Then the men repeat the dance more violently with the groom. I asked Gloria whether evangelicals typically danced like this at weddings. She blushed, "We call it 'playing' the viper, not 'dancing.'" She paused, then continued, "We really shouldn't have done it."

The desire to maintain harmonious relations with the larger community motivates Gloria to observe Catholic traditions at certain times. Her family runs a small stall selling thread and fabric in the municipal marketplace. At one end of the market building, a shrine to the Virgin of Guadalupe looks down at the merchants. Every year around the December celebration of the Virgin, a representative visits all the stalls asking for a contribution. Although all the other merchants knew a Baptist family owned the fabric business since they conspicuously close on Sundays, the representative stopped by to ask for a donation in honor of the Virgin. Gloria was helping customers at the time and feared embarrassment or hostility if she refused to give, so she quickly donated ten pesos. When the collector went to write down her name and contribution, Gloria urged her to stop. At other times, she participates willingly in Catholic rituals. During the Catholic fiesta of Day of the Dead, she regularly travels to the island of Janitzio to admire the colorful altars erected in the cemetery. None of this diminishes her standing as a lay leader in Pátzcuaro's Baptist congregation.

Members of several evangelical churches maintain Catholic customs years after conversion. During Tzintzuntzan's February Fiesta, two evangelical young women from La Colonia admired the carnival rides and shops set up outside the churchyard. They playfully snapped my photo on a disposable camera in the crowded plaza. At night during the weeklong fiesta, another member of the same congregation earned steady business selling tacos to the Catholic revelers. Ricardo and Norma's teenage daughters attended both Jehovah's Witness events with their parents and the Easter week theological chats led by a team of nuns. Ricardo himself played with his Catholic brother and other musicians in a band that entertained guests at Catholic weddings, fifteenth birthday parties, and baptisms. Like the evangelical taco vendor, Ricardo considered his participation in Catholic activities a necessary part of earning enough money to support a family.

While some evangelicals in Tzintzuntzan stop contributing to Catholic celebrations, I spoke with many converts who continue to pay the fiesta cooperaciones. All converts emphasize that they do not condone "pagan" Catholic customs, but recognizing their small numbers, they say donating to community events ensures the goodwill of their neighbors. In smaller communities like Tzintzuntzan and its surrounding settlements, the necessity of maintaining good relations with neighbors becomes even more critical. When the local authorities in Santa Fe expelled Dr. Cook from the community and prohibited his followers from worshipping there, Alejandra assured them that she and the other evangelicals would continue to pay the community cooperaciones. As she explained, "We know from the Bible that it's not good, but if we don't we'll be harming ourselves." In Santa Fe, paying the contributions demonstrates to the suspicious Catholic majority that the evangelical converts will not disrupt community traditions. Alejandra's appeal to the local authorities facilitated the quick return of evangelical services to Santa Fe.

Where evangelicals form a minority, paying the contributions helps prevent conflict with Catholic neighbors. Around 1980, Nestor, a carpenter, moved with the first wave of settlers from Tzintzuntzan to the suburb dubbed La Colonia. He later became the first person in La Colonia to leave the Catholic Church. Initially, his conversion to evangelical Christianity provoked mild hostility from his neighbors. Someone once threw eggs at his house, and another time his workshop was burgled. Rumors spread that he practiced satanic rituals and witchcraft. Eventually his neighbors came to tolerate him, but to avoid further disturbance, Nestor continues to pay the fiesta cooperaciones. He expresses confidence that God understands that he is not really supporting the Catholic Church. Moreover, Nestor uses the encounters with commissioners as a chance to evangelize. In one instance, a man who used to be one of Nestor's drinking buddies before he converted came to ask him to contribute for the celebration in honor of Tzintzuntzan's patron saint, Saint Francis. After giving his contribution, Nestor asked him if he had ever read the Bible. When the man replied he had not, Nestor told him that the Bible prohibits the adoration of images. The commissioner protested that the fiestas were traditions. Yes, Nestor countered, traditions of men. Rather than continue to debate, the commissioner moved on.

Another example comes from Tarerio, the indigenous community beyond Ichupio on the dirt road leading from Tzintzuntzan around Lake Pátzcuaro. Sara, her husband, Sergio, and their children are the only evangelicals in Tarerio. They attend services twice a week at the home of Nestor in La Colonia, but also worship on occasion with their neighbor Odilón. I asked Sara if her life had changed since joining an evangelical church. "Yes, our life has changed. We no longer go to fiestas. But we always give the cooperaciones so that other people don't get mad. Brother Odilón says we shouldn't contribute, but we do." She reasoned that maintaining good relations with her neighbors in Tarerio, where hers is the only evangelical family, outweighs Odilón's directive. She simply does not tell Odilón of her disobedience.

Even when evangelicals do not donate to the Catholic fiestas, they join their Catholic neighbors in offering cooperaciones for municipal improvements. In addition to soliciting funds for religious celebrations, communities like Tzintzuntzan ask residents to donate for school renovation and other civic projects. Despite their rhetoric of separation from the profane world, nearly all converts participate in their communities' activities and have an interest in better roads and schools. Moreover, as teetotalers, evangelical men like Sergio and Odilón are frequently called on as responsible representatives of their peers. When the state government placed a ban on fishing in Lake Pátzcuaro, the fishermen's union elected Sergio and Odilón—their only evangelical members—to argue their case in the state capital.

Another Catholic custom that converts retain is the tie of godparenthood. Until 1997, Sara and Sergio were Catholics. They did not go to Mass regularly before they converted, but they participated in the yearly cycle of fiestas in Tarerio, and Sergio drank his share of alcohol. As Catholics, they had asked Nestor to be the godparent at their eldest son's baptism. When the boy completed elementary school, they sent him to work in Nestor's woodworking shop. By that time, Nestor had become an evangelical and invited their son to attend the Sunday services with Pastor Orozco. Once their son began attending evangelical services, they became concerned. Sara told me that she worried: "'What is our son getting into? What will people say?' So three years ago we went to a service in La Colonia and have been going every Sunday since. God had a purpose for us." Like Odilón, who remains friendly with his godson's mother, Estela, Nestor maintained his godparent status even after converting. This reciprocal relationship helped him convince Sergio and Sara to join Orozco's evangelical congregation.

RESISTING BAPTISM

Converts achieve full membership in evangelical churches through baptism by immersion. From what I had seen in Cook's proselytizing sessions, a key component of evangelical faith is opening one's heart to Jesus. Certainly this is a prerequisite for attending worship meetings and being called a "sister" or "brother." But no matter how closely a convert follows biblical principles, she or he cannot be guaranteed salvation without baptism. It is in adult baptism that a convert becomes united with Jesus, so pastors place great emphasis on the event. Father Rogelio, following Catholic custom, baptizes only infants, who have no say in the matter. By baptizing only consenting adults, evangelicals stress that their members enter the faith willingly and in complete agreement with church doctrine. In every evangelical church I observed, the baptism ceremony occupies a central role as part of a spectacle designed as much to impress the undecideds as those about to be dunked. The Luz del Mundo mother church in Guadalajara features a baptismal pool in the center of the altar, as does Centro Cristiano Emanuel in Pátzcuaro. Dr. Cook times baptisms in his church to coincide with the yearly anniversary celebration of his ministry.

Whereas receiving Jesus often happens in a single burst of prayer, the step of baptism involves a much more considered decision. All the churches claim that they do not pressure members into baptizing, preferring to wait until they declare themselves ready. Pastors boast that, unlike leaders in the Catholic Church, they do not charge for the baptism ceremony. Still, the ritual comes at some cost for the volunteers. Several churches require candidates for baptism to attend a series of courses before the event, and all emphasize the seriousness of the decision. A member of Pastor Orozco's congregation in La Colonia remembered how difficult the decision was: "I was afraid. You have to leave behind this, leave behind that. I used to say a lot of swear words. But if you don't make the decision, you'll never leave it. God helped me. Baptism is a pact with God. You have to be an example to others." Baptism raises the stakes. Converts confirm their break from a sinful past and commit themselves to a life more in line with the Bible. Moreover, they serve as role models for other members of the congregation. During the weekly Jehovah's Witness Bible study, when no one responded to the leader's question, I often heard him imploring, "Come on, *baptized* publishers." The church expects more from its baptized members.

Pastors want all their members to become baptized since baptism lessens the likelihood of defection. If a convert has yet to be baptized in one church, it might be easier to justify attending services in another. Still, a significant number resist. As the pastor of Centro Cristiano Emanuel points out, from 20 to 30 percent of his congregation have not been baptized in that church. Unbaptized members worship with the rest of the congregation, give tithes, and even receive gifts of the Holy Spirit, but they cannot ascend to positions of leadership. In one Jehovah's Witness service in Quiroga, the congregation elders counted only twenty-eight of seventy-four worshippers present who

5.1 Pastor Orozco prepares four members of his church for baptism. He prays for them and invites any other unbaptized members on the bank of the creek to join them.

had been baptized. The preacher dedicated an entire forty-five-minute sermon to encouraging the unbaptized to become baptized and to minister door-to-door. He offered them both a carrot and a stick: God would reward their efforts for choosing baptism, but if they refused they would have to reckon with the approaching Judgment Day. Since evangelical churches baptize only consenting adults, the decision to postpone baptism indicates a conscious choice not to pledge full commitment to the church.

When Pastor Orozco baptized two of Nestor's sons and their wives, he took the opportunity to stress the need for everyone to be baptized. He stressed the importance of the event by scheduling it for a separate meeting during the middle of the week instead of part of a regular Sunday service. Orozco also signaled the uniqueness of baptism by inviting a family of traveling evangelical musicians to play their electrified hymns during the baptism. After several prayers and readings from the Bible, he asked the four young people to tell the crowd why they wanted to be baptized. They answered into the microphone with expressions of their determination to follow God's will. The congregation followed the four candidates to a nearby creek, lining the banks with anticipation. I had to jockey with several other photographers to capture the best angle (Figure 5.1). Pastor Orozco entered the waist-high water, fully clothed, with the four young adults. He made another plea for anyone else who wanted to be baptized. Quietly, an older woman removed her shoes and lowered herself into the water. This moment of surprise energized Orozco, but it became clear he would have no other takers. So, he prayed for each of the five, then submerged them backwards into the bracing water. When they reemerged, the crowd broke out into song: "My sins are erased. I am whiter than the snow."

In another service at La Colonia, Orozco took advantage of a sound system and musicians to hold amplified services in front of Nestor's house in plain view and earshot of the entire neighborhood. His culminating sermon turned into a plea for the unbaptized of the congregation to become baptized. He emphasized the eternal rewards that baptism would bestow:

> Jesus Christ won't stay in the heavens until you're ready to be baptized. The first letter to the Corinthians 15:35-58 says that in a blink heaven opens, Christ descends, and the dead are resurrected. We have to equal Jesus' behavior. In the end we'll have our compensation: eternal life. Be patient. Don't despair or stop coming to services. It's worthwhile to make the effort because one day we'll see Jesus Christ and receive our prize. You have to humble yourself to the Lord. You have to say, "Here's my life. I want to be liberated, healed, secure." Those who haven't made the decision to serve God, come forward. The Lord wants us all to be saved.

Orozco tried to rouse his congregation to serve God more rigorously. Accepting Jesus as one's personal savior is only the beginning of the conversion process. Next, members must submit themselves to God's will, humbling themselves as soldiers preparing for battle.

The band began playing softly in the background as Orozco repeated his call for those who had not made the decision to serve God to come forward. No one ventured toward the microphone. Orozco cajoled his flock, "You may say you've made a decision, but you need to show it with acts. We have many people here who aren't baptized. Don't be ashamed." One young woman stepped forward. Then a clump of eight more young women and a group of three men, who had been standing to the side, came to the front. Orozco prayed with them, his eyes closed and hands on their heads. The rest of the audience stood next to their seats, praying too. In Orozco's church, in addition to spiritual rewards, being baptized gives members the privilege of participating in the Holy Supper ceremony on the first Sunday of each month. Every time, Orozco reminds the unbaptized members that he will be happy to baptize them so they can participate in the next month's service.

Lay members also express reluctance to heed the pastor's call to proselytize. Once baptized, members follow the biblical injunction to spread the gospel of Jesus by devoting time to informing their neighbors about the church. When Orozco announced a campaign for souls, he asked members of his congregation to contact the municipal authorities in Tzintzuntzan, Pátzcuaro, and other locations for permission to install their band and microphone in the town plazas. Nestor spoke to Tzintzuntzan's mayor, a devout Catholic, who refused the request. The mayor advised that such a public display would not be in the Pentecostal church's interests because it might provoke a negative response. Hearing this from Nestor, I told him that sounded like a flimsy excuse for denying his constitutional rights to freedom of religion. Nestor saw my point, but did not bother to argue with the mayor. He reported to the congregation the next Sunday that they would not be able to hold an event in Tzintzuntzan.

Among the Jehovah's Witnesses in Tzintzuntzan, almost none evangelize door-to-door as requested by their religious leaders. Ricardo reasons that proselytizing is best left to those with a "talent" for rhetorical persuasion. His wife, Norma, feels that looking after young children occupies all of her time and so she cannot devote the required hours to "field service," as the church calls it. The Jehovah's Witnesses who do knock on doors with literature to distribute drive from the Quiroga congregation once a week. Given the potential for stirring resentment among Catholic Tzintzuntzeños, converts prefer not to proselytize to their neighbors as aggressively as their leaders encourage. They will express their opinions in informal conversations like the one between Norma and Yunuen, but converts in Tzintzuntzan value their personal transformations over following the wishes of pastors who do not live in the community. For all their power to regulate behavior, evangelical pastors have few methods to enforce their rules beyond public admonitions during sermons.

Most converts are conscientious about attending services, but they often attend more than one congregation. Sara and Sergio, the couple from Tarerio, worship in at least three evangelical churches. While their primary affiliation remains with Pastor Orozco in La Colonia, they also pray with Odilón and Antonia in nearby Ichupio as well as with Dr. Cook's ministry. "Pastor Orozco got upset when he found out we were going with other pastors," Sara says, "but Odilón says it's good to learn from everyone. Odilón has taken us to a few conferences, but we don't tell Pastor Orozco about this. We give him Sundays; then it's okay for us to do what we want on weekdays. It's the same what they say in Ichupio and La Colonia. We don't see it as bad. It's the same church." Even if it means disobeying the direct wishes of their pastor, they see no harm in multiplying religious influences.

A founding member of the Assemblies of God congregation in Pátzcuaro told me that before starting a congregation near her home, she would have to travel an hour to Morelia for services. When she did not have the money for bus fare, she would worship at Centro Cristiano Emanuel in Pátzcuaro. I asked her if she noticed a difference between her church and theirs. "No, it's the same songs, the same doctrine, and the same teachings. The only difference is that they have more members. Maybe it's because more buses pass by their location. In the end they have Christ in their hearts and have changed their character." The crossings between evangelical churches have become so commonplace that the minister who leads the Baptist congregation in Pátzcuaro started praying with Dr. Cook—rather than appealing to his own church hierarchy—to get medical and financial relief.

The ease and frequency with which converts participate in other denominations and in Catholic practices suggest that conversion is more complex than the shedding of Catholic beliefs in favor a new church's doctrine. Converts feel loyalty to a new church, but they do not limit themselves to following its doctrine without exception. As much as they respect their church leaders, evangelicals do not heed calls for spiritual exclusivity. While the evangelical message of salvation transcends particular places to apply to all believers across the world, harmonious community relations still matter for converts in Tzintzuntzan. Their faith gives them a powerful connection with the divine, but evangelicals still must maintain connections with their Catholic neighbors. When the pastors' demands to avoid fiestas, to become baptized, and to proselytize threaten converts' peaceful coexistence with Catholics, they diverge from doctrine.

DEFENDING TRADITION

For Catholics, fiesta celebrations crystallize community integrity by extending customs from the past into the present. While parishioners treat Father Rogelio with deference, they do not hesitate to ignore his wishes when they contradict desired goals like preserving tradition. Unlike the municipal president, who arises from within Tzintzuntzan, the parish priest derives his authority from his appointment by the bishop. Because of his link to the ecclesiastical hierarchy, Catholics know Father Rogelio will ensure the sanctity of their rituals. At the same time, his status as an outsider calls into question his commitment to the community and can undermine the effectiveness of his leadership. This weakness became evident during the fiesta of Corpus Christi in 2000.

Estela, who participates in every Catholic fiesta in Tzintzuntzan and several in other communities, calls Corpus Christi her favorite holiday. The fiesta, usually abbreviated in speech as "Corpus," aims to deepen believers' appreciation for the Communion Host and to affirm the community of the faithful—the body politic—in the symbolic body of Christ. It involves literally every sector of the parish in a celebration of the various professional groups: potters, wheat straw weavers, farmers, fishermen, merchants, and taxi drivers, each of whom decorates an altar in the churchyard with dangling bread and fruit, flowers, and candles. After a mid-afternoon Mass, the priest leads a procession through the churchyard holding a eucharistic wafer in a golden vessel. At each altar, he stops to recite a prayer and to ask Jesus to bless the work of each sponsoring group (Figure 5.2).

It is a time of playful inversion: men cook (and burn) tortillas over a fire in the churchyard while others, dressed as women, dance in the streets. On their procession to the churchyard, the fishermen ensnare cars in their nets. Many of the occupational groups hire bands, who compete with the firecrackers for the loudest display of devotion. Children outfitted as old-time pottery peddlers with crates strapped to their backs dance in front of the church. In some years, they erect a towering greased pole that young men attempt to scale for prizes. Most importantly, Corpus Christi features "throwing," a Tzintzuntzan tradition that the community cherishes.

When the procession ends and the consecrated Host has been returned to its locked case in the church, the men and women in charge of each altar gather in the back of flatbed trucks to throw items at the cheering crowd. They throw clay pots, Tupperware containers, mangoes, toys, carved wooden objects, reed mats, and wheat tortillas. I saw one woman, newly returned from the United States, flinging Levi's jeans to the crowd. Hundreds of young people swarm each truck, arms overhead to catch the falling objects. As one supply runs out, another group begins throwing in another section of the churchyard, so the crowd sprints to the next spot. Ceramic shards cut fingers while aggressive teenage boys push others to the ground. Euphoric chaos reigns.

At the first Corpus Christi I attended, in 1998, I waited around the churchyard for an hour after the procession had ended without seeing much activity of any kind. I began to suspect that all the talk I had heard about throw-

5.2 As part of the celebration of Corpus Christi 1998,
Father Rogelio, standing on the steps of the parish church,
blesses the *arrieros*, the muleteers who traditionally
brought pottery to sell in other parts of the state.

ing was exaggeration, but then I heard a commotion. I hurried to join the
swarm of people that moved toward the trucks, reaching for pots and baskets, but soon removed myself from the fray. Safe on the margins of the
crowd, I watched as young men and women squealed with horrified delight
as objects came sailing toward them. One group threw items from the bell
tower of La Soledad, showering plastic buckets on the masses below. For an
entire hour the crowd lunged for mangoes and reached for bread.

Before the fiesta in 2000, however, the priest made clear in his sermons
that he wanted to see an end to the throwing tradition. This practice, both
unhealthy and ungodly, displeased Father Rogelio. "God does not throw

miracles at his children. He hands them to us," the priest reasoned during one Mass. Word spread that the priest wanted the crowds to line up so that they could receive items from the cargo holders one at a time. As many Tzintzuntzeños pointed out to me, this method, if implemented, would no doubt result in even greater chaos. Perhaps the priest realized this too and had as his true goal ending the practice altogether, since it resembles a Native American potlatch ceremony more than a Catholic ritual.

Although Catholics all over Mexico celebrate Corpus Christi, people told me that only in the Lake Pátzcuaro region does throwing take on such a prominent role. Priests around the lake take different stances toward the event. In the 1940s, the Tzintzuntzan priest initiated the throwing with a symbolic first pitch, much as in the start of baseball season in the United States. In Pátzcuaro, I heard of a Catholic priest who tried to rationalize the practice, saying that by throwing the items toward the sky God blessed them before they came crashing down. Only Father Rogelio condemned the practice outright. In a conversation I had with him before Corpus Christi in 2000, I asked him what differences he saw between Tzintzuntzan and his previous parishes. "The people here," he replied, "are very rooted to their traditions. Their exterior manifestations of faith come from their ancestors. It is all right to have fireworks and bands. They may have to be purified a bit, but they are offerings to God." He made this comment to me on the eve of Day of the Dead, a Catholic holiday celebrated with local flair in Tzintzuntzan, but it took on added significance in June. He recognized the limits of his own power to eliminate a tradition, but he could seek to "purify" it.

Before the afternoon of Corpus Christi 2000, the community was abuzz with speculation about whether the representatives from different groups would throw. Father Rogelio appointed the commissioners in charge of each altar and set the time for the Mass, but his pronouncement against throwing faced unanimous opposition. One young man shook his head in disbelief. "He is crazy. If they hand them out, they'd be *aguinaldos*! Corpus is throwing." Aguinaldos are gifts that figure in the Christmas celebration of the Posadas. After the nightly reenactment of Joseph and Mary's search for shelter in Bethlehem, the families in charge of each neighborhood celebration distribute small bags of candies, fruits, and nuts to the children and string up a piñata. In those cases, children have to line up and calm down before receiving their treats.

The incredulous young man represented the feelings of a majority of Catholics, who considered throwing integral to the proper celebration of Corpus Christi. An older man, who attended Mass daily, also sided against the priest.

"People throw for happiness," he remarked. "It's a custom, and the customs here are laws. The priest is just passing through. He will leave in a few years. The fiesta is for the community." Many people subscribed to this logic: the priest was not from Tzintzuntzan, nor would he be staying there very long, so he had no right to meddle with the traditions that unified the community.

Others offered practical reasons why the proposed system would not work. As the elderly woman who headed the organization of volunteers that cleaned the parish church objected, "They've thrown for as long as I can remember. It used to be just the cargo holders of La Soledad who threw; now it's everyone. They can't just hand out the items. It would be so crowded." One man, who had thrown for many years with the potters, was the most adamant: "We're going to run this priest and his new ideas out of town!" In each case, Catholics placed more value on adhering to tradition than to the request of the priest.

One person I spoke with came to the defense of the priest: Marta, the schoolteacher who led the Prayer and Life Workshops. Significantly, she was not from Tzintzuntzan, either, nor did her hometown celebrate Corpus Christi with throwing. In the twenty years since moving to Tzintzuntzan, she had watched with disapproval as the throwing tradition expanded. "It's purely pagan. The Catholic Church set up a commission to study it and didn't find any religious meaning behind it. They only do it here around Lake Pátzcuaro." Despite her sympathy for Father Rogelio's position, she did not think it likely that the fiesta commissioners would obey him.

After the Corpus Christi procession ended in 2000, the priest lingered in the churchyard. Then he turned toward his house, adjacent to the parish church, with Marta and a few other female friends behind him. Within a few minutes, the first mango went flying.

The throwing in 2000 was not more extensive than I had seen two years prior, but it was certainly no less so. It continued for an hour of frenetic jumping and screaming. No one seemed to know for sure, nor could I count amid the disorder, but between six and eight groups threw items, sometimes simultaneously. The final and most sustained throwing came from the caretakers of La Soledad, who perched on the bell tower of the church and rained plastic buckets and fruit down on us. When it became clear that no new group would begin throwing, the crowd dissipated. Some went to the town plaza, where two bands hired for the occasion serenaded dancers. The usual greased pole did not materialize in 2000. Some speculated that this was another attempt by the priest to squelch tradition, but others claimed that the men in charge of the pole simply had been irresponsible. I went home as it was nearing dinnertime. For my second Corpus Christi I had mustered more bravery and entered the crowd. I was rewarded with several mangoes and a pair of sore hands. Estela's teenage sons proved far more successful. The plasticware they retrieved became integrated into the kitchen supply of containers, and we had mango shakes for dinner all week.

After the fiesta, I asked people who had participated in Corpus what the throwing symbolized. A young man who had elbowed his way into the crowd drew a parallel between the itinerant throwing and the travels of Jesus, who brought healing from town to town. A woman said vaguely, "God gives to his children." A young woman who had thrown with the potters did not try as hard to find a religious significance. "I knew the priest didn't want us to do it. But it's custom and it's fun." A man, originally from another part of Michoacán, who had thrown with the taxi drivers' group had not really thought about the symbolism of throwing until I asked him. "What is the meaning? It's to thank God or something. I don't know. But they've done it for all the years I've lived here. It's custom." Estela pointed out with her typical good-natured common sense, "Mangoes are very cheap right now, and what's a boy going to do with a plastic bucket? It's about having fun."

To an anthropologist's eye, the event looks like a holdover from the days when wealthy members of the community were saddled with high ritual expenditures to equalize income distribution. However, the commitment of equality no longer holds in Tzintzuntzan, and the event has come to represent the endurance of local tradition. Serving as a commissioner does not bankrupt a thrower. For one, not all the groups choose to throw. Those who do throw toss out items of very little value, as Estela noted. Potters discard their misfired or misshapen pieces; mangoes come for pesos a kilogram in the summer. Like the cargueros of the crosses, the Corpus commissioners share the expenses across nearly ten families and ask their neighbors and fellow professionals for contributions. What the Catholics fight to preserve is not the redistributive function of Corpus Christi, but its central role in a distinctly Tzintzuntzeño event. Without the throwing, Corpus Christi would resemble the Posadas around Christmastime or any other Mexican Corpus Christi fiesta and lose its unique character.

Fiestas, which have the potential for both awe-inspiring faith and explosive violence, generate particular controversy among the clergy. Evangelical leaders reject the fiestas and prohibit their followers from participating in them either financially or personally. Catholic priests sanction the fiestas but encourage a less rambunctious and expensive expression of faith. In his study on the techniques of social control operating in fiestas, Brandes (1988) concludes, "As for most of the people in Tzintzuntzan, participation must be satisfying because, in fiestas, they see their world reaffirmed. They have not absorbed any revolutionary notions by way of religious action" (184). Through humor and symbolism, religious rituals clearly distinguish acceptable from unacceptable behavior. Brandes contends that for all their chaotic movements and lavish display, fiestas fundamentally reinforce the existing order of the community. The upending of rules in a carnivalesque setting only serves to strengthen conformity to social norms during the rest of the year.

The priest never mentioned the throwing again. After the festivities in Tzintzuntzan, each of the three indigenous communities of Ichupio, Tarerio, and Ucasanastacua, which form part of the Tzintzuntzan parish, celebrated Corpus Christi on one of the following three Thursdays. Again, in all three fiestas the commissioners threw an assortment of food and artisanry to the crowd without heeding the wishes of Father Rogelio. However, in Tarerio, the commissioners made a minor concession by moving the throwing from the cramped plaza to the larger basketball court. In Ichupio, an enormous greased pole dominated the tiny concrete plaza. After Father Rogelio had made the circuit of altars, he quickly returned to Tzintzuntzan before the throwing and climbing began. Again, his quick disappearance seemed designed to save face rather than to confront his followers with their disobedience.

Most Catholics do not pretend that throwing holds any religious significance. They defend it on the basis of "tradition," not holiness. As Estela said when the priest first announced that since God delivers his blessings gently, so should we, "God may hand things to us, but that's God, and I'm not God." Catholics I met did not try to emulate Jesus Christ, only to live their lives in harmony with the community, which remains a focal point for their self-image. Similarly, evangelicals acknowledge by their actions that following Jesus Christ's teachings scrupulously requires superhuman fortitude. Their participation in Catholic fiestas and refusal to heed their pastors' strict sermons illustrate how the exigencies of life in Tzintzuntzan supersede blind doctrinal allegiance. When Father Rogelio declared that a local fiesta celebration should be modified, Catholics continued observing it with impunity because they interpreted the change as weakening the custom that affirmed their view of the world. They still showed respect for the priest, but made it clear that it was religion's role as a cementer of community bonds that ensured its continued relevance in Tzintzuntzan. Fiesta traditions, even if they have changed significantly over time, help maintain cohesion when so many other forces threaten it. With the diaspora of Tzintzuntzan residents and the increasing differences between them, distinctive Catholic traditions militate against the dissolution of community unity.

SIX | CONSIDERING THE CONSEQUENCES OF CONVERSION

WITHIN Mexico, Catholic observers commonly perceive evangelical churches as mere extensions of North American denominations with their conservative ideology. They accuse evangelicals of undermining the traditional structures of spirituality and participation that unite communities. To critics like Miguel, the local official in Santa Fe, converts consider the modern world sinful and withdraw from it into the protected world of prayer. Academic accounts of new religious movements in Latin America also claim that evangelical conversion will challenge the status quo represented by the fiestas. However, they are more sanguine about the prospect of upsetting Catholic authority, which to them represents a legacy of undemocratic politics and gender inequality. Scholars have seen in evangelical Christianity the ingredients to give voice to the voiceless and to tip the balance of power in favor of the poor. They frame the decision to join an evangelical church as a conscious step away from the anachronistic Catholic Church and toward "an induction into modernity" (Martin 1990:108).[1] Is the growth of evangelical churches part of a new Reformation, one that replaces the unprofitable concern with community with an entrepreneurial individualism?

One consequence of interpreting evangelical conversion as an entrance into modern life is the resulting portrayal of the Catholic majority as old-fashioned and ill-equipped to succeed in the modern, globalized economy. It also assumes that a convert's break with the community and the fiesta system is total. Predictions of evangelical churches' potential to effect social reform must be tempered with empirical accounts of how Catholics and converts *actually* live. On its surface, evangelical Christianity promises a radical break from the traditions of the Catholic Church and a return to a biblically pure past. However, converts practiced their faith in ways that contradict the idealized version offered by their leaders. Becoming an evangelical did not eliminate all contact with the Catholic world of fiesta contributions and godparenthood. They understood their faith on the level of individual health crises and community harmony, not on the level of social activism. With their concerns more locally directed, converts did not fulfill the promise for economic, political, and gender role reform that some scholars have predicted.

The ethnographic data I collected around Lake Pátzcuaro support the claims of evangelicalism's conservative nature and cast doubt on the ability of religious transformations to promote social change. One explanation for the conservative bent of evangelical churches could be their loyalty to right-wing interests in the United States that support them financially. However, foreign missionaries exert decreasing influence on evangelical congregations in Latin America. This is not to deny that conservative religious groups in the United States have offered ideological and financial support to missionizing efforts in Latin America (Brouwer, Gifford, and Rose 1996; Colby and Dennett 1995; Simons 1982). In many cases, converts internalized the conservative teachings preached in evangelical sermons or literature from abroad. Still, they framed their conversions neither as an effort to accommodate the democratic ideals represented by the United States nor as a retreat from them. The salient point of reference was the community itself and the desire to avoid conflict with their Catholic neighbors. In their acceptance of the status quo, converts express the continuity between their Catholic past and their evangelical present.

PURSUING PROGRESSIVE POSSIBILITIES

Academic observers of evangelical movements in Latin America give reasons for optimism that conversion has the potential to promote reform of both political and gender inequality. Since the largest conversion movements have taken place among the urban and rural poor, this reasoning goes, evangelical churches may form part of a larger strategy of resistance to the entrenched policies that support established hierarchies. Instead of an all-male leadership with an allegiance to Rome, evangelical faith substitutes a priesthood of all believers drawn from the women and men of the region. Instead of channeling faith in God through congeries of saints, sculptures, and clerics, it empowers individuals to come in direct contact with the divine. They suggest that it is possible that in evangelical churches, with their ecstatic worship, speaking in tongues, and personal testimony, the voiceless can gain a voice.

The pervasiveness of the idea that the growth of evangelical churches will reshape structures of power in Latin America attests to the enduring influence of Willems. His book, *Followers of the New Faith: Culture Change and the Rise of Protestantism in Brazil and Chile* (1967), portrays conversion as the regeneration of community ties that were disrupted by the dislocations of macroeconomic change. Through new religious communities, peasants uprooted by the dismantling of the traditional rural economy can forge new identities and organize for political action. Willems calls evangelicalism in Latin America "a protest movement, not just in the narrow theological sense, but a movement against the religious monopoly of the Catholic Church and its traditional ally, the ruling class" (1967:154). Proof of this oppositional spirit is that the denominations drawing the most followers are Pentecostals, whose form of worship is most distant from the norms of the dominant Catholic doctrine. Presbyterians and Methodists, Willems claims, resemble the Catholic Church too much to appeal to most disaffected migrants.

So, in this analysis, conversion emerges from conditions of change and then, in turn, creates change itself. Motivated by the desire to establish a more moral society, evangelical groups organize to participate in the political arena. Willems challenges the image of apathetic Christians who are unwilling to disrupt the status quo. He gives the examples of Pentecostals elected to legislative bodies in Brazil and Chilean Protestants who voted for the socialist Allende. Initial evangelical reluctance to enter the political fray stems not from doctrinal prohibitions but from the traditionally marginalized position of the poor (Cleary and Stewart-Gambino 1997). Other scholars cite Mexican converts as representative of evangelicals' ability to promote social change. In Mexico, conversion takes hold among people on the peripheries of society and gives them "tongue." Joining an evangelical church constitutes an "induction into modernity" for the poor, but a modernity of their choosing. They leave behind old constraints while acquiring organizational and technological skills that will help them survive and even improve their situation. According to this view, "Pentecostalism is a walkout from all that belongs to the status quo, especially the corruptions of the political arena, in order to create a space where local people run their own show" (Martin 1994:32).

Evangelical churches across Latin America emerge as politically engaged and willing to challenge the system to reach their goal of a more moral world. Congregations may even employ television and radio, the very media of the elite, to undermine the powers that be (Marty and Appleby 1991). The horizontal nature of evangelical leadership, the emphasis on public speaking, and the opportunity to take on responsibility may facilitate members' active involvement in civic life (Vera 1996). Postelection studies contend that evangelicals vote and participate in community groups in equal numbers to Catholics (Camp 1997; B. Smith 1998). Religious converts have won political office in several Latin American countries and offered crucial voting support to candidates who wooed them (Freston 1992; García Méndez 1997; Marostica 1994; Padilla 1992; Petersen 1997; Wilson 1994). Where legislators propose restrictions on religious freedom, evangelicals mobilize to oppose them. They take proactive stances as well, promoting structural change through institution building.

Evangelical participation in the political process does not follow predictably conservative principles. Nicaraguan evangelicals were stronger supporters of leftist Sandinistas in the 1990 election than the Catholic majority was (Lancaster 1988; C. Smith and Haas 1997). In Chiapas's Zapatista rebellion, evangelical religious groups paved the way for political action. Increased emphasis on participation in the congregations had the effect of "creating a space in which people could challenge the boundaries not just of gender and literacy, but of access . . . to formerly impenetrable domains of law and politics" (Collier 1994:59). When municipal authorities allowed the expulsion of 584 evangelicals from Chamula, Chiapas, the victims began a thirteen-month campaign of civil disobedience with marches through the streets and an occupation of the office of the Director of Indigenous Affairs in San Cristóbal.

This view also holds that where evangelical churches adopt an apolitical stance, they do so out of pragmatic, not religious, reasons. In some cases, when a church would like to distribute aid after a crisis, for instance, maintaining a neutral political position enables it to operate without government interference. A political scientist who surveyed evangelical organizations in Central America concludes that "converts to evangelicalism discover new dignity in their emphasis on a personal relationship with Christ and become less fatalistic about their helplessness in the midst of socioeconomic upheavals" (Hallum 1996:105). According to many scholars, evangelical churches' empowering message and active style of worship make participation in politics a natural consequence of conversion.[2]

The voices doubting the ability of evangelical religion to work toward social reform are less outspoken than are the followers of Willems in the academic literature. Those who do argue for the conservative effect of evangelical conversion trace their intellectual lineage to a contemporary of Willems, Lalive d'Epinay.[3] Like Willems, Lalive also views religious conversion in relation to the migration of peasants from their home communities to alienating metropolitan centers. They differ in how they envision those feelings of dislocation becoming manifest: in political action or political apathy. The title of Lalive's study sums up his position well: *Haven of the Masses* (1969). Leaving the once stable patron-peasant relationship of the hacienda, migrants to the cities seek to re-create their familiar, secure positions by joining hierarchical, male-dominated churches. There, they enter into relationships of dependence that heal the rupture experienced with the failure of the agricultural model, but that preclude active political participation.

Although evangelicals share with liberation theology the goal of fomenting social transformations through religious change, evangelicals uphold a more mystical vision of faith. Instead of achieving the desired society through political action, they aim to remove certain people from larger society, remake them, and then let the new morality percolate back. They believe that individual conversions, rather than structural solutions, will reshape Latin America (Stoll 1990). In Argentina under Pinochet and other countries governed by military dictators, Pentecostal groups forged patron-client relationships with the established powers. In exchange for their spiritual legitimacy, churches received necessary permits and tolerance. Deiros (1991:175) confirms that "even in cases of flagrant violations of human rights by military dictatorships," evangelicals "have consciously rejected any critical attitude toward the existing order."[4]

Despite their rhetoric of innovation, in practice evangelical churches endorse existing structures of power. Contrary to the image of an open, democratic church that gives support to the Zapatistas, some congregations suffer from repressive leadership hostile to change. "Traditional Latin American Protestantism remains an intimist, private form of religion, plagued by a dualistic view of the world, and lacking the impetus to transform Latin American societies" (Cavalcanti 1995:291). Given their peripheral status, many evangelical groups borrow from and reproduce local structures of authority to gain acceptance. In the case of the Presbyterian Church in Brazil, a caudillo-style leadership emerged, which was unwilling to propose any programs of social reform, preferring a call to internal salvation that kept their authority intact (Alves 1985). In an Assemblies of God congregation in Pernambuco, Brazil, the ranks of leadership are closed and exert undue influence on members' lives (Hoffnagel 1980). Faced with the dissolution of traditional social networks on the plantation, converts look to re-create a familiar relationship of dependence with their spiritual leaders.

In most cases, converts whom I observed spoke more enthusiastically about biblical-era events, personal physical change, or the afterlife than they did about contemporary issues. Sunday sermons in Mexican evangelical churches, usually fond of incorporating anecdotes from contemporary life, never mentioned rampant government abuses of power or even the 2000 federal elections, which drew international attention. The election dominated conversations I had with Catholics for most of June and July. The campaigning had begun the previous November, when the long-entrenched ruling party held its first-ever primary to choose a candidate to oppose opposition party nominees Vicente Fox and Cuauhtémoc Cárdenas. During the first half of 2000, all three major party candidates visited the Lake Pátzcuaro region at some point and papered over every streetlight and storefront with their campaign posters. The televised debates, only the second such event in Mexican history, drew large audiences from the Catholics in Tzintzuntzan.

Election Day fell on a Sunday, coinciding with a large fiesta dedicated to a figure of Jesus in the Quiroga parish church. Before I went to witness the procession in Quiroga, I accompanied Estela to the voting place in Tzintzuntzan. Anyone over eighteen with a valid credential could vote, and, judging by the final tally of more than fourteen hundred ballots cast in Tzintzuntzan, most every adult in the community did. Fox, who won the election, had been the most visible of the candidates in his expression of Catholic faith. At one rally, he used the image of the Virgin of Guadalupe as a banner. Nonetheless, the Catholic voters in Tzintzuntzan overwhelmingly favored candidates from the leftist Party of the Democratic Revolution (PRD), whose leader was the former governor of Michoacán. Estela, one of the few local Fox supporters, watched the early returns on the news that night, amazed that her candidate had won. The next morning, she told me the prospect of a Fox presidency had made her so excited that she could not sleep. In the middle of the night, she turned the television on again, saw the message "Congratulations, President Fox," and knew she was not dreaming.

By contrast, no convert expressed any interest in the election. In an informal survey of Jehovah's Witnesses before and after the election, I could not locate a single one who had voted. A convert in his late seventies told me with some pride that he had voted only twice in his life. He went on to declare solemnly, "Jesus will end all governments. It's all written in the Bible. The Book of Revelation gives us the reasons." When I asked some Jehovah's Witnesses about the election, their responses made me believe that was the first time they had given the matter thought. One man told me there was "no point" in voting. Another told me that although he had his voting credential, he did not vote. Some said that if they had participated, it would have been only to nullify their ballots.

Ricardo told me bluntly, "I don't vote anymore. We keep religion and politics totally apart. Religion tries to unite everyone; politics doesn't." When the significance of Fox's victory became clear, a Jehovah's Witness man explained the events in a biblical frame: "Scripture says there will be big changes in the last days. Scripture doesn't lie. The Book of Revelation says the beast, which is politics, will defeat the whore, religion. Then will come the reign of Jesus Christ." While his exegesis of Revelation may have been shaky, his disdain for politics was evident. And, although Jehovah's Witnesses are notorious political abstainers, members of other evangelical churches reacted similarly to the election. Evangelicals give relevance to worldly events only in the context of biblical prophecy and to the extent that they hasten the imminent Judgment Day.

The other area where scholars have predicted that evangelical religion will challenge the status quo is in gender relations. Sicilian Pentecostals, for instance, challenge the prevailing gender order by weakening its patriarchal bias. The new gender system that emerges retains vestiges of the old hegemonic system, but it allows greater freedom for women (Cucchiari 1990). Pentecostalism in Latin America also offers novel roles for female participation that may destabilize entrenched attitudes of machismo and signal its appeal to many women. For Mayan widows in Guatemala, evangelical Christianity provides "refuge from suffering and a space in which the women are able to reclaim some personal control over their lives" (L. Green 1993:162). In the supportive environment of a close-knit church, women replace their lost family members with a network of fictive kin. Similarly, for women evangelicals in Colombia, conversion redraws the expectations in a marriage to bring the male into the private sphere of the family. The husband remains the household head, "but his relative aspirations have changed to coincide more closely with those of his wife" (Brusco 1993:148). In Guatemala as much as Colombia, women often cycle through different churches or practice multiple theologies simultaneously. This does not indicate a lack of spiritual commitment, but rather a confirmation of how women turn to religion to protest conditions of misery.

Conversion to Pentecostal churches in Bolivia forms part of a strategy by indigenous women to resist the alienation of urban work. Theirs is not a political revolution but rather a symbolic opposition to the individualized, impoverished lifestyle they experience on moving to the city. Many women take jobs as domestic servants, which gives them little voice in organized labor movements and minimal contact with their peers. Joining a Pentecostal church "enables them to construct new social networks that are emotionally supportive and economically useful. . . . These ties replace ties with kin left behind in the countryside [and] offset the rigid hierarchy that domestic servants encounter at work. . . ." (L. Gill 1994:132). Indeed, the rhetoric of evangelical churches in Tzintzuntzan gives credence to the image of small, cohesive organizations guided by an ideology that the current world is sinful and that the church is equipped with the tools to do something about it. Yet, claims that the expansion of evangelical churches will introduce a more horizontal, inclusive style of leadership and empower women to participate in the public sphere overlook the ways evangelical congregations duplicate the rigid hierarchies that characterize the Catholic Church. Though different denominations follow different rules of worship, they all concentrate leadership in a single, charismatic male and systematically subordinate women.

Further, the personal control that conversion allows women to exercise over their familial relationships does not translate into public forms of power. Nearly all evangelical ministers are men, as in the Catholic Church. In cases like Alejandra's, where women lead congregations, they are subject to male superiors or are temporary substitutes for absent men. Certainly women in both Catholic and evangelical churches take on conspicuous positions of responsibility and fill the majority of the pews. However, ultimate authority to dispense the sacraments or invoke the Holy Spirit remains with the male.

The head of one Pentecostal church explained to me that "all church members are potential leaders," but it was clear that some leaders were more important than others. He has created an intermediate layer below himself of twelve congregation leaders, each of whom directs groups of twelve members in Bible study. Some women occupy the rank of group leader, but only if their husbands or another male relative also serves as a leader, and they guide only female followers. Then, the pastor sets the weekly themes and lessons by e-mailing the leaders a script to follow in their smaller groups. He remains the charismatic center of the congregation and the one who directs the supposedly more personalized study groups. During Sunday services with the entire congregation, the soaring music often induces spiritual trances in women sitting in the pews. Though they flail and mutter from the aisles, the pastor never cedes the microphone. Instead, from his position at the keyboard, he manipulates the music to calm the crowd so that they will retake their seats for his sermon.

When I visited a Baptist congregation one Sunday with Gloria's younger sister, she led the adult Bible study portion of the service. She chose her theme, the prophecies of Isaiah, and began preparing her lesson a week in advance. When I commented on her diligence, she remarked that she was particularly nervous because the pastor himself would be one of her pupils. I reassured her by saying that she was talented enough to be a pastor. "Oh no," she replied, "only men can be pastors." Although this church displayed a sign proclaiming that every member can be a minister, it is clear that male members are deemed more fit for this responsibility.

In the Catholic Church, the hierarchy of authority is made explicit through titles, privileges, and wardrobe. Leadership is supposedly more diffuse among the evangelical churches; Dr. Cook is fond of repeating, "If he could preach, I'd let my blind mule Methuselah be a pastor." However, in every evangelical congregation the pastor enjoys a position of authority akin to the Catholic priest's. For all the criticisms they levy against him in private, Tzintzuntzeños respect Father Rogelio. In his presence, parishioners use the formal address "*usted*" and temper their usual good-natured sarcasm. Pastors of evangelical congregations also receive respectful deference from their followers. Organizationally, the pastor occupies a position similar to that of the priest in a Catholic parish. Jehovah's Witnesses, for example, operate their international ministry along much the same lines as the Vatican. From the Jehovah's Witness headquarters in Brooklyn, New York, a president elected from an exclusive group of advisers oversees all doctrinal and publishing decisions. Underneath him (and it is by rule a he) descends a ladder of positions the equivalent of cardinal, bishop, and priest, each charged with administering a particular territory. To become a local leader, men have to endure a process akin to becoming a priest: spending years in lower positions, attending special schools, and currying the favor of church leaders.

As evangelical churches become more established, they bureaucratize their leadership. In 2000, Dr. Cook inaugurated a training center for pastors in a city near his compound. Before leading their own congregations, all aspiring pastors must pass through several years of schooling and serve as assistants. Even with the proliferation of assistant pastors, lay leaders, and guest sermonizers, authority clearly belongs to a tight cadre of men. At Nestor's in La Colonia, many members take turns hosting Sunday services in their homes while others pass in front of the pulpit to lead prayers or songs. However, members acknowledge that ultimate authority rests in Pastor Orozco by granting him the main sermon of each service and entrusting their donations to him.

At Luz del Mundo services in Pátzcuaro, the pastor always dresses in a three-piece suit, more formally than his audience. When he enters the congregation, members rise to attention. At the end, they allow him to exit before they file out, first the females and then the males. When they do speak to him, members always use the formal *"usted."* Just as an especially anointed man guides Catholics and the Jehovah's Witnesses, so does a spiritually endowed man lead the larger Luz del Mundo. Even in exile, Samuel, whose name appears alongside his father's in gold stenciled letters behind the pulpit in Pátzcuaro, claims to receive direct messages from God, which he then conveys to all the member churches. Whether invoking divine privilege or the miraculous gift of faith healing, evangelical leaders mediate how their followers communicate with God as much as Father Rogelio does.

Hopes for a transformation of gender roles hinge on the overwhelming female participation in evangelical churches; however, women also dominate the observance of Catholic faith. In Catholic families, women almost universally oversee the religious instruction of children and tend to the shrines and altars necessary for household protection. During Mass, women fill the pews and serve in the auxiliary roles; no one could remember the last time that the Tzintzuntzan parish boasted a male acolyte. The priest mingles with an all-female coterie of friends, and thirty women volunteer a day each month to clean the temple and sit watch. No man ever accepts this job, yet a waiting list of interested women forms to fill the spots when a current member dies or retires. While women read passages from the Old Testament and lead prayers during Mass, the priest reserves the main selection from the gospel (the one requiring all the parishioners to stand) for himself.

The pattern repeats itself in all the evangelical churches I visited. The Jehovah's Witnesses, Luz del Mundo, and Assemblies of God churches explicitly ban women from leadership roles, while other churches call women to the pulpit only irregularly. Unlike Catholic clergy, evangelical pastors marry, but their wives fill conspicuously secondary roles in the church: leading Sunday School classes for children, preparing the food for a feast, or singing backup in a choir. Evangelical churches retain clear divisions between male and female worshippers. In general, women cannot wear jeans, flashy jewelry, or gaudy makeup during services. Several congregations require that women cover their heads during worship. No similar rules apply to the men. Luz del Mundo congregations go as far as segregating male and female pews in their churches and require women to bring their donations forward at services apart from the men.

Taking into account women's reasons for conversion, it is not surprising that they content themselves with second-class status. After all, women who join evangelical churches often do so to make marriage to an alcoholic husband more bearable. They do not end their relationships, but rather seek ways to fulfill their traditional duties as spouse more effectively. Evangelical churches also eliminate all worship of the Virgin Mary, whose prominent place in Mexican Catholicism elevates the role of mothers and can even empower women (J. Rodriguez 1994). Evangelical leaders in Michoacán frown on any activity—be it veneration of Mary or electoral politics—that draws attention away from God's central theological importance. Overwhelming female participation, then, does not translate into additional strength. Their rhetoric of equality and societal uplift notwithstanding, evangelical churches closely resemble the Catholic Church in both hierarchical organization and male authority.

TESTING THE PROTESTANT ETHIC

When I began bibliographic research on the topic of evangelicals in Latin America, as expected I found relevant articles published in scholarly journals like *American Ethnologist, Journal of Church and State,* and *Latin American Research Review.* I also found references to magazines like *Forbes* (Marcom 1990) and *Business Week* (Ryser et al. 1990). After I had read the cited articles at the business school library, I understood why a finance publication would be interested in religious conversion taking place far from the centers of international capital.

Journalistic observers have found inspiration in Weber's work on the Protestant ethic to account for the religious transformations occurring in Latin America as a realignment of lives in accord with a capitalist ideal. The 1990 piece from *Forbes* is positively ecstatic about the prospect that Catholicism may lose its monopoly on Latin American faith. The reporter extols:

A new social atmosphere, one more flexible and more compatible with capitalism and democracy, is emerging. Upwardly striving urban poor are encouraged by religious teachings and support groups that preach the power of individuals to change their lives through faith. This contrasts sharply with the old attitude of resignation to one's fate and a glorification of poverty. The potential is quite literally revolutionary—more so than Fidel Castro or Che Guevara could ever be. (Marcom 1990:56–57)

The reporter detects an entrepreneurial spirit in evangelical faiths that he hopes will hasten a modernization of "semicapitalist, semifeudal" Latin America (Marcom 1990:64). Evangelicals, he claims, exhibit more disciplined behavior than Catholics, which makes them more fit for the conditions of employment in capitalist industry. To make the argument even more evident, a special advertising supplement follows, titled "Mexico: Dramatic Progress Ahead," which touts President Salinas's efforts to industrialize the country in an effort to woo foreign investors.

Another journalist heralds the "beginnings of a new Reformation" in Latin America, but with less glee than the financial commentators. Writing in the *Guardian Weekly*, Gott (1996) claims that religious conversion has stripped Latin Americans of their indigenous heritage, irreversibly hitching them to the economic superpowers. Weber also informs Gott's thinking, though he portrays evangelical faith as the final step in a process of integration into the capitalist marketplace that has been under way for several decades. "The contemporary appeal of Pentecostalism in Latin America," he writes, "is . . . precisely in its modernism. It is more about adjusting to society's changes—and even celebrating them—than a straightforward rebellion against the Catholic Church" (Gott 1996:12). The changes he refers to are shopping malls and McDonald's, signs of global capitalism that conversion to evangelical faith better prepares a person to accept.

Weber (2001 [1904–05]) identified the Protestant ethic as the precondition that made possible the flourishing of modern capitalism. In opposition to Marxist thinkers, who see religious forms as mere reflections of economic conditions, Weber documents how the emergence of Protestant faiths in the sixteenth and seventeenth centuries gave spiritual sanction to the pursuit of wealth. Ascetic Protestantism, particularly Calvinism, eliminated the possibility of salvation through the sacraments (as in the Catholic Church) in favor of the idea of predestination. To show their divine election, Protestants heeded a "calling" to devote themselves to God through good works and self-discipline. The rationality of the Protestant ethic imbued the accumulation of profit with moral purpose and, thus, enabled the growth of modern capitalism. Some authors note that a similar shift from the Catholic Church to Protestant churches in contemporary Latin America reduces the economic burden associated with both alcoholism and participation in fiestas. With the money saved and the strong emphasis on hard work, they suggest, converts function more successfully as workers in the capitalist system.

Anthropologists also have turned to Weber's notion of a Protestant ethic to explain the recent evangelical growth in Latin America. Annis began his fieldwork in the Guatemalan highlands intending to study the semiotics of women's weaving. But in his search for meaning, Annis finds in *God and Production in a Guatemalan Town* (1987) that Catholic and evangelical weavers in the same community understand their craft and their relation to the larger economy in significantly different ways. Differences carry over into farm production, political behavior, and even textile designs. To analyze how religion informs indigenous peoples' outlooks, Annis identifies two "logics" at work: the *milpa* logic expressed by most Catholics and the anti-milpa logic of most converts (1987:10). If a village person aligns herself with the traditionally "Indian" form of production embodied in the milpa plot of corn and beans, she expresses dependence on the land for production and an acceptance of a communal use of wealth through the distribution of ceremonial expenses. By contrast, the villagers with anti-milpa logic no longer expect to obtain sufficient land and look elsewhere for a means to support themselves.

Forces arose in the twentieth century to challenge the stability of the colonial model embodied in milpa logic. Intense population pressure, environmental degradation, spiraling inflation, expanded primary education, and political violence all made subsistence based on the cultivation of corn untenable. What evangelical faith provides is the blueprint for a new attitude toward production that gives anchor to peasants who no longer fit in the destabilized communal structure. Instead of investing surpluses to benefit the community, evangelicals seek personal enrichment along the lines of what Weber described as an ascetic commitment to hard work.[5] Annis draws the connection between a religious doctrine centered on personal testimony and a system of production that privileges personal advancement. "There *is* a Protestant ethic; and the draw of the new creed at the village level is closely related to the fact that it encourages personal rather than collective use of wealth" (Annis 1987:85, emphasis added).

As evidence for the evangelical emphasis on generating personal wealth, Annis offers examples of how converts in the community have devised more profitable livelihood strategies than the majority Catholics. Despite owning far more land than evangelicals, "Catholics do less well than Protestants in virtually every measure of agricultural productivity" (Annis 1987:104). Evangelicals buy plots with the best locations, plant higher yielding crops, and cultivate them more intensively. In terms of weaving, evangelical women participate more vigorously in the capitalist marketplace than their Catholic counterparts. Evangelical weavers display more entrepreneurial traits in selling their textiles and purchasing others' textiles to resell. They are also more likely to transfer the profit gained in craft selling to making capital improvements that will generate even more profit (Annis 1987:133–138). Both Catholics and evangelicals weave as a way to produce wealth, but for a Catholic weaver, the textile is wealth itself. It "expresses and celebrates the fusion of self and community," much as the milpa does. For an evangelical weaver, on the other hand, the textile is a means to wealth measured in currency negotiable outside the community. She invests only as much time in her weaving as needed to maximize profit (Annis 1987:123).

It follows, then, that converts find the elaborate and expensive village ceremonial life wasteful. In the same way that an evangelical woman will not invest in making a weaving any more intricate than necessary to earn personal profit, she sees no benefit in spending her earnings on community fiestas. Being Catholic in the Guatemalan highlands requires a significant outlay of ritual expenses, what Annis terms a "Catholic cultural tax." This tax—all for the benefit of the community—can deplete a quarter of a family's annual income (Annis 1987:94). Evangelicals where Annis lived refuse to pay the fiesta contributions to avoid the expenses associated with fiesta meals, costumes, and drinking. Consequently, they report a dramatic improvement in their financial situations after converting. They have found a religious worldview that enables them to adjust successfully to new economic imperatives. "By all accounts," Annis concludes, "it is 'cheaper' to be a Protestant than a Catholic" (Annis 1987:85). The old, "semifeudal" (as *Forbes* would call it) system of community investment seems wasteful in light of new capitalist incentives for personal gain.

This neat division between financially strapped community members who pay the Catholic cultural tax and those proto-capitalists who opt out does not hold for Tzintzuntzan. While some evangelicals do stop contributing to Catholic celebrations, many continue to pay the fiesta cooperaciones even if it means disobeying their pastor. I found no evidence that becoming an evangelical offers substantial monetary rewards; in fact, it may even impose an evangelical doctrinal tax. This tax requires a convert to spend additional income and time on religious activity, offsetting any savings from eliminating alcohol and drawing away resources from the pursuit of profit-making endeavors. The expense of evangelical faith makes it unlikely that converts are solely responding to macroeconomic imperatives to save money. It also calls into question the assertion that evangelicals have abandoned their commitment to community welfare in favor of personal gain.

Nearly all members of non-Catholic churches tithe 10 percent of their family's income. Those churches that do not obligate tithing strongly encourage voluntary donations. The Catholic Church also makes tithing a sacrament, but the custom has fallen into disuse. Around the time of February Fiesta, Father Rogelio makes pleas from the pulpit to give annual tithes, which he defines as a single day's earnings. Estela described to me how the tithes used to be much more substantial. In her parents' fields, the first fruits of the harvest always belonged to the priest, and in the past, some parishioners put eggs in the collection basket during Mass. But, in recent years, the priest made it clear that he prefers to receive cash. In Estela's mind, this marked the end of tithing among Catholics. "I harvest corn," her husband used to say, "not money."

Evangelical churches, like the one in La Colonia, make exhortations to tithe at every meeting. Pastor Orozco leads the services at Nestor's house every Sunday at 11 A.M. Congregants come from La Colonia, Pátzcuaro, and a host of tiny hamlets in between. Up to fifty people attend the Sunday services in Nestor's patio, the women in long skirts, the men in jeans, all carrying well-thumbed Bibles. Orozco requires tithing from his members to pay his own expenses and to support occasional visiting preachers or musicians. Yet, he recognizes that even faithful giving will not be enough to support his family, so he continues to work as a coppersmith in addition to ministering to three congregations. Collecting the tithe marks the halfway point in the service, after an hour and a half of singing and praying. It comes at a juncture after the latecomers have arrived and before the early departers have left. Both the lyrics of the hymns and the pastor's words reinforce the power of God to fulfill all requests. The service presents giving to the church as fitting gratitude for God's miracles and blessings. By having an assistant ask for donations, Orozco avoids looking as if he were seeking money for his own benefit. The pastor further encourages donations by emphasizing the believers' subordinate position in relation to the divine, who deserves tribute.

One member of Orozco's congregation explained to me how tithing had benefited his family. He had worked in Texas for several years as a landscaper, managing to save four thousand dollars before returning to Michoacán. Since he returned, he bought and drove a public transportation van in Pátzcuaro, supplementing this income with growing corn. When he first converted, he used to tithe whenever he felt like it. Since he committed to giving 10 percent of his weekly income regularly, he claimed to have received more blessings. The tithe, he said, merely returned to God what was rightfully his and multiplied the favors God granted him and his family. When I asked him where the donations went, he responded with a shrug. "I'm not sure, but I suppose Pastor Orozco takes from the offerings for his expenses."

In most evangelical churches, the collection arrives in the middle of the service, much as it does during the Catholic Mass. However, during Mass, the priest never announces the passing of the alms bowls; four young women acolytes quietly pass through the aisles while he prepares the Host for Communion. By contrast, evangelical groups all sing and pray over the offering of tithes. Some even have members recite relevant biblical passages that exhort donations, like Malachi 3:6–10 and 2 Corinthians 9:7. Orozco occasionally uses his sermons to chastise members who are not tithing faithfully, accusing them of withholding from the Lord what is his. The Jehovah's Witnesses do not require tithing, preferring to extract money from their members in more subtle ways, such as the sale of magazines. In addition to the bimonthly *Watchtower*, the Jehovah's Witness publishing house also produces a more general interest publication called *¡Despertad!* (Awake!). The twice-monthly magazines carry a suggested donation of three pesos per issue, which nearly everyone pays. One man told me he generally purchased twelve magazines every time they came out.

Worshipping with the Jehovah's Witnesses also requires purchasing their translation of the Bible, hymnals, supplementary texts used in the weekly Bible studies, and hardcover reference manuals. Most Jehovah's Witnesses consult publications other than the Bible and the *Watchtower* magazines infrequently, but nonetheless comply when leaders instruct them to make a "voluntary" purchase. Members who proselytize door-to-door buy multiple copies of these publications to leave with interested parties. As a constant target of their evangelizing, I received such short books as *The Greatest Man Who Ever Lived; The Bible: God's Word or Man's?; Life: How Did It Get Here? By Evolution or by Creation?; Knowledge That Leads to Everlasting Life;* and *Pay Attention to Daniel's Prophecy!* in addition to dozens of magazines. One Jehovah's Witness in Pátzcuaro, who could not read English, gave me his copy of a two-volume encyclopedia in English entitled *Insights on the Scriptures*. All these publications cost the donors money. In every Kingdom Hall (as the Jehovah's Witnesses call their worship places), every district and circuit assembly, and even in the room in the Tzintzuntzan home used for Bible study, the congregation leaders place donation boxes labeled with biblical citations in prominent places.[6]

Although my evangelical and Catholic friends never suggested that I donate to the weekly offerings, I felt awkward not doing so. In many cases, the collection baskets remain at the front of the room so the identity of who gives and who does not is conspicuous. In Mass, the acolytes walk by the end of every pew holding wooden bowls, so if I lacked small change I tried to avoid eye contact as they passed. During Catholic community fiestas, the parish makes public lists of the most generous donors and happily receives contributions from anthropologists. The researcher who was conducting an ethnographic census in Tzintzuntzan during February Fiesta in 2000 gave both for the fiesta music and for the maintenance of the church archives, where he gathered demographic data.

Non-Catholic worship involves a host of additional expenses that do not enter the church coffers directly. Converts may eliminate the alcohol-related costs associated with Catholic fiestas, but they have to spend money on their own fiestas. Every year Odilón and Antonia celebrate the anniversary of their introduction to the evangelical church, which took place during a visit to the state of Hidalgo in 1983. Every January 23, the pastor who welcomed them to his church travels to their home in Ichupio with members of his Hidalgo church for two days of prayer and celebration. On these occasions, Odilón and Antonia, as the only adult members of their congregation, supply lodging and food to more than thirty guests.

Similarly, Nestor and his family celebrate fiestas with Orozco's congregations throughout the year. Baptisms are particularly festive and costly occasions. Twice during the year I spent visiting Nestor and the Sunday services at his home, his church hosted a family of evangelical musicians from another part of the state. Orozco asked for extra offerings and more conscientious tithing to cover the expenses of the group. Members of the congregation volunteered to house and feed the visitors each time they stayed. During the musicians' first visit, the band plugged their electric instruments into enormous speakers, beginning the service with several earsplitting songs of praise. While we stood, clapping along, the leader of the band informed us, "It costs up to three thousand dollars to make a record. I'm not charging Brother Orozco a cent. Please give. The money is not for us, but to glorify the work of God." Then, he circulated a hat through the audience, warning—only half in jest—that the worshippers could not sit down until they had donated.

The Jehovah's Witness assemblies also involve considerable expense for Ricardo and Norma. District assemblies last for three entire days, requiring transportation, food, and the elegant clothes that distinguish Jehovah's Witnesses. Congregation elders encourage participation by keeping lists of who attends and who does not. I realized how much these events drain family resources when I heard Norma and other Jehovah's Witnesses talking about hosting a small dinner in honor of a visiting church leader. When they could not decide whether to hold the gathering, Norma suggested they wait until after the upcoming assembly to see if they had any personal funds left over.

The length and frequency of evangelical worship services point to an additional expense associated with conversion: the opportunity cost. The baptism ceremony Orozco conducted occurred on a Wednesday afternoon. Though it was hastily announced and in the middle of the workweek, the event drew at least eighty people. It took place in a remote community at the end of a dirt road nearly inaccessible to public transportation. For a fee, Nestor drove several families without a car. He picked me up at 11 A.M., and we did not return until 6 P.M.

Attending one hour of Mass a week qualifies a Tzintzuntzeño Catholic as devout. The very religious, who tend to be elderly women, go to Mass more frequently. One woman, who reads biblical passages from the pulpit during Mass and volunteers to help the priest give marriage chats to young couples, told me she started going to Mass every morning only after her husband died. Her new habits raised suspicion. "My children asked me, why do you go to Mass? I asked myself too. Is it to feel superior to others? Do I want to be in good standing with the priest, the people? Do I go with my heart?" She concluded that since she lived less than a block from the church, the 6:30 A.M. bells for Mass wake her. Given her proximity, she feels she is denying both herself and God if she does not go to Mass. Her devotion reaches such an extreme by Catholic standards that her own children question her motives. In most cases, a single one-hour session a week plus an annual confession and fiesta participation suffice to be considered a Catholic in good standing. By contrast, her regular visits to church would not elicit skepticism in an evangelical church. Non-Catholic churches require attendance at multiple weekly services, none of which is shorter than two hours long. Certainly, some members do not worship regularly, but even the average evangelical participant's commitment would match the most committed Catholic's.

Odilón and his family hold formal services three times a week. At first I wondered whether the four of them really abided by a fixed worship schedule given that the church members all live together. However, the times when I showed up unannounced, I found the daughter and mother with their heads covered, their Bibles in hand, while Odilón or his son preached from the pulpit. Typically, Sunday services with Pastor Orozco last from 11 A.M. to 2 P.M. followed by socializing and food. Nestor and the Tzintzuntzan area members also meet for two hours during the week for prayer without Pastor Orozco. Once a month, his three congregations hold a "Holy Supper," a special Sunday service that rotates between the three locations. These events include a modified wine and wafer ceremony (grape juice and crackers) and a forum for discussing church concerns. After four hours of song and prayer, few members can muster the energy to voice complaints, so they usually just sit down for tacos and beans.

All the evangelical services emphasize the importance of regular attendance. As a regular visitor and participant in several congregations, I too experienced the pressure to devote more time to group worship. After a two-week trip to Chiapas during my research year, I returned to a Sunday service at Nestor's house, slipping into a chair and offering a cheerful "God bless you" to the women on either side of me. I imagined no one had noticed my absence until Orozco began his sermon and promptly addressed me:

> Brother Pedro, how long have you been away? [I answered.] Psalm
> 133 says we must stay together. There are innumerable churches;
> we shouldn't put down any of them. But there are also many false
> churches. They twist the Word. Some *hermanos* come to service when
> they want to, read the Bible when they want to. Raise your hand if
> you have a responsibility to God. [Everyone raised a hand.] Raise
> your hand if you're fulfilling it. [Most everyone raised a hand.]

By singling me out in a way Father Rogelio would never do in Mass, Orozco made me aware that he noticed my irregular attendance. I felt further embarrassment when he used me as an example of a careless Christian, who fulfilled his responsibilities only when convenient. Participating in the services literally involves a life-or-death decision; on the unknown day when Christ returns to render judgment, I had better be attending church faithfully. Orozco's repeated biblical references give his instructions the ring of authority, even if the cited passages only awkwardly fit his message.

The Jehovah's Witnesses make explicit the importance of church attendance over all other activities, even money-making pursuits. They require all baptized publishers to spend at least fourteen hours a month on proselytizing and other religious activities, a discipline enforced by the regular collection of time cards. At the district assembly I attended in the Morelia soccer stadium, one church elder delivered a sermon that counseled us to remain constant in our faith even though we could not see God, since he certainly watched us. The suggestions he offered for fortifying our faith stressed regular attendance at church meetings and the rejection of an ethic of wealth accumulation. In a scripted exchange with another church leader, he placed church loyalty over economic success:

> *Speaker #1:* Strong faith helps us to preach to our neighbors and co-
> workers. It motivates us to attend all the meetings. Many have had
> to sacrifice, change to lower paying jobs as not to miss any meetings.
> Isn't that right?

Speaker #2: That's right. I had a good job. They gave me a raise and a scholarship to England. But they demanded more time from me that would have interfered with my church meetings, so I turned it down. In prayer, I was reminded of Hebrews 10:24 and decided to quit my job. I have no regrets. Jehovah provides for me. Three months later I found a job that pays enough to live on. Jehovah is real. [Applause from the audience]

Many sermons in evangelical churches express the same disdain for earning money. Pastors preach that an undue concern with money and material goods distracts believers from the true goal of salvation, which costs nothing. Quite the opposite from the Calvinists Weber wrote about, the evangelical Christians I met make poverty a calling.

All evangelical churches share the view that the pursuit of money is a worldly activity that followers of the Bible should avoid. A guest preacher one Sunday at the Jehovah's Witness congregation in Quiroga asked, "Does a rich man sleep well? No, he's worried about losing his wealth. Do millionaires die? It's nice to have money, but a relationship with God is more important. How much money does it take to buy life? You can't obtain salvation with money. What do you need for salvation? Faith and obedience." No amount of money guarantees salvation, and choosing to have Christ in one's heart costs nothing. He even speculated that in the terrestrial paradise awaiting faithful Jehovah's Witnesses, they would enjoy an eternity without money.

The sermon made me reflect on what another Jehovah's Witness had told me about his reasons for conversion. After identifying abstinence from alcohol as a reason to convert, he claimed that everyone had a desire to adore something—just look at the pre-Hispanic pyramids that loom over Tzintzuntzan. When we fill that spiritual hole with money, pleasure, or education, we go unfulfilled, he continued. At first, I interpreted his comments as an indictment of my own reluctance to be baptized and to continue studying with the Jehovah's Witnesses in California. When they pressured me to convert, I always used the excuse that my school commitments kept me very busy. With more experience, I saw that he did not address his criticisms to me specifically. Anyone engaging in worldly activities—advanced degrees, job promotions—could not simultaneously give full attention to religious concerns, which were the only ones that mattered.

The evangelical prohibition on making money extends to disapproval of migration to the United States. Again, pastors object that seeking material gain interferes with a believer's spiritual commitment, including the ability to attend frequent services. One Jehovah's Witness preacher devoted his Sunday sermon to the topic of migration:

> Many go to the United States when they have an economic problem. The Bible says it's good to work, earn money for food, but you need to seek a balance. In the United States they work exorbitant hours. The men abandon their families. Sometimes they send back money, but they lack the correct attitude. Philippians 3:7–8 tells us we need a good heart, not dollars.

Ricardo, for one, internalized the lesson of the sermon. After the service, he told me about a conversation he had with the taxi driver who had taken us to the Kingdom Hall that morning. "Did you hear," Ricardo asked me, "what they said about money today? That taxi driver said he earned three thousand dollars in three months working in Alaska and wants to go back for more. He already has two taxis. He's not poor. He thinks money is happiness." Other congregations discourage migration since crossing the border as an undocumented worker violates federal laws, which the Bible says to respect as much as ecclesiastical laws.

Although converts as much as Catholics migrate to the United States for material gain, they are more likely to downplay the importance of money in their lives. Evangelicals' distaste for wealth forms part of their overarching attempt to lead sanctified lives separate from any worldly influence. But, living only in the spiritual realm proves impossible. Everyone in and around Tzintzuntzan participates in capitalist markets. There is no equivalent to Annis's Catholic weavers, who imbue their crafts with markers of their shared indigenous identity. In Tzintzuntzan *all* artisanry represents a means to wealth, not wealth in itself, judging by how quickly artisans adopt decorative styles that sell well. Members of all churches work hard, often for little remuneration. Just as not all evangelicals espouse a Protestant ethic to earn money, neither does the Catholic Church oppose capitalist participation. Through its priests and publications, the Catholic Church in Michoacán promotes improvements in both the material and spiritual lives of its parishioners that equip them to succeed in the modern world.

Father Gilberto spent several years as a parish priest in Tzintzuntzan and Quiroga. In his role as cleric, he found no contradiction between ministering the Catholic sacraments and promoting economic success. He was born in Quiroga, a town now clogged with shops selling crafts by area artisans to tourists. But Quiroga was not always so commercially engaged. In 1934,

Gilberto's mother purchased a ceramic tea service from a potter in Santa Fe, leaving it on a table near the entrance of her house. A passing tourist offered to buy it, but she said it was not for sale. The tourist insisted, offering her five pesos. She sold the ceramics, then returned to Santa Fe to buy two more sets, both of which sold quickly. Soon, her neighbors in the town center began to copy her success. Gilberto's family came to own two small stores in Quiroga, and he intended to open his own business before a priest suggested he enter the seminary.

Father Gilberto brought his entrepreneurial experience to his role as priest in Quiroga. The parish always held the festival for its patron, San Diego, on November 13. Realizing this meant lower attendance from outsiders on years the fiesta fell on a weekday, Father Gilberto persuaded the organizers to move it to the first Sunday in November. To promote tourism further, he added a contest for the best *carnitas* (pork tacos) and best pozole. The first year of the contest, he took a risk by purchasing two tons of pork. He sold them all. Although the celebration moved back to November 13 after Father Gilberto left to direct the parish of Tzintzuntzan, he did persuade the organizers of the July fiesta to move that event permanently to a weekend. Stands selling carnitas still line the plaza in Quiroga.

When Father Gilberto first arrived in Tzintzuntzan, households let livestock roam the streets untethered. An older woman in Tzintzuntzan recalled how wandering pigs and chickens made the unpaved roads even dirtier. Father Gilberto taught his parishioners to build enclosures for their animals to promote hygiene and to protect their wealth. During World War II, when the United States was not receiving shipments of chairs from Japan, a young Father Gilberto used his pulpit to encourage capitalist participation. He organized a workshop where carpenters built chairs while other artisans wove reed seats. This arrangement gave employment to many crafts makers and filled orders for the North American market until the war ended.

Older Catholics in Tzintzuntzan remember Father Gilberto as an exemplary priest and maintain friendly relations with him in his retirement. His focus on commercial success is not peculiar within the Catholic Church. One study of Protestantism at a Maya site in Yucatán indicated that as the community participated more fully in capitalist markets, the majority remained steadfastly Catholic (Kray 1997). Official Catholic publications sold in Tzintzuntzan often contain articles praising the capitalist system. One magazine, *Inquietud Nueva* (New restlessness), appears every two months and is sold at the end of Sunday Mass in Tzintzuntzan. It compiles news stories about the pope and bishops alongside theological discussions of contemporary topics and readers' questions. One such question in the March-April 2000 issue asks, "Why does the Church reject communism?" The priest responding writes that capitalism is not an ideal system, but, "in capitalist countries, production is always superior to that in communist countries." He argues that "work," along with "supernatural gifts," make up the foundations of "eternal happiness."

The diocesan newsletter *Comunidad Cristiana* arrives every week in Tzintzuntzan, sold door-to-door. Each issue opens with an editorial by the archbishop of Michoacán and ends with an exegesis of that week's biblical texts. In between, writers report on parish activities. In some issues, the newspaper highlights industrial zones of the diocese complete with production statistics and workers' salaries. In the run-up to Mexico's presidential elections in July 2000, the paper carried several stories about the need for national reform. One article bemoaned that, from high-ranking politicians to shopkeepers, mediocrity reigned in Mexico. Most Mexicans, the writer claimed, live by the principle of least effort and lack the "spirit of work" necessary to achieve success. A photo of a disorganized stationery store accompanied the lament with the caption, "Our mediocrity is revealed in the disorder and bad service to the public." The author concluded with an invocation of Jesus and a message of individual effort that resembles the Protestant ethic: "Every human being can improve his situation if he wants and looks for the adequate means to do so."

Members of different faiths cannot be separated into the economic categories of semi-feudal and modern capitalists. As Weber concludes, the Protestant ethic "has escaped from its cage. But victorious capitalism, since it rests on mechanical foundations, needs its support no longer" (2001 [1904–05]:124). Catholics as much as evangelicals in Tzintzuntzan value work and strive to generate income for their families. For Catholics, the promise of participation in elaborate community fiestas justifies the often arduous pursuit of profit. For evangelicals, church dogma focuses exclusively on spiritual rewards, making excessive wealth undesirable. Unlike the Calvinist theology that characterized the Protestant Reformation, evangelical churches around Tzintzuntzan preach the irrelevance of money, instead focusing on salvation in the afterlife. By imposing intense schedules of worship on members and coercing them to tithe, evangelical churches undermine their members' ability to spend long hours earning money. Even venturing to the United States, a Protestant majority country, earns disapproval because working there would fulfill material goals while ignoring religious commitments. Still, evangelicals defy both their pastors' wishes and federal laws to enter the

United States in search of work. According to Weber, the Protestant ethic proved pivotal in lending legitimacy to capitalism when its acceptance was still uncertain. In the era of global capitalism, the relationship between economic and religious systems seems to be the reverse: the demands of acquiring capital require evangelicals to modify their religious practices.

Evangelical churches in Latin America have not fulfilled the promise of political activism and social reform. In some countries, converts have parlayed their theological concerns into campaign platforms, mobilizing members of their church to vote them into office. In other cases, converts have withdrawn from public debates and even given tacit support to dictators. Cox (1995) recognizes the inability of his fellow theologians to characterize the Pentecostal movement in Latin America, the fastest growing of the evangelical churches. "It is diverse, volatile, and mercurial. It will not sit still long enough for someone to paint its portrait, or stop changing long enough for anyone to chart its trajectory" (184). The binary model of conversion as either an accommodation to modern life or a retreat from it lacks the nuance necessary to describe this slippery phenomenon. The consequences of conversion for the economic, political, and social arena will not be the same for all of Latin America. As the example of Tzintzuntzan shows, members of evangelical churches take into account personal and community concerns more than societal wrongs.

CONCLUSION
Mobilizing Religion

The communities around Lake Pátzcuaro, much like the rest of Latin America, are experiencing an explosion of religious diversity. Evangelical Christian churches have arisen in the past thirty years to challenge the Catholic Church's centuries-old monopoly on Tzintzuntzeño spirituality. At the same time that international migration and economic integration with global capitalism have accelerated in Tzintzuntzan, its residents have embraced a wider range of religious identities. In other parts of Mexico and the world, the sharing of space between members of different faiths has occasioned outbreaks of violence. My ethnographic account of Tzintzuntzan examines an instance where the peaceful coexistence of two religious groups has been possible through a willingness to disobey doctrinal exclusivity and to share beliefs and practices.

Evangelical churches, particularly the more expressive and scripturally insistent denominations, have gained adherents from families in crisis. The call to a more ordered life, free from destructive behavior and pleasing to God, appeals to women who suffer the effects of alcoholic husbands. So pervasive is drinking in Tzintzuntzan that, when I first arrived, the community of three thousand people sponsored four chapters of Alcoholics Anonymous, with additional branches in La Colonia and Ichupio. Men drink publicly without any social sanction, and in most cases drink responsibly. However, alcohol abuse occurs and can bruise marriages. Since it is still unusual in Tzintzuntzan for a woman to leave her husband except under the most extreme circumstances, many wives appreciate the strong anti-alcohol message evangelical churches preach. Conversion narratives consistently describe a transformation from chaotic lives to more stable ones.

Most ethnographic accounts of how non-Catholic churches gain adherents assume that conversion entails a conscious decision to leave an outmoded faith and align oneself with a religion more relevant to modern life (Boudewijnse, Kamsteeg, and Droogers 1991; Chesnut 1997; Earle 1992; Lewis 1964; Roberts 1968). They envision a religious bazaar where converts are finicky consumers searching for the best possible product to meet their needs and discarding what no longer works. Some theorists refer to this method as a bricolage, or "spiritual toolbox," in which believers select the faith most appropriate for their present circumstances (Hervieu-Léger 1996; Willaime 1996).[1] What appears as the secularization of modern society, they say, is in reality the restructuring of religious life to fit a more individualized culture. They apply the economic concepts of "market" and "deregulation" to the religious field, where individuals have the power to choose between competing brands of faith.

This model does not adequately describe the people I spoke with in Michoacán. The concept of the spiritual toolbox suffers from two weaknesses. First, it depends on an overly functionalist interpretation of religion. In this view, people mobilize religion to serve specific needs at certain times, often during crisis. So, if a child is sick, his parents will take him to a medical doctor, make a vow to a patron saint, and visit an indigenous healer. Sometimes the problem is a general state of anomie that leaves a person uncertain and disconnected from a supportive community. Religion becomes just one of many wrenches that parents take out of their toolbox, hoping it will be the right size to fit the loose bolt. But religious faith is never so limited to a single problem, even in the cases of evangelical converts with alcoholic husbands. Nor is it something external to the individual, to be picked up and used at appropriate moments, then put away at other times. For the Catholics and evangelicals around Lake Pátzcuaro, faith is omnipresent, marking the sale of the first freshly squeezed juice in the morning and blessing the grandchildren before they go to bed at night. Its presence is not always as a benign protector; at times Catholics assume expensive ritual obligations that increase their debt, and evangelicals follow strict rules of conduct that deny them many physical pleasures. The model of a toolbox captures the multiplicity of influences that shape faith, but in privileging the selection of the most appropriate tool, it underestimates the pervasiveness of religious faith.

My other objection to a consumer model of faith is the implied fragmentation of the resulting identity. Each spiritual tool remains discrete and separate, incapable of producing a single, coherent system of belief. Mutual borrowing of ideas and practices, as I have described for Catholics and evangelicals in Tzintzuntzan, does not preclude primary identification with one church. The Catholic who reads Jehovah's Witness literature and participates in the solstice ceremony nonetheless considers himself a Catholic. The Baptist woman who visits the cemetery on the Day of the Dead feels no less a connection with her Protestant faith, even though her actions contradict received doctrine. Even the term "syncretism" does not fully capture how believers maintain a single spiritual affiliation while disobeying the strictness of their leaders' wishes for exclusivity. Theories that categorize beliefs and practices as either orthodox or unorthodox foster an incomplete understanding of how Tzintzuntzeños perceive their religious identities. The model that emerges is both more inclusive and less functionalist than the toolbox metaphor. Choosing a faith has less to do with testing many "products" than with appreciating the positive attributes of all religions.

Other scholars working in Latin America describe the same fluidity both between and within churches. Lesley Gill (1994) borrows the term "religious mobility" from Murphee (1969) to account for the conversion of Aymara women in La Paz, Bolivia, to Pentecostal churches. Over the course of their lives, the domestic servants in Gill's study move from church to church. "Yet even as impoverished immigrant women flock to Pentecostal churches, their commitment is not always as great as their mentors desire. Religious identity must be thought of as a dynamic, continually evolving process that takes place over an individual's entire lifetime" (Gill 1994:136). A former Brazilian Catholic explained, "All religions are good, but there is an occasion for each one" (quoted in Rostas and Droogers 1993:1). He had joined a Spiritist group, but continued to worship the saints and hoped to return eventually to the Catholic Church.

From a range of ethnographic sources, a picture of creative reconfiguration emerges. In the Mexican state of Puebla, evangelical churches incorporate Catholic customs like godparenthood into their worship to forge an "indigenous Protestantism" (Garma Navarro 1987). Nineteenth-century Mexican American Methodists similarly mixed their Anglo-American faith with their cultural heritage to become a "truly indigenous, authentic, and empowering faith tradition" (Barton 1999:10). Whether it is to ensure the survival of a child (L. Green 1993), to maintain smooth community relations (Juárez Cerdi 1995), or to preserve indigenous culture (Sullivan 1998), evangelical converts rework the doctrine preached to them according to their own interests and traditions.

By showing how conversion supplements rather than supplants previous religious beliefs and practices for many evangelicals, my goal is not to deny the depth of their faith. There is no confusion about who belongs to the Catholic Church in Tzintzuntzan and who does not. Oftentimes, evangelicals distinguish themselves sharply from Catholics, who pray to what they consider idolatrous images and drink copious amounts of alcohol. Frequent admonitions from their pastors to avoid sinful behavior reinforce converts' sense of difference from the Catholic majority. Yet, in the balance between accepting the message of separation from the world and retaining community cohesion, converts around Lake Pátzcuaro implement their beliefs in ways that their literal-minded pastors do not sanction. Under the model of religious mobility, it is insufficient to consider religion as a response to an isolated crisis. A person's religious identity takes shape over the course of a lifetime and not always in agreement with doctrinal rules. These flexible interpretations of faith do not weaken spiritual commitments, but rather strengthen them by inserting them in a larger social context.

Starting with the reforms of the Vatican's Second Ecumenical Council, Catholics have responded forcefully to the loss of parishioners. No longer may priests in Latin America take for granted the loyalty of their followers. Even without the progressive rubric of liberation theology, clergy in Michoacán have energized their pastoral efforts and instituted programs to deepen understanding of the catechism. Parishioners used to an aloof, paternalistic church scarcely recognize their own religion in new activities like the Prayer and Life Workshops or marriage retreats, suspecting evangelical affiliations. After overcoming their initial doubt, Catholics applaud the Church's revitalizing efforts and experience a renewal of their faith. They demonstrate the continued significance of the Catholic Church by calling on its familiar forms when new challenges, like undocumented migration, put them in danger. While I expected to be the target of evangelical proselytizing in Tzintzuntzan, I found that Catholics rallied just as persistently to convince me to join their religion.

I would not have predicted much cooperation between evangelicals and Catholics on the basis of the official discourse of each church. Both doctrines claim an exclusive path to salvation and the damnation of nonfollowers. As much as Catholic priests support the fiestas, evangelical pastors rail against their sinfulness; in contrast to evangelical encouragement of personal communication with God, the Catholic Church favors prayer to intercessory saints. Despite their leaders' seemingly irreconcilable pronouncements, however, evangelical and Catholic followers put aside theological differences to

endorse mutual priorities. Community stability is one priority that Tzintzuntzeños of all faiths share. When their religious leaders give instructions that
threaten community stability—be it to proselytize door-to-door or to eliminate throwing from Corpus Christi—evangelicals and Catholics respectfully
disobey. In all the congregations where Tzintzuntzeños worship, the leader
either comes from another part of Mexico or, if locally born, reports to a
more powerful outsider. Their followers trust these sophisticated and charismatic men to convey the intricacies of religious doctrine and to administer
the sacraments, but they do not trust them to have the best interests of Tzintzuntzan in mind.

The well-documented recent history of Tzintzuntzan shows why the preservation of community is so cherished by evangelicals and Catholics alike.
When Foster first arrived in Tzintzuntzan, he encountered a community ruled
by the logic of limited good, where a religious hierarchy ensured the masking of class differences. In the past fifty-eight years, Tzintzuntzan has benefited from an improved standard of living, increased reliance on migration
and tourism, and the breakdown of the illusion of equality. Throughout these
transformations, Tzintzuntzeños have remained proud of their once glorious
precolonial capital. Foster suggested to me that the continuous presence of
anthropologists has helped generate an esprit de corps among Tzintzuntzeños, who have come to understand that they are worth studying. When Foster's original 1948 ethnography of Tzintzuntzan appeared in Spanish, he
made sure that every household in Tzintzuntzan received a copy. On more
than one occasion during my fieldwork when I arrived at a house unannounced, I would find people reading the four-hundred-page book or ex-
amining the photographs. As Tzintzuntzeños, both Catholic and evangelical,
continue to emigrate from Tzintzuntzan, three generations of anthropologists
have performed a reverse commute, returning to Michoacán year after year.
The cycling of visits by migrants and researchers strengthens the viability of
a sense of community in Tzintzuntzan.

Lest I overstate the impact of anthropologists' presence in Tzintzuntzan,
I also believe that the preoccupation with preserving community helps deter
interference from the state. In Talea, Oaxaca, Nader (1990) identified a prevailing "harmony ideology" that informs how community members interact
even though they are extremely litigious. Dispute settlement, however, occurs
entirely within local courts and ignores the state-run district court. Taleans
understand how the government since colonial times has used the law as
a tool of political control. By resolving conflicts internally, the community
limits opportunities for the state apparatus to intrude on their lives and to en-

force its political and cultural hegemony. For Tzintzuntzeños, the avoidance of interreligious conflict helps to achieve this same local autonomy. Previous attempts to limit intracommunity difference through income redistribution are no longer effective. Instead, Catholics and evangelicals downplay the divisions between them so as not to provoke government intervention.

During the initial years of Foster's fieldwork, an ideology of equality characterized the social context in Tzintzuntzan. Public religious practice reflected the denial of differences by encouraging wealthy members of the community to take on expensive ritual burdens. However, with increased migration to the United States, further opportunities for education, and increased challenges for artisanal production, that mentality became untenable.[2] Over the course of my visits to different churches around Lake Pátzcuaro, I heard a new mantra: "All religions are good." Catholics repeated this to me explicitly, while evangelicals affirmed it through their willingness to retain Catholic traditions. In contrast to the disapproving tone some official Catholic publications and sermons take against evangelical churches, Catholics in Tzintzuntzan see the benefits of other faiths. One Catholic woman who had taken her husband to a hospital in Morelia attended an evangelical service there while praying for him to recuperate. "They gave us a Bible. They sang very beautifully. I liked how they explained things, with lots of devotion. Then I went to Mass in the Cathedral. It's the same God."

In addition to appreciating evangelical beliefs and practices, Catholics express skepticism about the rectitude of their own. The inordinate expenses and drinking associated with the fiestas generate particularly harsh criticism. Ricardo's brother, a Catholic, runs a small grocery store and sees both men and women go into debt spending money on alcohol. The poverty present in Tzintzuntzan, he says, is not a product of scarce resources, but of shortsightedness. Even he feels the pressure to conform to Catholic customs. Rather than invest in renovating their home, he and his wife decided to spend fifty thousand pesos on a fifteenth birthday party for their daughter. "Good or bad," he remarks, "it's our belief." He remains close to his brother despite their different churches. When Ricardo and Norma's fifteen-year-old daughter left home to marry another teenager, her parents objected because they wanted her to continue her schooling. Ricardo sent his brother to mediate with the boy's parents, but the young woman refused to return home.

On a short follow-up visit to Michoacán in August 2001, I found that while all the evangelical churches had stayed active, no new converts from Tzintzuntzan had joined them. Ricardo recognizes how difficult it is to give up the saints and traditions of the Catholic Church. He tells his brother that paper images of saints are just that and nothing divine, but Ricardo has become resigned to his lack of success in proselytizing. "Many people say their parents taught them their religion, and that they'll die with it. Everyone is free to choose. It's right to practice the religion that suits you." By proclaiming that "all religions are good," Tzintzuntzeños justify their own liberal borrowing of ideas from different spiritual sources. At the same time, they affirm that differences in religious denominations do not qualify as a reason for conflict.

In the open-minded reception I received as a Jew, I understand what people mean when they say, "All religions are good." Catholics and evangelicals alike are curious to hear about Jewish belief and worship beyond what they know from the Old Testament. I became a living fossil of sorts, parsing out the differences between Christianity and Judaism for my interrogators. Soon, I found myself stressing the similarities in worship services and holiday celebrations, as eager as they were to affirm that "all religions are good." Members of all the churches I visited expressed interest in my Jewish heritage, reminding me that indeed it was all the same God and that believing in him was what mattered. This tolerance did not prevent members of all churches from seeking to convert me, but they listened respectfully when I explained my reasons for declining.

Unfortunately, Catholics and converts have not achieved the same peaceful existence in other parts of Mexico. Community leaders in Chamula, Chiapas, backed by the state, exercise control through the administration of fiesta sponsorships and alcohol sales. There, opting out of the fiestas delivers a direct blow to caciques and their government sponsors, so conversion has sparked clashes that have left members of both religious groups dead, wounded, or homeless. In places like Tzintzuntzan, which have experienced greater integration with the global economy, the religious hierarchy that created a class of prestigious fiesta sponsors has given way to a system of shared community financing. This is not to say that communities in Chiapas are sealed off from outside influences that may hasten the breakdown of the cargo system. Highland Chiapas has also hosted teams of anthropologists engaged in decades-long research, although in a more geographically dispersed pattern than in Tzintzuntzan (Vogt 2002). Also, the presence of natural resources like oil lures multinational corporations to Chiapas. However, Chiapas has yet to develop the same circuits of migration that have reshaped life so fundamentally in Tzintzuntzan.

Around the world, seemingly irreconcilable religious beliefs and practices held by opposing groups have provoked deadly conflict. In the name of their

God, religious factions mobilize to defend against the potential threat of other faiths. As my grandmother, horrified by the latest suicide bombing in Israel, asked me, would the elimination of religious divisions also remove the impetus to fight? Though the context of each situation is important, an anthropological perspective can help arrive at an answer. Religious expression shows no signs of disappearing in the modern world and has grown even more diverse. But its continued vitality does not necessarily foretell continued conflict. In the case of Tzintzuntzan and its neighbors around Lake Pátzcuaro, the presence of evangelical churches has not sparked hostility among the majority population of Catholics. This tolerance owes much to a willingness of both groups to further common goals of community harmony and to acknowledge the fundamental goodness of adhering to religious principles of any kind. Religious belief connects Tzintzuntzeños to a larger body of the faithful and an overarching conception of the universe, yet it remains rooted in the realities of everyday life.

Preface: Confronting Interreligious Violence

1. The categories "mainline," "evangelical," "Protestant," and "Pentecostal" are used inconsistently across academic literature, government statistics, and everyday speech. Scholars divide Protestant faiths into mainline and evangelical denominations. The mainline churches, like Methodists and Presbyterians, can trace their lineage directly to the Protestant Reformation in Europe. Their form of worship is more sedate and their internal organization more hierarchical than the evangelical churches that have gained adherents in Latin America since the 1960s. The evangelical churches I discuss have a more recent origin and are often indigenous to Mexico. They include denominations like the Jehovah's Witnesses, who were founded by Charles Russell in 1872, and Pentecostals, who date from a revival movement in 1906. Because of their particular histories and theologies, some of these evangelical churches are considered para-Protestant. The tenets of evangelicalism—centrality of the conversion experience, literal interpretation of the Bible, and active proselytizing—have grown so popular within all Protestant traditions that it has become difficult to sustain the distinction between mainline and evangelical (Freston 2001). Following the terms that believers themselves use, I will refer to all those non-Catholic Christian churches that engage in proselytizing activity as evangelical.

2. Many of the church's proselytizing techniques mirror the cult recruitment tactics described by Singer (1995:Chapter 5). She emphasizes that anyone, no matter how educated or self-confident, can be vulnerable to the lures of cult membership at certain times. The evangelical churches diverge in that cult leaders tend to foster veneration of themselves, while evangelical leaders encourage veneration of God.

1. Sharing the Burden of Fiestas across Borders

1. Kemper (1977) analyzes the activities of migrants from Tzintzuntzan in Mexico City.

2. All names, except for those of some of the religious leaders, have been changed for the sake of privacy.

3. William Christian's *Local Religion in Sixteenth-Century Spain* (1981) describes the religious landscape from which the Spanish evangelizers emerged.

4. Scholars have disagreed on the antecedents of this redistributive system, with some tracing its origins to the colonial era (Carrasco 1961), some to the post-Independence years (Chance and Taylor 1985), and some to the early twentieth century (Rus and Wasserstrom 1980).

5. *Posadas,* meaning "lodgings," take place on the nine nights preceding Christmas. Each night a different street in the community hosts a procession in which images of Joseph and Mary are shown to reenact their search for shelter in Bethlehem. After Joseph and Mary find lodging for the night, the commissioners distribute bags of sweets, and children break a piñata. For the history of the event in Tzintzuntzan, see Chapter 8 of Brandes (1988).

6. Not everyone in Tzintzuntzan considers cargueros' motives so pure. Although the responsibilities associated with each religious post are expensive, the positions also present opportunities for financial gain. Even the cargueros of La Soledad admit that contributions to the church generate a steady income of three thousand to six thousand pesos a month, which belongs solely to the cargueros. One Catholic man recalled the time his neighbor served as carguera of La Soledad. He knew she had to spend all her time at the church, so she could not work. Still, she and her family bought new items for their house. "She told us God helps them so they don't lack for anything. But it's not God. They steal. They don't give any alms to the priest. They don't do any projects. When the cargueros finish their duty, people say to them, 'Where will you take from now?'" He is not alone in his cynicism, which many people also direct toward the many municipal officials who purchase new cars after their terms end.

7. Similar patterns are evident for migrants from many parts of Michoacán. During fiesta time, communities like Cherán would swell with men dressed in Chicago Bulls jackets who pinned twenty-dollar bills on the image of the patron saint (Martínez 2001). The ethnographic film *Oaxacalifornia* (Ziff and Stevens 1994) follows a Mexican family from Fresno, California, to its natal community in southern Mexico, where the parents have agreed to sponsor a fiesta.

2. Drinking and the Divine in Chiapas and Tzintzuntzan

1. The original museum label reads: "A partir de la década de 1960, se han promovido nuevas creencias religiosas e iglesias distintas, opuestas al viejo sistema de cargos, las cuales buscan adeptos entre los pueblos campesinos. La presencia de estas iglesias ha desencadenado divisiones en las comunidades, aunque en la realidad sólo encubren los motivos económicos y políticos que se encuentran en el fondo de los conflictos."

2. Significantly, in the parts of Chiapas where Urbina did not install local leaders, religious cargos have remained relatively inexpensive and paid for cooperatively (Rus 1994:296 n. 46).

3. According to some observers, Oaxaca, an adjacent state in southern Mexico where indigenous law and custom have been institutionalized, has suffered even more incidents of interreligious conflict than Chiapas (Gross 2001).

4. Working with Jehovah's Witnesses in Guadalajara, Fortuny Loret de Mola (2001) identified the same preoccupation with restoring order in a chaotic life.

5. Jehovah's Witnesses do not pledge allegiance to national flags, and they excoriate the United Nations. One member told me the organization maintains a team of lawyers

in Mexico City to defend church members who have been expelled from school for not observing secular rites. Penton (1985:149–151) highlights a contradiction: although church leaders prohibit membership in any political party or the military, they allow male Mexican church members to bribe government officials or purchase counterfeit certificates that state they have completed the required one year of military service.

6. All biblical translations come from *The New Oxford Annotated Bible* (Metzger and Murphy 1991).

7. "Tata" is a Purépecha term of address for a man, indicating great respect. It is roughly equivalent to the Spanish "Don," but I heard it used more sparingly and only for the truly revered, like Vasco de Quiroga and Lázaro Cárdenas.

8. Even ethnographers who are not focusing on the role of alcohol cite the desire to stop drinking as a reason for leaving a natal church. See Finkler (1983), Fortuny Loret de Mola (1995), López Cortés (1990), Mariz (1990), Mintz (1960), Rosenbaum (1993), Simmons (1979), Swanson (1994), and Vázquez Palacios (1991).

9. Later a church member in Pátzcuaro would explain to me that this represented a branch from the story in Numbers 17 in which God asks Moses to collect a rod from each of the twelve tribes of Israel. When Moses places them in the tent where he met with the Lord, he finds that only the offering from Aaron, a member of the Levi clan, flowers and bears almonds. This indicates God's favor.

10. Luz del Mundo members have not held their leadership to the same high standards, however. Samuel, though revered by his followers, has brought scandal to the church. In the wake of the Heaven's Gate mass suicide in the United States, researchers and journalists in Mexico paid closer attention to cult activity. After psychologists diagnosed Samuel with paranoid delusion, stories emerged of his sexually abusing younger members of the church (Masferrer Kan et al. 1997). Samuel refused to grant interviews. Instead, he took out a full-page ad in five Mexico City newspapers denying the charges and denouncing the calumny of his detractors. A Luz del Mundo convert in Pátzcuaro told me that Samuel now spends most of his time visiting congregations in South America in what sounds like a self-imposed exile. It is a testament to their strong focus on personal transformation that church members countenance such egregious transgressions in their leaders.

3. Accounting for Missionaries and Money

1. Other scholars see continuity between the waves of Protestant churches. In Brazil, mainline Protestants and charismatic Pentecostals share similar organizational features (Lehmann 1996:119).

2. I saw Cook treat one patient who complained of chronic headaches. She had gone to a private doctor in Quiroga, who charged her eight hundred pesos (about eighty-five dollars) for an X-ray that revealed nothing. With a few questions, Cook determined that she suffered from simple sinus problems; he gave her a box of Claritin pills, which cured her pain.

3. For legal reasons, he incorporated his churches into a religious association called Nueva Vida en Cristo, or New Life in Christ Ministry.

4. Responding to the Minority: Catholic Self-Improvement

1. See Brandes (1976) for a discussion of how a Catholic community in Spain interpreted those innovations as the attempt of the parish priest to do away with religious traditions.

2. A comprehensive study of the religious life of twenty-three hundred Latinos revealed that in each successive generation born in the United States, the percentage of Catholics decreases while the percentage of evangelicals increases (Lobdell 2001).

5. Responding to the Majority: Doctrinal Disobedience

1. Similarly, in a study of urban evangelicals in Chile, Dixon (1992) found that conversion helps men and women contend with alcoholism but does not significantly alter their previous relationships.

2. The renovated Catholics she mentions refer to a branch known as "Charismatics." Though scarce around Lake Pátzcuaro, Catholic Charismatics play a significant role in the diocese of Zamora, Michoacán (Juárez Cerdi 1997). Charismatics operate under the supervision of the parish priest, but with a separate corps of lay leaders, who claim special spiritual gifts. Like Pentecostals, Charismatics emphasize faith healing, prophecy, and ecstatic prayer in their services. Both groups attract primarily lower-class women by offering them opportunities for leadership and strict guidelines for behavior. Although part of the Baptist church, a mainline denomination, Gloria refers to herself as an "evangelical," further demonstrating the difficulty of assigning specific and consistent terms to religious groups.

6. Considering the Consequences of Conversion

1. See Carlsen (1997), Denton (1971), Goodman (1991), Kanagy (1990), Mintz (1960), Muratorio (1980), and Sexton (1978) for analyses that tie evangelical growth in Latin America to a desire among converts to accommodate changing economic conditions.

2. A. Gill (1994) contends that religious diversity increases political action not by mobilizing converts themselves but by forcing the Catholic hierarchy to adopt membership retention strategies that undermine government attempts at repression.

3. In Garrard-Burnett (1992), Glazier (1980), and Soneira (1991), Willems and Lalive d'Epinay play the roles of intellectual forefathers in the discussion of religious conversion in Latin America.

4. In an analysis of Pentecostalism in Brazil, Mariz (1994:151) suggests that political passivity may still belie substantial emotional change. "Of all the religions analyzed here, [Pentecostalism] was the one that most encouraged people to face up to the frustrations created by the absence of material resources and the impossibility of increasing those resources."

5. In most cases, anthropologists who agree with this theory accompany their analyses with a sense of nostalgia over what is being lost. However, Clawson (1984) and Weigert, D'Rogelio, and Rubel (1971) are unabashedly cheerful about the end of noncapitalist Catholic activity.

6. The omnipresent collection boxes read, "Contributions to the global work, Matthew 24:14."

Conclusion: Mobilizing Religion

1. A study of tin miners (Nash 1979) describes how Bolivians, though nominally Catholic, may draw on devil imagery and mythical animals to conceive of their place in the world. Rather than synthesize the different and often contradictory ideologies, miners assign each a separate place and day of the week.

2. Despite the evident class, ethnic, and gender distinctions around Lake Pátzcuaro, some residents still cling to the illusion of equality. In one recent study of a local junior high school (Levenson 2001), students deflected every suggestion of difference with the refrain, "We are all equal." Their vehemence suggested to the researcher that they were trying to convince themselves as much as the questioner that it was true.

Alcala, Fray Jeronimo de
1981   [1541] *Relación de las ceremonias y ritos y población y gobierno de los indios de la provincia de Michoacán.* Morelia, Michoacán: Fimax Publicistas.
Alves, Rubem A.
1985   *Protestantism and Repression: A Brazilian Case Study,* trans. John Drury. Maryknoll, N.Y.: Orbis Books.
Amatulli Valenti, Flaviano
1984   *Diálogo con los protestantes.* Mexico City: Apóstoles de la Palabra.
Anderson, Thor
1988   *Sacred Games: Ritual Warfare in a Maya Village.* 60 mins. Berkeley: University of California Extension Media Center.
Annis, Sheldon
1987   *God and Production in a Guatemalan Town.* Austin: University of Texas Press.
Báez Camargo, Gonzalo, and Kenneth G. Grubb
1935   *Religion in the Republic of Mexico.* London and New York: World Dominion Press.
Baldwin, Deborah J.
1990   *Protestants and the Mexican Revolution: Missionaries, Ministers, and Social Change.* Urbana: University of Illinois Press.
Barton, Paul T.
1999   In Both Worlds: A History of Hispanic Protestantism in the U.S. Southwest. Ph.D. dissertation, Religious Studies, Southern Methodist University.
Bastian, Jean-Pierre
1980   Protestantismo y política en México. *Revista Mexicana de Sociología* 43 (special issue): 1947–1966.
1989   *Los disidentes: Sociedades protestantes en América Latina.* Mexico City: El Colegio de México, Fondo de Cultura Económica.

1990   Heterodoxia religiosa y cambio social: El impacto regional de las sociedades religiosas no católicas en México. In *La política y el cielo: movimientos religiosos en el México contemporáneo,* edited by Rodolfo Moran Quiroz, 23–40. Guadalajara: Editorial Universidad de Guadalajara.

1992   Protestantism in Latin America. In *The Church in Latin America 1492–1992,* edited by Enrique Dussel, 313–347. Kent: Burns and Oates.

1996   Violencia, etnicidad y religión entre los mayas del estado de Chiapas en México. *Mexican Studies-Estudios Mexicanos* 12 (2): 301–315.

Beals, Ralph L.

1969   The Tarascans. In *The Handbook of Middle American Indians.* Vol. 8, edited by Evon Z. Vogt, 725–773. Austin: University of Texas Press.

Beck, Marilyn, and Stacy Jenel Smith

1999   Director: To Vatican, Film Is like "JFK" for Warren Commission. *Times-Picayune* (New Orleans), August 24, F-5.

Bonicelli, Paul Joseph

1993   Serpent-Doves and Sons of Thunder in Mexico: Comparing the Politics of Latin American Evangelicals. Ph.D. dissertation, Political Science, University of Tennessee, Knoxville.

Bonner, Arthur

1999   *We Will Not Be Stopped: Evangelical Persecution, Catholicism, and Zapatismo in Chiapas, Mexico.* Available on-line: UPUBLISH.COM.

Boudewijnse, Bárbara, Frans Kamsteeg, and André Droogers, eds.

1991   *Algo más que opio: Una lectura del Protestantismo Latinoamericano y Caribeño.* San José, Costa Rica: Editorial Departamento Ecuménico de Investigaciones.

Bowen, Kurt

1996   *Evangelism and Apostasy: The Evolution and Impact of Evangelicals in Modern Mexico.* Montreal, Kingston: McGill-Queen's University Press.

Brandes, Stanley H.

1976   The Priest as Agent of Secularization in Rural Spain. In *Economic Transformation and Steady-State Values: Essays in the Ethnography of Spain,* edited by Joseph B. Aceves, Edward C. Hansen, Gloria Levitas, 22–29. Queens College Publications in Anthropology. Flushing, N.Y.: Queens College Press.

1988   *Power and Persuasion: Fiestas and Social Control in Rural Mexico.* Philadelphia: University of Pennsylvania Press.

Brouwer, Steve, Paul Gifford, and Susan D. Rose

1996   *Exporting the American Gospel: Global Christian Fundamentalism.* New York: Routledge.

Brusco, Elizabeth

1993   The Reformation of Machismo: Asceticism and Masculinity among Colombian Evangelicals. In *Rethinking Protestantism in Latin America,* edited by Virginia Garrard-Burnett and David Stoll, 143–158. Philadelphia: Temple University Press.

1995   *The Reformation of Machismo: Evangelical Conversion and Gender in Colombia.* Austin: University of Texas Press.

Bunzel, Ruth

1940   The Role of Alcoholism in Two Central American Cultures. *Psychiatry* 3: 361–387.

Burdick, John
1993   *Looking for God in Brazil: The Progressive Catholic Church in Urban Brazil's Religious Arena*. Berkeley: University of California Press.
Cahn, Peter S.
2000   De la fresa a la pesca. *La Opinión* (Los Angeles), January 14.
Camp, Roderic Ai
1997   *Crossing Swords: Politics and Religion in Mexico*. New York: Oxford University Press.
Cancian, Frank
1965   *Economics and Prestige in a Maya Community: The Religious Cargo System in Zinacantán*. Stanford: Stanford University Press.
1992   *The Decline of Community in Zinacantán: Economy, Public Life, and Social Stratification, 1960-1987*. Stanford: Stanford University Press.
Carlsen, Robert S.
1997   *The War for the Heart and Soul of a Highland Maya Town*. Austin: University of Texas Press.
Carrasco, Pedro
1961   The Civil-Religious Hierarchy in Mesoamerican Communities: Pre-Spanish Background and Colonial Development. *American Anthropologist* 63 (3): 483–497.
Cavalcanti, H. B.
1995   Unrealistic Expectations: Contesting the Usefulness of Weber's Protestant Ethic for the Study of Latin American Protestantism. *Journal of Church and State* 37 (2): 289-308.
Chance, John K., and William B. Taylor
1985   Cofradías and Cargos: An Historical Perspective on the Mesoamerican Civil-Religious Hierarchy. *American Ethnologist* 12 (1): 1-26.
Chesnut, R. Andrew
1997   *Born Again in Brazil: The Pentecostal Boom and the Pathogens of Poverty*. New Brunswick, N.J.: Rutgers University Press.
Christian, William
1981   *Local Religion in Sixteenth-Century Spain*. Princeton: Princeton University Press.
Clawson, David L.
1984   Religious Allegiance and Economic Development in Rural Latin America. *Journal of Interamerican Studies and World Affairs* 26 (4): 499-524.
Cleary, Edward L.
1992   John Paul Cries "Wolf": Misreading the Pentecostals. *Commonweal*, November 20, 7-8.
Cleary, Edward L., and Hannah W. Stewart-Gambino, eds.
1997   *Power, Politics, and Pentecostals in Latin America*. Boulder, Col.: Westview.
Cohen, Jeffrey H.
1999   *Cooperation and Community: Economy and Society in Oaxaca*. Austin: University of Texas Press.
Colby, Gerard, and Charlotte Dennett
1995   *Thy Will Be Done: The Conquest of the Amazon: Nelson Rockefeller and Evangelism in the Age of Oil*. New York: HarperCollins.

Collier, George

1997   Reaction and Retrenchment in the Highlands of Chiapas. *Journal of Latin American Anthropology* 3 (1): 14–31.

Collier, George, with Elizabeth Lowery Quaratiello

1994   *Basta! Land and the Zapatista Rebellion in Chiapas.* Oakland, Calif.: Food First, Institute for Food and Development Policy.

Conferencia del Episcopado Mexicano

2001   Proyecto Pastoral de la CEM 1996–2000. Electronic document, http://www. cem.org.mx/documentosepiscopado/planpast.htm, accessed February 7.

Conover, Ted

1987   *Coyotes: A Journey through the Secret World of America's Illegal Aliens.* New York: Vintage.

Cox, Harvey

1995   *Fire from Heaven: The Rise of Pentecostal Spirituality and the Reshaping of Religion in the Twenty-first Century.* Reading, Mass.: Addison-Wesley.

Creighton, Frank Whittington

1926   *The Bishop's Journal.* Mexican Manuscript 1729. Bancroft Library, University of California, Berkeley.

Crump, Thomas

1987   The Alternative Economy of Alcohol in the Chiapas Highlands. In *Constructive Drinking: Perspectives on Drink from Anthropology,* edited by Mary Douglas, 239–249. Cambridge, U.K.: Cambridge University Press.

Cucchiari, Salvatore

1990   Between Shame and Sanctification: Patriarchy and Its Transformation in Sicilian Pentecostalism. *American Ethnologist* 14 (4): 687–707.

Darling, Juanita

1992   Ancient, Modern Beliefs Clash in Hills of Chiapas. *Los Angeles Times,* May 7, A-32.

de la Torre Castellanos, Renée

1995   *Los hijos de la luz: Discurso, identidad y poder en La Luz del Mundo.* Mexico City: Instituto Tecnológico y de Estudios Superiores de Occidente.

1999   El catolicismo: ¿Un templo en el que habitan muchos dioses? In *Creyentes y creencias en Guadalajara,* edited by Patricia Fortuny Loret de Mola, 101–131. Mexico City: Centro de Investigaciones y Estudios Superiores en Antropología Social.

Deiros, Pablo A.

1991   Protestant Fundamentalism in Latin America. In *Fundamentalisms Observed,* edited by Martin E. Marty and R. Scott Appleby, 142–196. Chicago: University of Chicago Press.

Denton, Charles F.

1971   Protestantism and the Latin American Middle Class. *Practical Anthropology* 18 (1): 24–28.

DeWalt, Billie R.

1975   Changes in the Cargo Systems of Mesoamerica. *Anthropological Quarterly* 48 (2): 87–105.

De Witt, Addison
1998   Exploiting Religion in Chiapas: The PRI as Puppetmaster. *New Leader* 81 (9): 7–10.
Dixon, David E.
1992   Popular Culture, Popular Identity and the Rise of Latin American Protestantism: Voices from Santiago *Poblacional*. Paper presented at the Latin American Studies Association Seventeenth International Congress.
Earle, Duncan
1992   Authority, Social Conflict, and the Rise of Protestantism: Religious Conversion in a Mayan Village. *Social Compass* 39 (3): 377–388.
Eber, Christine
1995   *Women and Alcohol in a Highland Maya Town: Water of Hope, Water of Sorrow.* Austin: University of Texas Press.
Finkler, Kaja
1983   Dissident Sectarian Movements, the Catholic Church, and Social Class in Mexico. *Comparative Studies in Society and History* 25 (2): 277–305.
Flores, Leo
2000   Religious Brawl. *The News* (Mexico City), January 11, 2.
Fortuny Loret de Mola, Maria Patricia
1995   On the Road to Damascus: Pentecostals, Mormons and Jehovah's Witnesses in Mexico. Ph.D. dissertation, Department of Social Anthropology, University College, London.
1996   Mormones y Testigos de Jehová: La versión mexicana. In *Identidades religiosas y sociales en México*, edited by Gilberto Giménez, 175–215. Mexico City: Instituto de Investigaciones Sociales, Universidad Nacional Autónoma de México.
1999   [ed.] *Creyentes y creencias en Guadalajara.* Mexico City: Centro de Investigaciones y Estudios Superiores en Antropología Social.
2001   Looking for a System of Order in Life: Jehovah's Witnesses in Mexico. In *Holy Saints and Fiery Preachers: The Anthropology of Protestantism in Mexico and Central America,* edited by James W. Dow and Alan R. Sandstrom, 87–116. Westport, Conn.: Praeger.
Foster, George M.
1965   Peasant Society and the Image of Limited Good. *American Anthropologist* 67: 293–315.
1967   *Tzintzuntzan: Mexican Peasants in a Changing World.* Boston: Little, Brown.
1979   *Tzintzuntzan: Mexican Peasants in a Changing World.* New York: Elsevier.
1988   *Tzintzuntzan: Mexican Peasants in a Changing World.* Prospect Heights, Ill.: Waveland.
Foster, George M., assisted by Gabriel Ospina
2000   *Los hijos del imperio: La gente de Tzintzuntzan,* trans. Reynaldo Rico. Zamora, Michoacán: Colegio de Michoacán.
Freston, Paul
1992   In Search of an Evangelical Political Project for Brazil: A Pentecostal "Showvention." *Transformation* 9 (3): 26–32.
2001   *Evangelicals and Politics in Asia, Africa, and Latin America.* Cambridge, U.K.: Cambridge University Press.

Frye, David
1996   *Indians into Mexicans: History and Identity in a Mexican Town.* Austin: University of Texas Press.
Galarza, Ernesto
1964   *Merchants of Labor: The Mexican Bracero Story.* Charlotte, N.C.: McNally and Loftin.
Galindo, Florencio
1994   *El "fenómeno de las sectas" fundamentalistas: La conquista evangélica de América Latina.* Navarra, Spain: Editorial Verbo Divino.
García Méndez, José Andrés
1997   Entre el apocalipsis y la esperanza: La presencia protestante en Chiapas. *Eslabones* 14 (July/December): 102–119.
Garma Navarro, Carlos
1987   *Protestantismo en una comunidad totonaca de Puebla, México.* Mexico City: Instituto Nacional Indigenista.
Garrard-Burnett, Virginia
1992   Protestantism in Latin America. *Latin American Research Review* 27 (1): 218–230.
Gill, Anthony
1994   Rendering unto Caesar? Religious Competition and Catholic Political Strategy in Latin America, 1962–79. *American Journal of Political Science* 38 (May): 403–425.
Gill, Lesley
1990   "Like a Veil to Cover Them": Women and the Pentecostal Movement in La Paz. *American Ethnologist* 17 (4): 708–721.
1994   *Precarious Dependencies: Gender, Class, and Domestic Service in Bolivia.* New York: Columbia University Press.
Giménez, Gilberto
1988   *Sectas religiosas en el sureste: Aspectos sociográficos y estadísticos.* Mexico City: Centro de Investigaciones y Estudios Superiores en Antropología Social.
1996   [ed.] *Identidades religiosas y sociales en México.* Mexico City: Instituto de Investigaciones Sociales, Universidad Nacional Autónoma de México.
Glazier, Stephen D., ed.
1980   *Perspectives on Pentecostalism: Case Studies from the Caribbean and Latin America.* Lanham, Md.: University Press of America.
Goldin, Liliana R., and Brent Metz
1991   An Expression of Cultural Change: Invisible Converts to Protestantism among Highland Guatemala Mayas. *Ethnology* 30 (4): 325–338.
Gómez, Fernando
2001   *Good Places and Non-Places in Colonial Mexico: The Figure of Vasco de Quiroga (1470–1565).* Lanham, Md.: University Press of America.
Goodman, Timothy
1991   Latin America's Reformation: The Waning of Catholicism: The Coming of Capitalism? *The American Enterprise* (July/August): 41–47.
Gott, Richard
1996   Protestant tidal wave sweeps Latin America. *Guardian Weekly,* January 14, 12–13.

Gossen, Gary H.
1989   Life, Death, and Apotheosis of a Chamula Protestant Leader: Biography as
          Social History. In *Ethnographic Encounters in Southern Mesoamerica: Essays in
          Honor of Evon Zartman Vogt, Jr.*, edited by Victoria R. Bricker and Gary H.
          Gossen, 217-229. Albany, N.Y.: Institute for Mesoamerican Studies.
Green, Duncan
1991   *Faces of Latin America*. London: Latin American Bureau.
Green, Linda
1993   Shifting Affiliations: Mayan Widows and Evangelicos in Guatemala. In *Re-
          thinking Protestantism in Latin America*, edited by Virginia Garrard-Burnett and
          David Stoll, 159-179. Philadelphia: Temple University Press.
Greenberg, James
1981   *Santiago's Sword: Chatino Peasant Religion and Economics*. Berkeley: University
          of California Press.
Gross, Toomas
2001   Community and Dissent: A Study of the Implications of Religious Fragmenta-
          tion in the Sierra Juárez, Oaxaca. Ph.D. dissertation, Department of Anthro-
          pology, University of Cambridge.
Hallum, Anne Motley
1996   *Beyond Missionaries: Toward an Understanding of the Protestant Movement in
          Central America*. Lanham, Md.: Rowman and Littlefield.
Hernández Castillo, Rosalva Aída
1989   Del Tzolkin a la Atalaya: Los cambios en la religiosidad en una comunidad
          Chuj-K'anjobal de Chiapas. *Religión y Sociedad en el Sureste de México* 2 (162):
          123-225.
Hervieu-Léger, Danièle
1996   Por una sociología de las nuevas formas de religiosidad: algunas cuestiones teó-
          ricas previas. In *Identidades religiosas y sociales en México*, edited by Gilberto
          Giménez, 23-45. Mexico City: Instituto de Investigaciones Sociales, Universi-
          dad Nacional Autónoma de México.
Hoffnagel, Judith Chambliss
1980   Pentecostalism: A Revolutionary or Conservative Movement? In *Perspectives
          on Pentecostalism: Case Studies from the Caribbean and Latin America*, edited
          by Stephen D. Glazier, 111-124. Lanham, Md.: University Press of America.
Ingham, John M.
1986   *Mary, Michael, and Lucifer: Folk Catholicism in Central Mexico*. Austin: Uni-
          versity of Texas Press.
Internet Movie Database
2000   Movie/TV News. Electronic document, http://us.imdb.com/SB?20000204#7,
          accessed September 15.
Jeffrey, Paul
1997   Evangelicals and Catholics in Chiapas: Conflict and Reconciliation. *Christian
          Century* 114 (6): 195-200.
Jordan, Mary
2001   Immigration on Mexican Agenda; Bush and Fox to Discuss Change in Treat-
          ment of Illegal Workers. *Washington Post*, February 16, A-1.

Juárez Cerdi, Elizabeth

1995   *¿De la secta a la denominación? El caso de los presbiterianos en Yajalón, Chiapas.*
          Mexico City: Instituto Nacional de Antropología e Historia.

1997   *Mi reino sí es de este mundo.* Zamora, Michoacán: El Colegio de Michoacán.

Kanagy, Conrad L.

1990   The Formation and Development of a Protestant Conversion Movement among
          the Highland Quichua of Ecuador. *Sociological Analysis* 51 (2): 205-217.

Kearney, Michael

1970   Drunkenness and Religious Conversion in a Mexican Village. *Quarterly Jour-
          nal of Studies on Alcohol* 31 (1): 132-152.

Kemper, Robert V.

1977   *Migration and Adaptation: Tzintzuntzan Peasants in Mexico City.* Beverly Hills,
          Calif.: Sage.

2002   From Student to Steward: Tzintzuntzan as Extended Community. In *Chroni-
          cling Cultures: Long-Term Field Research in Anthropology,* edited by Robert V.
          Kemper and Anya Peterson Royce, 284-312. Walnut Creek, Calif.: AltaMira
          Press.

Kray, Christine Anne

1997   Worship in Body and Spirit: Practice, Self, and Religious Sensibility in Yuca-
          tán. Ph.D. dissertation, Department of Anthropology, University of Pennsylva-
          nia.

La Farge, Oliver

1947   *Santa Eulalia: The Religion of a Cuchumatán Town.* Chicago: University of Chi-
          cago Press.

Lalive d'Epinay, Christian

1969   *Haven of the Masses: A Study of the Pentecostal Movements in Chile.* London:
          Lutterworth.

Lancaster, Roger

1988   *Thanks to God and the Revolution: Popular Religion and Class Consciousness in
          the New Nicaragua.* New York: Columbia University Press.

Lehmann, David

1996   *Struggle for the Spirit: Religious Transformation and Popular Culture in Brazil
          and Latin America.* Cambridge, U.K.: Polity Press.

Lernoux, Penny

1982   *Cry of the People: The Struggle for Human Rights in Latin America—The Catho-
          lic Church in Conflict with U.S. Policy.* New York: Penguin.

Levenson, Bradley A. U.

2001   *We Are All Equal: Student Culture and Identity at a Mexican Secondary School,
          1988-1998.* Durham, N.C.: Duke University Press.

Lewis, Oscar

1964   *Pedro Martínez: A Mexican Peasant and His Family.* New York: Random House.

Limón, Francisco, and Abel Clemente

1996   From Zapata to Zapatistas: Protestants, Politics, and Social Struggle in Mex-
          ico. In *In the Power of the Spirit: The Pentecostal Challenge to Historic Churches
          in Latin America,* edited by Benjamin F. Gutiérrez and Dennis A. Smith, 119-
          128. Lexington, Ky.: Presbyterian Church.

Lobdell, William
2001   Latino Exodus From Catholic Church Rising, Study Says. *Los Angeles Times,*
            May 5, Metro part 2, p. 1.
López Cortés, Eliseo
1990   *Pentecostalismo y milenarismo: La Iglesia Apostólica de la Fe en Cristo Jesús.*
            Iztapalapa, Mexico: Universidad Autónoma Metropolitana.
Maccoby, Michael
1972   Alcoholism in a Mexican Village. In *The Drinking Man,* edited by David C.
            McClelland et al., 232–260. New York: Free Press.
Macín, Raúl
1983   *Lutero: Presencia religiosa y política en México.* Mexico City: Ediciones Nuevo-
            mar.
Marcom, John, Jr.
1990   The Fire down South. *Forbes,* October 15, 56–71.
Mariz, Cecília
1990   Pentecostalismo y alcoholismo entre los pobres de Brasil. *Cristianismo y Socie-
            dad* 28 (105): 39–44.
1994   *Coping with Poverty: Pentecostals and Christian Base Communities in Brazil.*
            Philadelphia: Temple University Press.
Marostica, Matthew
1994   La iglesia evangélica en la Argentina como nuevo movimiento social. *Sociedad
            y Religión* 12: 3–16.
Martin, David
1990   *Tongues of Fire: The Explosion of Protestantism in Latin America.* Oxford, U.K.:
            Basil Blackwell.
1994   Evangelical and Charismatic Christianity in Latin America. In *Charismatic
            Christianity as a Global Culture,* edited by Karla Poewe, 73–86. Studies in Com-
            parative Religion. Columbia: University of South Carolina Press.
Martínez, Rúben
2001   *Crossing Over: A Mexican Family on the Migrant Trail.* New York: Metropoli-
            tan Books.
Marty, Martin E., and R. Scott Appleby, eds.
1991   *The Fundamentalism Project.* Chicago: University of Chicago Press.
Masferrer Kan, Elio, et al.
1997   *La Luz del Mundo: Un análisis multidisciplinario de la controversia religiosa que
            ha impactado a nuestro país.* Bosques de Echegaray, Mexico: Publicaciones para
            el Estudio Científico de las Religiones.
McGreal, Chris
1989   Mexican Indians Made to Pay for Allegiance to New Religion. *Independent*
            (London), March 29, 10.
Metz, Allan
1994   Protestantism in Mexico: Contemporary Contextual Developments. *Journal of
            Church and State* 36 (1): 57–78.
Metzger, Bruce M., and Roland E. Murphy, eds.
1991   *The New Oxford Annotated Bible.* New York: Oxford University Press.

Meyer, Jean A.
1976   *The Cristero Rebellion: The Mexican People between Church and State 1926–1929.* Cambridge, U.K.: Cambridge University Press.
Miller, Phil
1999   Catholics Outraged by "New Exorcist." *Scotsman* (Edinburgh), September 11, 5.
Mintz, Sidney W.
1960   *Worker in the Cane: A Puerto Rican Life History.* New Haven: Yale University Press.
Muratorio, Blanca
1980   Protestantism and Capitalism Revisited in the Rural Highlands of Ecuador. *Journal of Peasant Studies* 8 (1): 37–60.
Murphee, M. W.
1969   *Christianity and the Shona.* London: Athlone.
Nader, Laura
1990   *Harmony Ideology: Justice and Control in a Zapotec Mountain Village.* Stanford: Stanford University Press.
Nash, June
1960   Protestantism in an Indian Village in the Western Highlands of Guatemala. *Alpha Kappa Deltan* 30 (1): 49–53.
1979   *We Eat the Mines and the Mines Eat Us: Dependency and Exploitation in Bolivian Tin Mines.* New York: Columbia University Press.
Ottawa Citizen
1999   Critics, Church condemn *Stigmata. Ottawa Citizen,* September 13, A-4.
Padilla, C. René
1992   Latin American Evangelicals Enter the Public Sphere. *Transformation: An International Evangelical Dialogue on Mission and Ethics* 9 (3): 2–7.
Penton, M. James
1985   *Apocalypse Delayed: The Story of Jehovah's Witnesses.* Toronto: University of Toronto Press.
Petersen, Douglas
1997   Towards a Latin American Pentecostal Political Praxis. *Transformation: An International Evangelical Dialogue on Mission and Ethics* 14 (1): 30–32.
Reck, Gregory G.
1978   *In the Shadow of Tlaloc: Life in a Mexican Village.* New York: Penguin.
Riding, Alan
1985   *Distant Neighbors: A Portrait of the Mexicans.* New York: Knopf.
Roberts, Bryan
1968   Protestant Groups and Coping with Urban Life in Guatemala City. *American Journal of Sociology* 73 (May): 753–767.
Rodriguez, Jeanette
1994   *Our Lady of Guadalupe: Faith and Empowerment among Mexican-American Women.* Austin: University of Texas Press.
Rodriguez, Richard
1992   *Days of Obligation: An Argument with My Mexican Father.* New York: Viking.

Rosenbaum, Brenda

1993   *With Our Heads Bowed: The Dynamics of Gender in a Maya Community.* Albany, N.Y.: Institute for Mesoamerican Studies, the University at Albany, State University of New York.

Rostas, Susanna, and André Droogers, eds.

1993   *The Popular Use of Popular Religion in Latin America.* Amsterdam: Centre for Latin American Research and Documentation.

Rouse, Roger

1991   Mexican Migration and the Social Space of Postmodernism. *Diaspora* 1 (1): 8–23.

Rus, Jan

1994   The "Comunidad Revolucionaria Institucional": The Subversion of Native Government in Highland Chiapas, 1936–1968. In *Everyday Forms of State Formation: Revolution and Negotiation of Rule in Modern Mexico,* edited by Gilbert M. Joseph and Daniel Nugent, 265–300. Durham, N.C.: Duke University Press.

Rus, Jan, and Robert Wasserstrom

1980   Civil-Religious Hierarchies in Central Chiapas, A Critical Perspective. *American Ethnologist* 7 (3): 462–478.

1981   Evangelization and Political Control: The SIL in Mexico. In *Is God an American? An Anthropological Perspective on the Missionary Work of the Summer Institute of Linguistics,* edited by Søren Hvalkof and Peter Aaby, 163–172. Copenhagen: International Work Group for Indigenous Affairs; London: Survival International.

Ryser, Jeffrey, and et al.

1990   Latin America's Protestants: A Potential New Force for Change. *Business Week,* June 4, 79.

Sandoval, Ricardo

2000   Spreading the Word in Chiapas: Missionaries Respect Native Ways. *Boston Globe,* January 9, A-19.

Sarmiento, Socorro Torres

1999   Buscando El Gasto: Tzintzuntzeño Immigrant Income-Generating Strategies. Ph.D. dissertation, Department of Social Science, University of California, Irvine.

Selby, Henry A.

1974   *Zapotec Deviance: The Convergence of Folk and Modern Sociology.* Austin: University of Texas Press.

Sexton, James D.

1978   Protestantism and Modernization in Two Guatemalan Towns. *American Ethnologist* 5 (2): 280–302.

Simmons, William S.

1979   Islamic Conversion and Social Change in a Senegalese Village. *Ethnology* 18 (4): 303–323.

Simons, Marlise

1982   Latin America's New Gospel. *New York Times Magazine,* November 7, 45–47.

Singer, Margaret, with Janja Lalich
1995   *Cults in Our Midst*. San Francisco: Jossey-Bass.

Smith, Brian H.
1998   *Religious Politics in Latin America: Pentecostal vs. Catholic*. Notre Dame, Ind.: University of Notre Dame Press.

Smith, Christian, and Liesl Ann Haas
1997   Revolutionary Evangelicals in Nicaragua: Political Opportunity, Class Interests, and Religious Identity. *Journal for the Scientific Study of Religion* 36 (3): 440–454.

Smith, Christian, and Joshua Prokopy, eds.
1999   *Latin American Religion in Motion*. New York, London: Routledge.

Smith, James F.
2000   New Chiapas Governor Initiates Process to Release Rebels. *New York Times*, December 9, A-3.

Smith, Waldemar R.
1977   *The Fiesta System and Economic Change*. New York: Columbia University Press.

Soneira, Jorge
1991   Los estudios sociológicos sobre el Pentecostalismo en América Latina. *Sociedad y Religión* 8 (March): 60–67.

Stoll, David
1982   *Fishers of Men or Founders of Empire? The Wycliffe Bible Translators in Latin America*. London: Zed Press with Cultural Survival.
1990   *Is Latin America Turning Protestant? The Politics of Evangelical Growth*. Berkeley: University of California Press.

Sullivan, Kathleen
1998   Religious Change and the Recreation of Community in an Urban Setting among the Tzotzil Maya of Highland Chiapas, Mexico. Ph.D. dissertation, Graduate Faculty in Anthropology, City University of New York.

Sutro, Livingston
1989   Alcoholics Anonymous in a Mexican Peasant-Indian Village. *Human Organization* 48 (2): 180–186.

Swanson, Tod D.
1994   Refusing to Drink with the Mountains: Traditional Andean Meanings in Evangelical Practice. In *Accounting for Fundamentalisms: The Dynamic Character of Movements*. Vol. 4, edited by Martin E. Marty and R. Scott Appleby, 79–98. Chicago: University of Chicago Press.

Taylor, William B.
1996   *Magistrates of the Sacred: Priests and Parishioners in Eighteenth-Century Mexico*. Stanford: Stanford University Press.

Thompson, Ginger
2000   In a Warring Mexican Town, God's Will Is the Issue. *New York Times*, August 13, A-3.

Valderrey, José
1987   La cuestión de las sectas religiosas en la prensa mexicana. In *De sectas a sectas: Una aproximación al estudio de un fenómeno apasionante*, edited by Angel Saldaña. Mexico City: Claves Latinoamericanos.

van Zantwijk, R. A. M.
1967   *Servants of the Saints: The Social and Cultural Identity of a Tarascan Community in Mexico*. Assen, The Netherlands: Royal VanGorcum Ltd.

Vázquez Palacios, Felipe
1991   *Protestantismo en Xalapa*. Xalapa, Mexico: Gobierno del Estado de Veracruz.

Vera, Rodrigo
1996   Democracia, horizontalidad y tolerancia. *Proceso* (Mexico City), May 6.

Verástique, Bernardino
2000   *Michoacán and Eden: Vasco de Quiroga and the Evangelization of Western Mexico*. Austin: University of Texas Press.

Vogt, Evon Z.
2002   The Harvard Chiapas Project: 1957–2000. In *Chronicling Cultures: Long-Term Field Research in Anthropology*, edited by Robert V. Kemper and Anya Peterson Royce, 135–159. Walnut Creek, Calif.: AltaMira Press.

Weber, Max
2001   [1904–05] *The Protestant Ethic and the Spirit of Capitalism*, trans. Talcott Parsons. London and New York: Routledge.

Weigert, Andrew J., William V. D'Rogelio, and Arthur J. Rubel
1971   Protestantism and Assimilation among Mexican Americans: An Exploratory Study of Ministers' Reports. *Journal for the Scientific Study of Religion* 10 (3): 219–232.

Willaime, Jean-Paul
1996   Dinámica religiosa y modernidad. In *Identidades religiosas y sociales en México*, edited by Gilberto Giménez, 47–65. Mexico City: Instituto de Investigaciones Sociales, Universidad Nacional Autónoma de México.

Willems, Emilio
1967   *Followers of the New Faith: Culture Change and the Rise of Protestantism in Brazil and Chile*. Nashville: Vanderbilt University Press.

Wilson, Everett A.
1994   Latin American Pentecostalism: Challenging the Stereotypes of Pentecostal Passivity. *Transformation: An International Evangelical Dialogue on Mission and Ethics* 11 (1): 19–24.

Wolf, Eric R.
1959   *Sons of the Shaking Earth*. Chicago: University of Chicago Press.

Ziff, Trisha, and Sylvia Stevens
1994   *Oaxacalifornia*. 58 min. Berkeley: University of California Extension Media Center.